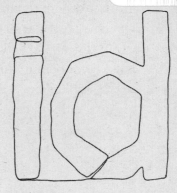

id

the quest for
meaning in
the 21st century

SUSAN
GREENFIELD

SCEPTRE

First published in Great Britain in 2008 by Sceptre
An imprint of Hodder & Stoughton
An Hachette Livre UK company
First published in paperback in 2009

1

A CIP catalogue record for this title is available from the British Library

ISBN 978 0 340 93601 6

Typeset in Sabon by Hewer Text UK Ltd, Edinburgh
Printed and bound by Clays Ltd, St Ives plc

Hodder & Stoughton policy is to use papers that are natural,
renewable and recyclable products and made from wood grown in
sustainable forests. The logging and manufacturing processes are expected
to conform to the environmental regulations of the country of origin.

Hodder & Stoughton Ltd
338 Euston Road
London NW1 3BH

www.hodder.co.uk

CONTENTS

PREFACE

I was a Baby Boomer, born into a world of unprecedented and expanding realms of consumerism, health and education, from where the future always beckoned as a bright, shiny place. And the innovation and iconoclastic march of the 1960s reinforced the idea that, for my generation, anything was indeed possible, from material gain to personal development to social progress. At that time it wasn't so much that I was 'interested' in the future from an academic stance – I was simply dying to be a part of it. Then my world tilted.

In the 1970s the economic gloom was reflected in Britain in strikes, a three-day week and national power cuts. Meanwhile, at the personal level there was suddenly real work to do: after wonderfully unstructured undergraduate days of self-indulgent thinking, reading, writing and dreaming in a library, there were now long hours of routine slog in an unlovely research lab, battling with practical problems and the caprices of grinding experimental procedures. Nature gave up her secrets grudgingly and very, very slowly; most days, things went far from according to plan. And so it was in the wider world. Deaths in Vietnam, then deaths in Northern Ireland, rendered the 1960s' vision a tinny, tarnished absurdity, as captured in a play we all saw at the time: *Kennedy's Children*, by Robert Patrick, in which a handful of characters in a New York bar don't actually interact, but deliver monologues about how their individual lives have been shaped by the era. We were indeed all on our own.

The material confidence of the 1980s was somehow unmatched, at least from where I was standing, by a corresponding mindset that could cope with it. Carried away by Filofaxes, shoulder pads, City careers and the mandate to succeed, none of us was really fulfilled for very long, and most of us were anxious. The 1990s were worse in that the personal insecurities continued, undermined further by far less consumer comfort and a scary new high-tech takeover of all aspects of our lives, including even attitudes and expectations.

When I wrote *Tomorrow's People* not long after the millennium, discussion of new technologies and the lifestyle they could bring was far less rehearsed, and therefore seemed to me to be completely crucial to examine – which is what I did. But even over the relatively brief period of time since then, much of what seemed at the time startling has already crept into the warp and weft of our daily lives and raised concerns that everyone now acknowledges, from obesity to literacy standards to then unheard of and unimaginable screen crazes such as *Facebook* and *Second Life*.

Back in 2002, I felt it necessary to flag some of the possible outcomes of an increasingly pervasive and invasive technology. But such predictions as I ventured then tended to be rather negative: the perhaps unhelpful message that things might well be different for the next generation could have been construed as somewhat Luddite as well as lacking in passion and compassion. I was by no means sure of where we as a society, and as individuals, might want to go, given the extraordinary time and facilities and longer lifespan that the new developments were making possible. But since then, these issues have become mainstream.

In April 2006, we had a debate in the House of Lords on the impact of the latest technology on the way young people might think and learn differently from preceding generations. The diversity of the contributions, with many different issues being raised, convinced me that the time was ripe to face up to the future technologies and explore the impact they would have, in the broadest possible sense, on those born in this century. The big question, it seemed to me, did not stop at how our children and grandchildren might learn: the implications went more deeply, into what *kind* of people they might become. Would they have options open to them, both good and bad, that had never before confronted humanity? And this issue of a new type of identity in the future inevitably raised questions about our identity today.

The more I thought about it, the more fascinated I became with how we define ourselves and others, which in turn relates to how fulfilled we are as individuals, which then, or so my fevered thinking ran on, brings us to the big and ancient topics of happiness and the meaning of life. In this book, I want to see if neuroscience can make an important contribution in helping us with the truly big questions, and even offer new insights on the eternal problems that have been with us humans for over a hundred thousand years.

In his recent book, *The Meaning of the 21st Century*, James Martin argues that we shouldn't just ask what is going to happen in the future, but how we are going to shape the future. Neuroscience, I firmly believe, is perfectly positioned as a discipline not only to help explain why we are as we are, but to explore how we might change and be changed. My recurring theme is the dynamism, the 'plasticity', of the human brain and the wonderful benefits and terrifying threats that that malleability brings. I want to show how our identity *is* our brains, or rather our minds: as such we are highly vulnerable, but at the same time could be potentially fulfilled as never before, by future technologies. Lofty goals, agreed – but ones that our children and grandchildren might never forgive us for shunning.

One of the inevitable challenges of applying brain research beyond its normal context is striking the right balance between the necessary technical detail on the one hand, and on the other, couching somewhat rarefied neuroscientific findings in terms that are clear, relevant, interesting and above all understandable to the non-specialist. Such an exercise can never satisfy everyone, and I ask the forgiveness of my more purist colleagues who could feel offended that I have not given certain scientific nuances the attention they might otherwise deserve. Similarly, I really hope that the general reader will see that there *is* a point, in the early chapters, in first getting to grips with the basic neuronal nuts and bolts of brain functioning, and the neuroscientific story so far.

Given the extremely multidisciplinary nature of the subject, I have had to turn to many colleagues and friends for advice and help. In alphabetical order, I would therefore like to thank: Peter Brown, Gordon Claridge, Guy Claxton, Ellie Dommett, Michael Hill, Paul Overton, Jonathan

Sharples, Nick Shea, John Stein, Kathleen Turner, Jack Velero, Katja Weich, Martin Westwell and Russell Wilcox. I'm also indebted to Emma and James Arbuthnot for putting up with me as the most anti-social house guest ever when, over Easter 2007, I commandeered their study to press on with the writing, emerging only at mealtimes. Younger friends have also helped, without knowing it, on giving a perspective on the preoccupations of the next generation: Alice Arbuthnot, Phoebe Collins, Merryn Hurley-Rawlins and Amy Irvine.

I'd also like to thank my publishers Rowena Webb and Helen Coyle for their enormous support and unstinting enthusiasm throughout.

Finally, however, the biggest debt of gratitude goes to my wonderful friends, for just being there throughout and whenever. In particular, Carolyn and John Lloyd-Davies deserve a special mention. As I write these words, they are facing the biggest challenge, the most overwhelming journey of their lives, as they come to terms with serious illness. I dedicate this book to them, in admiration of their great courage, love, dignity and, above all, humour.

Susan Greenfield
Oxford
December 2007

THE FUTURE

The twenty-first-century is promising and threatening much. We now live in a world and at the beginning of an era where nothing, other than huge changes, can be taken for granted. The dire consequences of global warming are finally permeating everyone's mindset, while the technology now assumed as indispensable and integral to our daily existence is actually becoming ever more pervasive, invasive and startling. But although the instability and insecurity of the environment is a current, constant topic of debate, the impact of twenty-first-century technologies, not so much on our outer lives but on our inner ones – our minds – is not really being questioned. Yet just look at us, and how we are changing.

Daily the press shake their collective head over binge-drinking teenagers, feral and dysfunctional, of obesity reaching epidemic proportions, and of gun crime and murder among a generation that should have ahead of them a life that is longer and more stimulating than at any previous time in history. Even for the great majority who don't hide behind hoods, and who do make it routinely to school, there's a big question mark over what to teach, and how. Increasingly children are turning to sources of authority that they have never met, searching on the internet, socializing on the screen, spending on average six hours a day in two dimensions.

Meanwhile many older people are facing the prospect of long lives with no obvious purpose. Increasingly freed up from fatal or debilitating diseases, they see decades of post-retirement time stretching out into a solitary and empty end-game. For others less lucky, there is the spectre of neurodegenerative disease, in particular of conditions such as Alzheimer's disease and the most frightening prospect of all, loss of the mind – of everything that makes you so unique and special.

And then there's my generation, the ones in the middle, living life like hamsters in a wheel, bombarded with aspirational goals, desperately worried about how we match up, what we look like, what others think; many are asking, above all, why they are not happy. In his recent survey of global wellbeing, *Affluenza*, the psychologist Oliver James blames many of such ills in Western society on 'selfish capitalism', an unfettered consumerism that has arisen from our shifting, almost a century ago, to a market economy. We have been cajoled all too often into buying things that we don't need but only want. And the reason we crave more clothes, cars, goods, brands and so on is that they will 'say something' about us – symbolize our distinct, preferably superior, identity. But as with all arms races, there is no happy finishing post. Small wonder that the most prevalent disease soon will be not AIDS but depression: the World Health Organization predicts that as the twenty-first century unfolds a staggering one in four people will succumb.

And small wonder, then, that alternative paths seem highly attractive – paths uncluttered by consumer goods and paved out straight before us, with no confusing diversions or side tracks. In itself, such an option is far from new: the twentieth century was arguably a battleground between a blatantly decadent consumerism and tougher, purer, simpler lifestyles dictated by the blueprints of ideologies, be they political, religious or some cult cocktail of the two. Whether the emphasis lay in the genes, as the Nazis would have it, or the environment, as Marxism preferred, the individual has in both cases been cast in a predictable mould: identity shifts away from the unique person with their idiosyncratic personality in favour of the collective persona, the collective narrative. Now such single-minded devotion has taken on a ferocity and extremism that might even eclipse the gut-wrenching inhumanity of those previous, more overtly political ideologies.

What do these very different black scenarios none the less have in common? In a word: identity. In two words: identity crisis. How do you see yourself? What defines you? What makes you happy? What do you want from life? These questions, naïve and unoriginal though they may sound, are in my view right up there with the current crisis of climate change as we contemplate how we are going to live out the next few decades and beyond. But this particular problem relates not so much to the outer world as to the inner landscape of the human mind: how you see yourself, and how you think others perceive you.

Many of the current spate of gun attacks in inner cities are allegedly triggered by an imagined slight, some facial expression or gesture perceived as an insult. Could the far more widespread phenomena of obesity and binge drinking stem from the same basic issue of status? Over-eating or over-drinking might be precipitated by disappointment and frustration in what or who you are, or perhaps by the lure of a pure escapist, hedonistic thrill of anonymity, or by peer pressure or, most likely, by all of the above. If so, as with the more extreme cases resulting in violent crime, such behaviours would all none the less be traceable to the idea of the self, to how that person sees themselves in relation to others. Similarly, the quest for the perfect body, or the perfect home, also reflects an identity defined by a highly specific, though by no means universal, Western cultural manual. Meanwhile, the fulfilment and pleasure of defining oneself in the robust and fixed terms of a fundamentalist rulebook have always been equally, if not more, reassuring.

But now we can add to the mix a new type of devotion. Now we have a way of subsuming individual identity, or perhaps of developing a false persona, or maybe even of losing one's identity altogether. Information technology, nanotechnology and biotechnology are already transforming our lives, and they will be pervasive and invasive in unprecedented ways. But there is no point in either hyping or fearing these new technologies as factors that will impinge on the minds of generations to come until we can place them in the context of the workings of the brain itself.

The cyber-world is already with us, of course. For the moment cyber-technologies are in the main screen-based, be they a mobile, a laptop or an iPod. You might well argue that the TV is, and always has been, a screen and that we've managed to accommodate it without human nature undergoing any apparent cataclysmic makeover. But there *is* a big difference from twentieth-century TV: twenty-first-century screen technologies, including the television, are interactive. This means you can be involved in the world on the screen and play a part in the ongoing narrative to greater or lesser extents. Soap operas, so called because of the industry that originally sponsored them, started out on American radio in the 1930s; they were to prove an early introduction to the experience of living a life vicariously, albeit many stages removed from real life. But still, good enough to offer a sanitizing alternative.

Reality TV has been the next big pull, going one better by using real people rather than actors, and therefore bringing the events on the screen even greater credibility while still offering the protection of a second-hand voyeurism. The cyber-experience of *Second Life* is perhaps the ultimate in this line of screen escapism. Emphatically not a computer game, *Second Life* offers a complete new world, one in which you live out a completely different existence directly, though again not as your 'real' self.

But the new technologies and software are doing more than softening our sense of identity; they are particularly powerful simply because they are so pervasive. In the late twentieth century no one really questioned whether the ability to record TV programmes and the opportunity to log missed phone calls was changing our mentality too much. Taken for granted though the VHS recorder and the Ansaphone now are, at the moment of their original appearance they freed us up for the first time from the inconvenient happenstance of life. We started to be more in control of our *time*. It was the first step, perhaps a small one, towards piecing together our own individual reality.

Now the mobility of the cellphone, the iPod and the laptop have empowered us further, this time in relation to freedom over our *space*. The portable screen has put us continuously in touch with one another, interacting and controlling. Increasingly the global cyber-world, accessible at fingertip touch whenever we wish and wherever we are, promises a more reassuring, safer option than the messy, haphazard world of the in-your-face three-dimensional life: a real life of banana skins and elephant traps, however metaphorical.

But the information technologies are perhaps already blurring the cyber-world and 'reality'. One particularly depressing anecdote I heard just after 9/11 was that there were some who couldn't really believe that the planes crashing into the Twin Towers, and the instant conflagration, were actually 'real', so similar were the events to some games. This conflation of the cyber and real worlds is starting to impact on two very different aspects of our lives that until now I, for one, have taken pretty much for granted: fun and privacy.

First, let's think about having fun. A very understandable current concern is that a whole range of erstwhile demanding intellectual activities are becoming obsolete in favour of the quick fix of a laugh, a rush of adrenalin and the immediacy of the next sensory kick. The worry is that the challenge of understanding Dostoyevsky will be evaluated and found wanting against the new universal yardstick of how much fun you're having. Just as text messaging doesn't tap into our abilities to exercise the wide range of vocabulary and expression of previous letter-writing generations, could it be that our very understanding, our sense of reasoning, might now also be diminished and brutalized by the simplistic sensory sensations of the screen experience?

Fuddy-duddy quibbling though this may sound, we should not dismiss such worries out of hand as being out of step with the lifestyle of today and tomorrow. Having fun has always been on the human agenda, but, intriguingly, not all the time. Just as we might feel sorry for someone who claims they never have any fun, so we would feel a similar sense of sadness for someone who boasted that their life was just one long round of it. But perhaps this balance *is* shifting in favour of the kind of activities that are normally associated with having easy fun rather than thinking deeply.

This is not to say that thinking deeply isn't enjoyable – but the pleasure is of a different type from that of surrendering to sensations. My own view is that the enjoyment of reading Shakespeare or Joyce involves an appreciation and savouring of 'meaning': some cerebral light flashes on as you start to see one thing in terms of something else, and place an event or behaviour in a new, wider context. Really 'understanding' something, be it in science or literature, usually devolves from that 'Aha' moment, from making a connection: by contrast, having fun is usually based on the opposite, on *dissolving* connections, splitting the here-and-now moment from the past and the future, splitting the sensational taste of the ice cream or chocolate from the 'significance' of unhealthy food, splitting the thrill of downhill skiing from the associations of injury, and above all splitting the sense of self, of a particular identity, in favour of abandonment to the raw sensory experience. You 'let yourself go'. This idea might seem a little far-fetched as my opening premise; but it is a provocative one, and one which we should (as we shall shortly) be considering seriously. Let me be blunt and ask up front: is screen culture jeopardizing good old-fashioned abstract thought?

The second area that we have taken for granted, at least until recently, is privacy. And the reason that a private life used to be such a clear and unambiguous concept was that until the end of the twentieth century the technology simply wasn't there to challenge our privacy on a systematic, mass scale. Of course, phone-tapping, private detectives and amoral journalism have been around for as long as there's been 'modern' life. But in the previous century the privacy of the average citizen, conscientiously living out a normal, everyday existence, was assured. Not any longer.

In the shadow of the current debate in the UK on the desirability or otherwise of identity cards, we are resigned to cyber-profiling as we shop online, as search engines start to collate data on us in our innocent curiosity, as the unscrupulous devise ever more ingenious ways of accessing our credit cards. All of us, all of the time, now have our privacy under siege. We need to take active measures to protect it and be alert to situations where it might be eroded.

Yet with the advent of cyber-pastimes such as chatting on *Facebook*, a way of life for many teenagers and young adults, such precautions are becoming ever harder to take. (Just in case you haven't yet been initiated by your children, *Facebook* is a social networking site which links friends and strangers and enables them to share conversations, photos, videos and games.) However, such otherwise normal com-munication is now only conducted via a screen, rather than face to face: more significantly still, it is out there on the web, public. A sixteen-year-old intern in our lab, Amy, introduced my research group of twenty-something-and-upwards geriatrics to *Facebook*. She summed up her reaction to using it herself like this: 'I can see that *Facebook* makes you think about yourself differently when all your private thoughts and feelings can be posted on the internet for all to see. Are we perhaps losing a sense of where we ourselves finish and the outside world begins?'

Until now these technologies have been screen-based, essentially visual. In and of itself this is an interesting issue: what impact might such a biased input of fast-moving icons to the brain have on the way we think? Yet soon voice-activated devices will be with us, as will computation embedded in clothing, jewellery and spectacles. It seems bizarre to imagine a world of endless spoken cyber-conversations, a kind of wrap-around, purely auditory Google. And while it might stretch credibility to the limit to envisage why you would ever need to ask your sweater the date of the Battle of Hastings or the height of Kilimanjaro, surely it is possible that future technology would enable you to interrogate anything already being carried around on your body – from watches to coat-sleeves – for oral updates, music, price quotes, directions and more.

No longer anchored to a screen and keyboard, unencumbered by bulky devices, you will meander in a three-dimensional space that is increasingly shaped by a fourth, cyber dimension. The firewall of brain and body will weaken as it is breached each moment by the spoken word monitoring and guiding each step. Will there now be time and place ever just to stand still?

But it doesn't stop there. The ever more pervasive becomes invasive, as nanotechnology – devices on the scale of a billionth of a metre – enters our lives. To gain some idea of the vast implications of its arrival, imagine trying to explain the potential of plastics to the medieval inhabitant of a wattle-and-daub hut or a castle. But it's not just that the material world will have very different properties and possibilities. The impact of nanotechnology touching, as it will, on every aspect of life from crime prevention to energy conservation to healthcare is almost too breathtaking and impossible to contemplate.

One of the strangest scenarios is that of a brain and body now really opened up to the outside, as nanotechnological devices beyond your skin ensure that levels of hormones, glucose and protein, and blood pressure, are all fed into a second-by-second read-out of the state you are in. Nano-technology is not promising, or threatening, nanorobots or molecular doctors beavering away in your bloodstream; but it *does* offer the prospect of completely novel ways of treating disease and devices for precise, targeted drug delivery. Thanks to the unprecedentedly tiny size of the microscopic implants, drugs might in some cases be con-tinuously delivered over long periods of time, revolutioniz-ing treatment.

Brain cells – neurons – appear to flourish on silicon chips. And this unlikely liaison can also work the other way around: silicon implants can have a powerful effect on brain malfunction. We shall see in more detail later how an implant in the brain can transform the life of a quadriplegic by intervening at the erstwhile mysterious and elusive step from thinking to action. But for now, perhaps it is enough just to ponder on the wide-ranging implications of crossing this final frontier. 'Between the idea and the reality . . . falls the Shadow' runs the line in T. S. Eliot's famous poem 'The Hollow Men'. Could neuroscience finally be shortening that shadow?

The brain itself has until now been the final bastion against medical science, not only in clinging on to the secrets of schizophrenia, depression and dementia but more immediately in resisting treatments. Walled in as it is within the thick bone of the skull, the brain is also isolated less obviously, but much more powerfully and subtly, by tight-fisted blood vessels that barricade against indiscriminate trafficking of chemicals with the rest of the body. Yet now not just nanotechnology but biotechnology is overcoming this final hurdle. Drugs acting as Trojan horses can sneak medication into the brain to go only as, where and when it is needed; genetic technologies can help with the conceptualization of new types of treatment; stem cell therapy is introducing a whole new 'regenerative' approach, by which ailing cells can be replaced by healthy new ones; and all in all the number of strategies for pharmacological treatment of disease is set to rise tenfold, from some four hundred basic targets for medication throughout the whole body to approximately four thousand.

Needless to say, it's not all plain sailing into a clear, bright horizon. One of the many ethical issues that biotechnology is forcing upon us is the question of where to draw the line between therapy and lifestyle: for example, is it best *never* to be sad? And what goals or scenarios do we actually wish to reach in our lifestyle – assuming they were ever technically possible – by having a better memory, by being more clever or by being less shy? And what, after all, would mental and physical perfection actually be?

Yet even assuming that biotechnology *could* deliver a completely healthy human, with no physical defects and a bright brain, the questions don't stop there. Modern medicine will ensure that the usual cruel criteria for assessing someone's age – health and appearance – will no longer be so instantly revealing; but other milestones of passing through life will be removed as well. Take reproduction, until now limited to the generations between adolescence and middle age, and again easily demarcating the different phases of life. Perhaps in the not too distant future, genetic material will be extracted from any cell in the body of anyone of any age: by IVF then, at least in theory, anyone of any age or sexual orientation would be able to have a child with anyone else. Leaving aside for the moment the obvious ethical debate that such a scenario mandates, an important knock-on effect would be the homogenizing of generations. Imagine an adulthood stretching over decades where everyone was healthy, looked similar, had children of highly variable ages and had similar, more standardized experiences, mainly removed from the 'real' world in favour of its cyber-counterpart.

In ways, then, that we could never have imagined, the technologies of the twenty-first-century are challenging the most basic compartments by which we have made sense of our environment, and lived as individuals within it. Information technology, nanotechnology and biotechnology are blurring or even breaching every dichotomy that has until now transcended any particular culture, and held firm for every human society: the real versus the unreal; the old versus the young; the self versus the outside world.

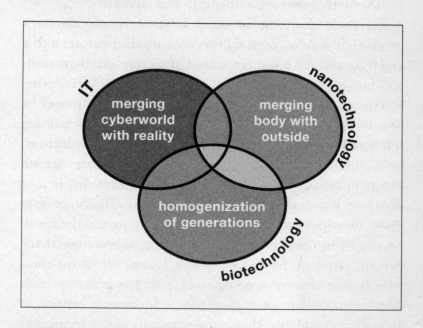

Perhaps the *simultaneous* blurring of all these compartments could have still wider implications for how we see the world, our lives and our identities. So where do we go from here? There is no precedent in the history of our species that might give us a clue as to what might happen, and what would now be the best course of action. Yes, of course the situation could be alarming – but only if we allow it to be so. The early twenty-first century could also be one of the most exciting eras to be alive – the first era in which we have the time and the technological tools to determine the kind of society that will realize our full potential as individuals, to the maximum.

First are the immediate issues of education, work and healthcare: what do we actually wish to achieve? But tied in closely with these monumental, and deceptively simple, questions is the issue of what kind of people the next generation will be, what will be their needs, their problems and their abilities? And what kind of society will they want, and be able, to form?

The reason any options at all can even present themselves here is that the human brain is not like the heart or the liver, fixed and predictable in what it delivers from one century, or even from one millennium, to the next. Rather, we are about to see how the brain, especially of humans, is in a constant dialogue with the outside world, evaluating everything that happens in terms of previous personal experience, and in turn being updated by the happenings of the present moment. So if, as I'm suggesting, life in the mid-twenty-first century is going to be radically different from anything that has ever gone before in human history, it follows that we, or rather the generations about to succeed us, will be very different too.

You and I are about to set out on a wildly ambitious journey where we try to discover not so much 'how the brain works', but rather how your brain and mine gives each of us a sense of unique individuality. We shall trace how banal brain cells develop into a holistic brain, a brain that in turn becomes personalized into a 'mind'. Then we'll see just how sensitive and therefore vulnerable that mind is to the happenstance of your particular life narrative.

These steps will be key to exploring one of the most important questions of all for our current world: how the new technologies might impact on our brains in completely novel ways, thereby actually transforming us as people. There will be a range of possible future scenarios, the potential for different types of identity. One possibility is that human nature is inviolate and that, after all, we shall stay as we are, as struggling individuals. Let's call this scenario the 'Someone' option. But then the new technologies, saturating and penetrating your brain and body as never before, could offer the alternative of endless fun, of physical ease and sensual gratification, as the passive recipient of the senses. I'm calling this the 'Nobody' scenario. Finally, as an alternative to either egoism or hedonism a collective identity with a clear narrative and direction might seem much more appealing. This is the 'Anyone' scenario.

Some, perhaps all, of these options will turn out to be radical and unprecedented, perhaps even unpalatable, or, then again, exciting. But what is certain is that if at least we try to understand them and their potential we shall have more chance of shaping the kind of society more specifically to become the kind of individuals, who will truly make the most of the twenty-first century.

2

THE BRAIN

What am I expecting? It's over thirty years ago, and I'm edgy and uncomfortable. Unforgiving fluorescent strips remorselessly show up every grey square metre of the practical class laboratory. There is a whiff of disinfectant chemicals wafting in the air. Banks and banks of benches stretch out to blank walls festooned with the familiar essentials: safety posters, cupboards of tubing and funnels and glass measuring cylinders, the occasional sink. And there we all are, kitted out in stiff white coats, paradoxically excited and cynical, awaiting our first hands-on class in neuro-anatomy. Or, to be more specific, our first dissection of the human brain.

I hadn't realised you *could* study the brain in any meaningful way: surely it was just there, a constant presence behind your eyes and between your ears, encased and inaccessible in your skull. Unlike the heart or lungs, the head has no mechanical moving parts. I don't understand how cutting up a dead brain is going to reveal how it 'works'.

So, what am I expecting and hoping to know? Agreed, the phrase 'how the brain works' trips off the tongue easily enough; yet if you think about it, the question as it stands is really quite meaningless. After all, it's not like asking how a car works, or even a computer. In the case of machines there is a clear output, the end result of a chain of tangible, observable, predictable events. But the brain doesn't have to have an observable output. It's 'working' when you're just thinking and when you're asleep – though there's surely an enormous and intriguing difference between what must be going on in conscious versus unconscious states.

It's actually hard even to specify what the brain 'does', what function it has – because it does everything, or at least underpins everything going on in your body. Throughout your life, twenty-four hours a day, seven day a week, your brain is monitoring the dips and surges of glucose in your blood, the distension of your stomach, the pressure in your bowels, the beat of your heart. And every single moment it's coordinating the interplay of your vital organs, inter-facing with your immune and hormonal systems, and orchestrating the tens of thousands of chemical reactions and interactions that enable you not just to stay alive but to run for a bus, dream, remember, reason, plot, grieve, fantasize and love. Above all, your brain gives you that unique consciousness that no one else can hack into, and on top of that a self-consciousness: a continuing experience of your own special identity.

Enter the demonstrators with trolleys of white plastic Tupperware-type tubs, now being handed out, one to each pair. They instruct us to put on the surgical gloves from the cardboard boxes in front of us, a tight second skin that immediately dulls the intimacy of my hands with the outside world. We're wearing gloves because the tubs contain the brains that are bathed in formalin, a colourless but highly toxic liquid. Formalin will preserve the dead brain for ever, and simultaneously has converted it from its original state of soft-boiled egg consistency to something much firmer and thus easier to dissect. We prise open the lids of our tubs. I roll up my starched sleeve above my elbow and plunge my hand into the reeking contents, my groping fingers making contact with an object. And now I am holding in one hand what was once the essence of a human being.

What would happen if I wasn't wearing the gloves? If the brain tissue, though firmed up by the formalin, none the less gave way under my inexpert heavy hand and some of it lodged under my fingernail? Would that have been what someone loved with? Or perhaps it was a memory, or a bad habit. . . . The enormity of the task ahead makes my mind reel: how to explain how we think and feel, to understand how we are so very different from each other, how we live out tragic, wonderful, boring and courageous life stories all sealed up in this banal off-white substance that could so easily disintegrate under a fingernail.

Little did I know then that I was at the start of the intellectual journey of a lifetime. And the first, most important concept I was to grasp that morning long ago was that the unique aspect of the brain in my hand, indeed of my brain too, was the power to learn, interact and develop a mind of its own. For more than a hundred thousand years, what has made the human brain so special is our astonishing talent to learn, and thus to change. We don't run particularly fast, we aren't particularly strong, we don't hear or see as well as many other species: but where we excel in the animal kingdom is in our ability to adapt to our environment. No surprise, then, that we occupy more ecological niches than any other species on the planet. This adaptability gives each of us the potential to be different: if you have individual experiences, then you become an individual.

Just think for a moment about, say, the goldfish. If your children had a pet goldfish, and it sadly died, then you could save them from becoming completely traumatized with a kind deception. While they were at school, you could sneak off to the pet shop and purchase another goldfish of similar size and colour: your offspring would know no difference. Callous though it might sound, let's face it, goldfish don't have highly developed personalities. They exhibit no individual repertoire of behaviour that would distinguish one from another. The same could not be said even about a hamster that might have become used to being handled: and you certainly couldn't pull the same trick with a pet cat or dog, nor indeed – however much your child might hope – with their brother or sister.

This shift away from the stereotyped, narrow dictates of the genes is not a crude dichotomy of Nature versus Nurture, but rather a continuum along which genes and the environment impact and influence each other to greater or lesser extents. The goldfish is towards one end of the spectrum, we humans are at the other. Human brains are constantly being shaped through incessant changes in the dynamic configurations of the connections between brain cells, by the ceaseless interaction of genes, diverse factors in the micro-environment of the brain, and in turn by events and chance in the wider, external world. Contrary to what you might occasionally read in the sensationalist press, the genes themselves do *not* set an autocratic agenda but rather are key players in a complex interaction. In fact, while we might expect that a characteristic like being witty or being good at cooking is *not* trapped miraculously inside the interstices of the DNA molecule, it's surprising how even traits that one might assume were impervious to interference from the environment are none the less influenced by it.

A really striking example of Nurture interacting closely with Nature can be seen in a seemingly unlikely observation made a few years ago by Anton Van Dellen and his colleagues, working at the Department of Physiology at Oxford University. The experiment involved mice genetically engineered to have the mouse equivalent of the hereditary movement disorder Huntington's Chorea. This distressing disease is named after the Greek for 'dance' (as in choreography), as the patient is helplessly driven to generate wild, involuntary flinging of the limbs in a grotesque caricature of dance. The underlying problem is the slow but inexorable loss of brain cells in a key brain area relating to movement; this loss or 'neurodegeneration' is in turn directly linked to a single rogue gene. If either of your parents passes the genetic aberration on to you, you yourself are 100 per cent certain of suffering from the disease later in life. Accordingly, Huntington's Chorea is known as a 'single gene' disorder, the only such disorder that specifically causes a problem with the function of the brain.

None the less, this astonishing study demonstrated that, despite the seemingly tight and inextricable link between a gene and a malfunction, the environment could after all make a difference. One group of genetically engineered 'transgenic' mice were kept in 'standard' laboratory housing; but another group, genetically identical and thus equally doomed to develop the mouse equivalent of Huntington's Chorea, lived a different life, spending their days in an 'enriched' environment. Enrichment for a mouse does not of course mean that they are whisked off to some Caribbean resort, but rather allowed happy access to ladders, wheels and other mice.

Before we look at how living the more stimulating life actually made a difference for the mice, a brief note of caution about this 'enrichment' treatment itself. Many behavioural psychologists point out that, for the average rodent living outside a lab cage, such an interactive environment would be normal. The flip-side of this argument is that the animals in the 'standard' lab housing are actually undergoing a form of under-stimulation – in human terms, even deprivation! Yet the important point here is still valid, namely the *difference* between the two environments, and the difference that the two very different experiences might have on how well the mice moved as they aged. What could be the point of such an experiment? After all, the dysfunctional movements that characterise Huntington's Chorea are due to one rogue gene only. Anyone, human or mouse, that has that gene is destined eventually to develop the distressing and debilitating signs.

But now for the surprise: despite the fact that in Huntington's Chorea, unusually for a brain dysfunction, only one gene is at fault, the mice exposed to the more stimulating conditions showed a far more modest impairment, and a far later onset. Even here, therefore, in the case of a single aberrant gene, a mere mouse brain and some unspectacular environmental influences, the interaction with the environment was the key determining issue. The results showed that the mice exposed to the enriched environment took twice as long to develop the same degree of disability as their non-enriched counterparts and, most importantly, remained at that level; meanwhile the under-stimulated mice became five times worse.

But it would be as dangerous now to discount genes, Nature, and swing to the opposite extreme in favour of pure Nurture. Genes *are* necessary for correct functioning of body and brain, but when it comes to determining the individual chemical and anatomical landscape of each individual brain it is important not to confuse necessity with sufficiency. The activation or switching on of a gene will result in the manufacture of a large molecule, a protein. However, we now know that this apparently simple cause and effect is actually far from simple. Even in the humble fruit fly, the activation of one gene can result in any of thirty-eight thousand different proteins. And just as a gene doesn't have a complete function, or dysfunction, locked away inside its molecular framework, neither does any one of the proteins that it eventually ends up making.

Instead, the critical issue is how that particular protein in turn works within the circuitry of the brain, how it changes the communication between certain brain cells known as neurons. Once the cross-talk between neurons changes there will be a knock-on effect in the dynamics of ever larger networks of brain cells, and eventually in a whole brain region.

So before we can go any further, we're going to need a kind of Executive Summary of how brain cells, and hence brains, work. Since it seems so natural to use the analogy of 'talking' and 'networking' of neurons when describing the basic operations of the brain, I've been really tempted to push the analogy of conversations and relationships to its limits. Once I started to jot down the similarities between a person and a neuron, I was myself surprised at how far the parallels would stretch. Neurons and individuals are isolated units, complete in themselves, with their own internal life support systems, so they can adapt to change, and most of the time are in close interaction with others.

Similarities between neurons and people

Neuron	Person
Basic Unit of Brain	Basic Unit of Group/Organization
Contains organelles	Contains organs
Generic yet individual	Generic yet individual
'Plastic'	Adaptable
Gradually makes connections (synapses)	Gradually builds relations
Indirect contact via transmitter, direct touching can occur but rarer	Indirect contact via language, direct touching can occur but rarer

But neurons, like people, can only just about survive – and certainly don't flourish – in isolation. 'No man is an island, entire of itself', John Donne's famous meditation on the interconnected nature of the human condition could just as easily apply to neurons: the brain works through its billions of cells ceaselessly networking with each other. When a neuron is active it generates an electrical blip, a minute electrical voltage lasting a thousandth of a second, that will enable the cell to communicate with its neighbour.

But the first conceptual hurdle here is actually a gap. The problem is this: in the most standard scenario, neurons don't really make contact with each other but are separated by a gap called the synapse, and the electrical blip just cannot breach across this tiny void. An intermediary is necessary to cross between one neuron and another, so a chemical messenger or transmitter is released from one cell and activates the next. As the electrical blip zooms into the end of the neuron it triggers the release of the transmitter, which sails across the synapse and docks into the target cell; and this molecular docking sets off a new electrical blip. The ultimate building-block of brain operations, and therefore the basis of your uniqueness, is this chain of electrical-chemical-electrical events.

Basic analogies between brains and societies

Neuron	Person
Synapse	Relationship
Transmitter	Language
Neuronal Network	Tribe/School/Business
Different Brain Regions	Different Cultures
THE BRAIN	**GLOBAL SOCIETY**

Although I've just compared the physical action of a transmitter to that of a boat, its actual function is much more like a language: an indirect means of communication. Transmitters, like languages, come in many different types, and like languages fit into a taxonomy – though in the case of transmitters this is based on chemical identity, from a tiny gas such as nitric oxide to a large fragment of a protein, a peptide such as the natural opiate enkephalin. But the most important point in all this biochemical chicanery is that the neuron is much more than a passive relay station. When people talk, very few of their conversations consist merely of passing on words, like Chinese Whispers: rather, every conversation is modifying how the listener may subsequently think and behave. And so it is in the brain.

Neurons are designed to have an analogous, proactive role. Inputs from as many as a hundred thousand other neurons can converge on a single cell, so it has to perform some very sophisticated integration of this incoming tide. This means that there will be a massive dilution of any one of the original inputs as it becomes just one of tens of thousands of further inputs; the integrated signal will in turn itself become yet one of tens of thousands of inputs to the next neuron along. So every synapse is refining the final net message, the final collective output from a large group of neurons.

And just as the more you talk to someone the stronger your relationship becomes, so it is with neurons. This strengthening of synapses the more they function was first proposed as a hypothetical mechanism in the nervous system over half a century ago by the visionary psychologist Donald Hebb. Thanks to the neuroscience techniques of the last few decades, we now know much more about the biochemical mechanisms that enable this remarkable phenomenon of strengthening-through-use to come about. Most importantly for our current exploration, the consequences of this adaptability mean that we can start to see how the brain might become personalized. By having different experiences, different connections will strengthen, thereby differentiating one brain from another.

Similarities between synapses and relationships

Synapses	Rrelationships
Strengthen through use	Strengthen through use
Grow stronger with more intense input	Grow stronger with more intense input
Constantly changing	Constantly changing
Most changeable when young	Most changeable when young

Just as a person can change and evolve to an astonishing degree as they live out their life story, so can neurons be highly changeable: neuroscientists refer to this dynamism of neurons as plasticity. Of course this term is technical rather than literal and doesn't mean that neurons, or anything else in the brain, are literally made of plastic: the derivation is from the Greek adjective *plastikos*, to be moulded. And just as we are constantly evolving as people, changing as a result of the subtle, all-important interplay between our genetic predisposition and the diverse events in our environment, so too do the individual neurons in your brain respond, and change, according to the type, strength and frequency of inputs.

Recently there have been some fascinating examples of this neuronal plasticity. Perhaps the best-known study, which captured the attention of the British media a few years ago, concerned London taxi drivers. Unlike most taxi drivers throughout the world they have to pass a very special test, ominously referred to as The Knowledge. The Knowledge is an unusual examination in that it is entirely oral and relies completely on memory. In brief, the benighted candidate has to remember all the streets of central London and to have learnt by heart all the one-way systems and road connections. The expectation is that a passenger will merely need to say, 'Take me to X', and the driver will be able to do so by taking the optimum route, without recourse to a manual but using just their working memory.

The idea behind this study was that the brain might be sufficiently plastic for the brains of London taxi drivers to show up differently in scans compared to those of other people of the same age. More specifically, the question was whether an area of the brain related to working memory (the hippocampus) might be different in the brains of London taxi drivers. And it was. It was bigger. Nor was it the case that perhaps having a larger than normal hippocampus, by serendipity, predisposed you to being a London taxi driver: the difference was more marked the longer the drivers had been engaged in their job.

Another, still more intriguing example of the malleability of our brains comes from a study on an activity far more widespread than driving London taxis: playing the piano. It involved three groups of adult volunteers, none of whom could play the piano. The first group, the controls, as always given the least exciting role, merely coexisted in the same room as a piano for the experimental sessions, which lasted five days. The second group were taught to practise five-finger piano exercises: incredibly, even over the short period of the study their daily brain scans, compared with those of the controls group, showed a significant increase in functional brain territory related to the movement of their digits. But the most astonishing effect of all occurred with the third group: its members were not required to play the piano physically but to imagine that they were performing the exercises. Quite remarkably, the scans of this group were almost indistinguishable from those of the group actually engaged in piano playing. Here, then, is surely an example of a thought or mental event having virtually the same effect – modification of neuronal circuitry – as a physical one, in this case piano playing.

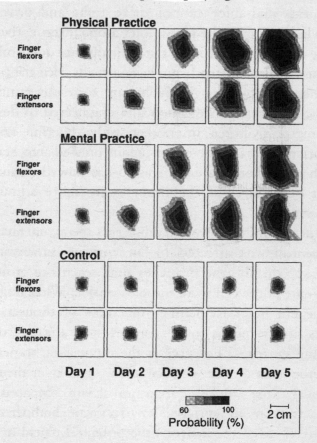

Brain scans showing effects of practicing piano on brain plasticity, and the impact of 'mere' thought

What had actually happened to the neurons in the taxi drivers' and rookie piano players' brains? Brain scans just can't get to that level of detail and obviously, it would be impossible to open up the heads of healthy people and take biopsies. Instead, we can only make progress indirectly by looking in the brains of rodents. Since rats and mice cannot drive taxis and pass The Knowledge or play the piano – let alone imagine they are doing so – a comparable but appropriate form of stimulation is used instead. We have already seen the power of a special type of environment for subverting the genetic destiny of mice genetically engineered to develop Huntington's Chorea. In another study, this time on rats, an enriched environment was again pressed into service. On this occasion, the idea was to see how the synapses might be changed if the brains were more stimulated than usual.

It turned out that even in adult rats the actual shape of the neuron was affected by an enriched environment; more specifically, the branches that reach out from the main part of the cell were more extensive. What might be the benefit here? Remember that tens of thousands of inputs are trying to make contact with the neuron by forming synapses. The greater the number of branches it has, the greater the surface area of that neuron, so obviously the more connections will be possible. Interacting in an enriched environment had therefore effectively given the neurons the potential to make more connections.

Although the rats in this study were adult, such neuronal dynamism is even more remarkable in the younger brain.

Similarly, we humans are at our most impressionable when young, and have the most changeable shifts in quantity and quality of relationships in early childhood. As with people, so it is with neurons. In the young brain, the branches (dendrites) are themselves growing and thus will be most malleable according to whatever inputs are most hardworking and in whatever brain areas.

But we don't just communicate with people in our immediate vicinity: the impact of our conversations has effect over longer distances and to wider audiences. Beyond our nuclear family and close circle of friends, we are also part of a much greater community. This greater community is organized as a kind of nested hierarchy of intimacy, composed of groups of friends and families, in ever wider groupings that feed into each other. Similarly with neurons: each of the immediate synaptic configurations feeds into larger and larger groups, neuronal networks that eventually form part of a distinct brain region, which interlocks with all the other regions to make up the holistic brain.

Similarities between structures of brains and societies

Brain Region	Culture/Tribe/Organization
Distinct, large structure constituted from nested hierarchy of cells-synapses-networks	Distinct, large structure constituted from nested hierarchy of networks
Quasi-permanent, but can be modified by occasional large-scale event (e.g. stroke)	Quasi-permanent, but can be modified by occasional large-scale event (e.g. flood/strike)
Together, make up whole brain	Together, make up global society

i.d.

And the different brain regions, or rather the dynamic neuronal networks of which they are constituted, work in ways comparable to an organization responding to market forces. As an organization grows, it becomes less dependent on the momentary fluctuations of chance events in the outside world, since it has an internal cohesion and strength; similarly with the mature brain. Instead of momentary events leaving their mark equally and unconditionally on the brain connections, a brain with connections already present will mandate more of an interaction. The dynamics of environment and neuronal malleability give rise to an ever-evolving identity, one that is unique and individual, yet an individuality that is constantly transforming.

Similarities in the development of identity

In the mind . . .	In the organization . . .
Neurons become increasingly specialized as network grows	People become increasingly specialized as network grows
. . . and more resistant to change in general function	. . . and more resistant to change in general function
Supernumerary connections atrophy via underuse	Friendships/non-essential posts fade/redundant when not active/needed
Transition from omnipotence of external influences to interaction with environment	Transition from omnipotence of external (e.g. market) forces to interaction with inner resources
Balance of network–environment interaction constantly shifting	Balance of internal-external forces constantly shifting
A unique identity of a brain evolves into a mind	An organization evolves a unique identity

The analogy between brains and groups or organizations can even extend to scenarios when things go wrong. For example, as we shall see in greater detail later, a central problem in schizophrenia is that the patient has an effective excess of a particular transmitter called dopamine. To continue the analogy with language and transmitter, a parallel might be an organization that is ailing because too much time is spent on discussion in meetings. Depression, meanwhile, results from a paucity of a group of specific transmitters such as a chemical cousin of dopamine called serotonin: an analogous situation would be an organization with not enough communication.

Then there is actual death of brain cells; a comparable scenario here would not be, let us hope, necessarily the actual death of key members of the workforce, simply that they leave. But there are two different situations that could result. In the case of diseases such as Alzheimer's or Parkinson's which involve neurodegeneration, the remorseless loss of more and more cells, the situation would become terminal as everyone left and the workforce declined to zero. On the other hand, if the workforce became smaller because of a planned downsizing, then the remaining staff would presumably be expected to compensate and perhaps expand their repertoire.

In the brain, a stroke is far from planned; but the similarity to, say, a downsized workforce is that the surviving neurons can compensate. Why some neurons in some brain regions can retaliate in this way, while other neurons appear so defenceless and vulnerable, is one of the big questions which we shall be examining very soon. And the bigger issue still, the whole starting point of our

Similarities in the process of decline

Dysfunction of Brain	Of Organization
Schizophrenia/depression: a problem caused by too much/too little transmitter	Malfunctional organization: a problem caused by too much/ too little communication
Neurodegeneration: a problem caused by atrophied neuronal connections	Potentially terminal scenario when key individuals leave
Stroke: compensation by remaining neurons possible, depending on extent and location of neuronal loss	Downsized workforce: compensation by remaining employees possible, depending on extent and types of jobs lost

forthcoming journey, is how the generic brain, which as we have just seen is so dynamic, can be personalized into an individual mind. This mind then grows into a thinking self, an individual identity then will last a lifetime. . . . Or will it?

We are going to be looking at the latest cyber-, bio- and nanotechnologies and exploring how they could have an unprecedented impact on our thoughts and feelings. In this way we shall be able to imagine what kind of people our grandchildren might be – or, to be more accurate, we shall be able to speculate on the various options that might be open to them. But before we can do that, we shall have to have an idea of how that oh-so-precious yet elusive individual human mind has, until now, usually developed, or 'lost', or 'blown'. And in order to do that, we shall first need to see how the mechanical workings of the generic brain itself can be subverted.

MANIPULATING THE BRAIN

The burgeoning technologies of the twenty-first century have the potential for bending the brain in new ways and opening it up to manipulation as never before in the history of *Homo sapiens*. The biggest question, at least for me personally, is whether the result of such unprecedented brain changing might be reflected ultimately in an unprecedented transformation in human identity. I am not certain whether, in the long run, such a change would be desirable or not. But I *do* know that the more we question and reflect on the possible long-term, often far-fetched, implications of new ways of intercepting brain operations the greater our chance of harnessing them for the benefit of the generations to come.

The most obvious starting point nowadays in any metamorphosis of humanity is genes; some extreme views assert that it probably ends there too. After all, by intercepting the links between aberrant genes and disease current biotechnology is already opening up vast new possibilities. Molecular biology, coupled with sophisticated and almost instantaneous processing of massive quantities of information ('informatics'), and indeed with computer-driven automation in the experiments themselves, has enabled swift analysis and 'mapping' – the linking of identified genes to specific traits like Huntington's Chorea.

For several decades now, the strategy has been to target the respective rogue genes responsible for the illness in question: so-called gene therapy. But there remains one very big stumbling-block. In order to treat a patient, the therapist would have to access the faulty gene in each one of the tens of trillions of cells that constitute the human body! Various strategies to overcome this problem are currently underway, such as marrow transplants, the use of viruses as Trojan horses (vectors), and bolistics, in which DNA is mixed with tungsten and fired into cells at high speed.

Another, much more remote, possibility is an artificial twenty-fourth chromosome to complement the twenty-three pairs we already have, and which would act like an extra coathanger for genes. This additional chromosome would help make the notion of enhanced genes more feasible at the practical, if not at the dreamed of, functional level: if the new gene were to reside on the new chromosome, it would eliminate the current problem of gene therapy which is that the viral vectors – those viruses acting like Trojan horses – may damage the natural chromosome or interfere with its otherwise normal gene function.

But a far more effective way still of manipulating DNA is to tamper with what is known as the germ-line – to access the genes directly early on in life, in either the sperm or egg, and thereby ensure that any offspring will also have that modified DNA in all the cells of their body. The transgenic mice we met in Chapter 2, all destined to develop Huntington's Chorea, had been so engineered. However, germ-line engineering in humans – the production of transgenic humans with immortalized genetic modifications – is considered unethical and is understandably illegal.

Even so, the problems of targeting non-sperm or non-egg cells might soon become obsolete in the face of a new technology for one-generation germ-line engineering. The new, desirable gene would be introduced into the germ cells (egg or sperm), along with another gene for an enzyme that would destroy it. But for the time being, this killer gene would be switched off. When it came to the moment you wished to reproduce you would take a pill that activated the killer gene, so that the 'unnatural' gene was ejected from your sperm or eggs and therefore not passed on to your baby.

Were such an opportunity to become an everyday reality, the ethical issues and the ensuing regulatory minefield are hard to contemplate in all their ramifications. Who would decide on whether or not the killer gene should be activated? How would we, or 'they', evaluate the implications of allowing the trait to pass on to the next generation? Would such facilitated enhancement be available to all, at taxpayers' expense, or just to the rich? And were the gene to be allowed to 'enhance' the next generation too, would that next generation then have to revisit the issue and review again whether to activate the killer gene? A crucial question, and one without a clear-cut answer, is where to draw the line between remedying a problem and improving on 'normality' – whatever that is.

But you may wish to go one better and not only eliminate a disease: as a prospective parent, might you not jump at the chance of cherry-picking the genes that made up your offspring's character in general? Here, even aside from the very weighty bioethical questions, the most basic issue is the conceptual one of how we relate genes to brain function in the first place. The notion of the gene for almost anything from good housekeeping to being witty is a vastly simplistic shorthand that has insidiously crept into the collective social psyche. In a society which aspires to acquire or avoid a gene for a specific mental trait we could drift towards further, even more radical, lifestyle treatments inspired by genetic technologies.

Now that the monumental scientific milestone of the mapping of the human genome has been achieved, a perhaps understandable enthusiasm has grown for linking genes directly, not just to specific diseases where a glitch in the DNA may well have caused the malfunction, but by extension to sophisticated mental traits. Crucially, for the questions we're asking in this chapter, we would need to know just how much the brain and its processes, and hence your thoughts and feelings, could be swayed by modifying genes. But there is already a huge elephant trap opening up at our feet.

The end-product, a trait, may well be a malfunction that can be traced to a particular genetic cause, rather like a malfunctioning car might be explained by a faulty spark plug. But it is impossible to conceptualize in the opposite direction. Given an isolated spark plug, there would be no intrinsic clues as to how that component might eventually contribute to a fully operational car. By the same token an isolated gene, and the tens of thousands of proteins that can be expressed once it is activated, give little clue as to how those proteins might work in the brain to contribute to a sophisticated predisposition, attitude or personal agenda – eventually your personality.

Such a direct link is only possible when something is

wrong, with highly infrequent single-gene disorders such as Huntington's Chorea; and even then, we've just seen in Chapter 2 how powerfully environmental factors can intervene. An aberrant gene might well be like a faulty spark plug and be the ultimate cause of an aberrant trait; but that doesn't mean to say that the trait depends *exclusively* on that one gene, any more than the complexity of a car can be reduced to an isolated component.

For example, the geneticist Tony Payton has recently related cognitive decline to deviations in genes linked not directly to mental activity itself, but to malfunctioning in a transmitter, serotonin. Yet we still cannot trace the precise sequence of events between the release and action of this particular transmitter at different synapses throughout the brain, and final mental function. The bad spark plug prevents the car working, but there is far more to a car than that. Genes are as necessary to mental function as spark plugs are to cars, but not in themselves sufficient.

An amusing but persuasive analogy that illustrates this highly indirect link between genes and mental function – one introduced to me by the geneticist Gaby Dover – is the ingenious self-opening umbrella originally devised by Rube Goldberg. This highly impractical invention enables an umbrella to open automatically when it rains: you do not need your hands at all, though there is a high price to pay . . . Rain falls on a prune, (a crude analogy with gene activation) which swells and thereby pushes up a lever which flicks on a lighter which lights a candle, which in turn boils water in a kettle. When the steam from the kettle blows a whistle, it scares a monkey who jumps on a swing. As the swing rocks back and forth, so a scythe attached to the string cuts through a string anchoring a balloon, which consequently rises in the air. Since the balloon is also attached to strings tied to a cage door, the door opens. Little birds then fly out of the cage, and since they are tied to the umbrella, the umbrella opens! In our analogy, this is equivalent to any specific mental trait.

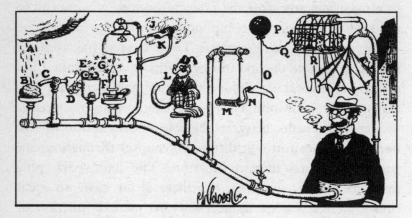

An analogy for the highly indirect link between gene activation and conscious states of mind

So, when everything is just fine, how could we ever go about linking a gene directly to a nebulous character trait? One approach is twin studies: identical twins are, after all, human clones with identical genes – in contrast to non-identical twins who originated from different fertilized eggs and therefore have different sets of genes. In such investigations, the idea is to try and disentangle the influence of the environment by studying the relatively rare cases of twins reared apart.

However, the rationale is tricky to apply. For example, in a comparison of identical twins living apart, original estimates of the inheritability of IQ were around 70 per cent. If the comparison was between sets of identical and non-identical twins where each pair lives together, the environment in each case would be standard. Any respective difference between the sets of twins, the rationale runs, would therefore have to be genetic: in this case the estimate of the inherited contribution is 50 per cent. This number falls even lower when considering an important, but often overlooked, factor: if you include in your calculations the issue that all twins, even those reared apart, do have a shared environment for a short but highly critical time – the same womb – then the degree of IQ attributed to genes falls to some 20 per cent!

Moreover, it is surely likely that each twin would have been brought up in a similar socio-economic background and in the same country. Eerie anecdotes of twins reared remotely yet having similar dispositions and identical choices in clothes or cars don't seem to take account of the contribution of similar cultural influences; nor indeed is there ever mention of the behaviours, choices and tastes that the twins do *not* share.

But that said, surely genes *do* play a part in our mental make-up. After all, certain talents and dispositions, for example musical ability, seem to run in families; moreover, child prodigies are just that because they have abilities not seen at such a tender age in their peers. Their talent, including the motivation, say, to practise six or seven hours a day, couldn't be something that they were simply taught. Such initial proclivities often seem to come 'from nowhere': it is likely that the one-off admixture of that particular child's genes might be a relevant factor, rather than any one isolated, autonomous gene. But in any event, the inextricable interaction of highly indirect and multiple genetic dispositions with a conducive and supportive environment would be impossible to deconstruct. Not only that; not *all* musicians, writers, and artists have come from families where those abilities were prominent, or where the talents shone through at a premature stage.

In any case, if even a concept such as IQ is complex and controversial – which it is – how can we define different and specific 'mental' traits? It is almost impossible to describe being witty, for example, in terms of a simple behaviour or a standard test that could in turn relate directly to a brain mechanism such as arousal, or activation of serotonin systems, or a hyper-functioning brain area. And even if we could do that, such a mechanism or brain region activity could not reduce to a single gene. Further, we must be careful not to lump all mental traits together equally. Can we be sure that exceptional musical talent is describable in the same way, by the same genre of biological brain mechanisms (even if we knew what they were), as being kind or being witty?

A mental trait such as 'creativity' or 'being kind' is usually an umbrella, operational definition for a whole raft of talents, reactions, interactions and end results. The educationalist Howard Gardner attempts in *Extraordinary Minds* to discover the all-important features common to figures such as Mozart, Freud and Virginia Woolf. He rejects the idea that special ability is even attributable in isolation to any individual, but argues instead that 'extra-ordinariness' emerges as a result of the interaction of the individual with his or her discipline, and indeed with others who will then evaluate the contribution in question and appreciate that it really *is* special. Freud, for example, changed his area of scientific focus several times, most notably from neurology, before embracing and making his own the fledgling discipline of psychoanalysis; only then did his unique talents become widely recognized.

Genes are necessary but not sufficient and, as we saw just now, are inextricably interdependent on factors in the environment. But as the twenty-first century unfolds these key considerations will not stop some attempting to select traits during IVF, before the embryo is implanted in the womb, nor stop others from selling their genes – their sperm or eggs – on the assumption that whatever physical or mental prowess they might have would be guaranteed to the would-be parent purchaser. Similarly, others might dream in the future of genetic enhancement of a desired trait, such as a higher IQ, even though we've just seen how it is impossible to trace a direct link between a single gene and a complex mental trait such as any cognitive ability.

But although such ideas are still not a practical reality for the healthy, when it comes to specific diseases biotechnology is none the less opening up new approaches to diagnosis and therapy which could manipulate the brain and be with us much sooner. One of the most hotly debated at the moment is stem cell therapy.

Stem cell therapy offers a particularly exciting and realistic prospect of a completely new type of treatment, as well as providing a very valuable tool to gain a better understanding of diseases such as Parkinson's, with the ultimate goal of developing more effective drugs. The rationale is completely different from conventional treatments, however: not to treat the symptoms, but to harness regenerative biological mechanisms so that new cells are produced and ailing cells are supported by the natural chemicals that are subsequently produced. This approach really could amount, not just to a treatment, but actually to a cure. It would not merely be replacing the chemicals that are lost as a result of cell death, but the cells themselves, from the microscopic ball of some two hundred that make up the early-stage embryo. Embryonic stem cells are extraordinary as they have the capacity to produce every single type of cell in the body. Many of the chemical and micro-environmental signals that determine their fate are now known. Thus we are able to manufacture the type of cells that degenerate in Parkinson's disease, and the different type of cells that are lost, in a different part of the brain, in Alzheimer's. By introducing such cells into the appropriate environment within the brain, the idea is that they will effectively *become* those lost neurons.

But there are potential technical problems which, in the heat of the debate on ethical issues, are often overlooked. One possible difficulty is that stem cells, in an uncontrolled state, might divide and so proliferate and constitute a tumour. To date there is no clinical evidence that this has occurred, and in any event strategies to overcome the problem are well advanced: for example, it could be possible to manipulate stem cells so they only divide at a few degrees hotter than would normally be the case in the living brain. Another way would be the initiation of neuronal 'suicide genes' if the cell attempts pathological division.

Yet a further issue is that the chemical messengers produced by the implanted stem cells may be excessive and inappropriate compared to the normal levels otherwise produced in the brain. On the other hand, it is more likely that brain cells, once they are in place, will behave like their naturally occurring predecessors, and release chemicals at normal levels, as and when they are stimulated and interacting in their normal environment. And in any event, the excessive amounts of chemical messenger released as a result of conventional drugs would be far more likely to go beyond the range seen with stem cells.

Finally, the method of delivery might seem to be problematic, surely necessitating major brain surgery. In fact this is not the case. With so-called stereotactic neurosurgery, the procedure can be performed under local anaesthetic. Only a small hole is made in the skull, and a fine needle introduced, using precise three-dimensional coordinates – a little like drilling for oil: the diseased area can be specifically targeted and the injection of cells kept strictly localized.

However, the general problem remains that the special location of the brain, locked away as it is in its bony fortress, prevents a simple importing of the technologies and strategies otherwise viable elsewhere in the body: stem cell therapy for the brain thus presents unique technological constraints and challenges. But this is where nanotechnology might have answers. This relatively new science, which we touched on in Chapter 1, involves the study and application of materials that have at least one surface less than a billionth of a metre thick: it is the science of materials so small that they acquire unusual properties, and can be used in highly novel ways.

But even beyond changing the properties of matter, nanotechnological devices could sneak into parts of the body that larger objects or chemical systems just couldn't reach. For example, nanoparticles could deliver substances to the brain when standard drugs cannot penetrate easily. Alternatively, there are nanoshells linked to specific antibodies that target tumours. These nanoshells comprise an ultra-thin metallic – for example, gold – layer that enables an optimally sensitive reaction to light: when hit by infra-red light, they heat up to destroy the growths selectively. Still further into the future, nanotechnology is promising not merely novel medicines and novel access but the potential for new types of monitoring and screening devices that could signal key genes being activated at a certain time, or could detect other types of suspect disease-related substances in the body.

But we needn't wait for nanotechnology in order to invade the brain. Implanting silicon chips into the brain is already increasingly plausible, as is the converse of placing brain cells on chips. Strange though it might sound, this carbon–silicon interfacing occurs quite readily. Neurons are superbly efficient electronic components: they have had the whole of evolution to become so, to develop the properties required to generate the minute and varied voltages – those electrical blips – that they use for signalling to each other. Moreover carbon, an essential part of all living matter, and silicon, the mainstay material of the integrated circuit, are actually close neighbours on the Periodic Table of the chemical elements. It might come as no surprise, then, that neurons can now actually be grown on integrated circuits, forming the prototype for what in the future might be regarded as a workaday 'neurochip'.

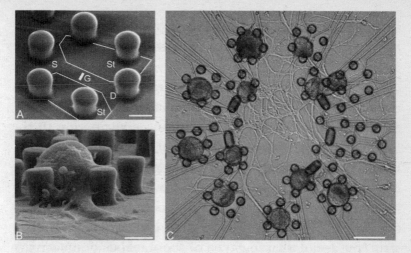

A nerve cell in contact with silicon microstructure (B) on a standard circuit board (A) and an overview of several such clusters (C).

And if brains on chips are possible, what about chips in the brain? A technique developed by Brazilian neuroscientist Miguel Nicolelis consists of implanting a microchip into the brain to translate the nerve pulses into electrical pulses, making it possible for the recipient to 'will' the movement of robotic prosthetic arms. Studies in rats and monkeys now show the animals 'willing' a robotic arm to move to achieve a certain task, rather than physically exerting their own muscles to gain the same reward.

Do you remember from Chapter 2 the effects on the brain of merely imagining playing the piano? Amazingly, a mere thought appears to be able to drive the growth of those all-important neuronal branches (dendrites), so that neurons can then make more connections, just as happens with rats in an enriched environment. But what is it about a thought itself, a highly subjective process, which translates into a physical change in the brain? How might 'just thinking' operate a robotic arm, or over a few days change the landscape of brain scans as with the imaginary piano players?

A clue to answering this very tricky question came a while ago from some classic experiments from the American Benjamin Libet. Libet's enduring contribution to the brain sciences has been to show that the electroencephalograph (EEG) recording brain wave patterns will change a fraction of a second before a subject 'decides' to press a button. It is this change in activity which has been subverted by Miguel Nicolelis for indirectly driving a robotic arm. But could the same type of spontaneous brain activity also apply to understanding the 'imagination'?

The answer has to be a qualified 'Yes'. First, we know that when we dream and are doing nothing, receiving nothing from our senses, our brains are perfectly capable of generating a rich inner world dependent presumably on no more than residual, intrinsic neuronal activity. In fact, thanks to the work of Stephen Kosslyn we already know that certain brain regions are active – albeit different from those involved in dreaming – when we imagine something. Once a group of neurons are active, they will release transmitters and activate other neurons; a network will be established which, if it persists and works hard, will eventually change the strength of the synapses or drive the proliferation of branches (dendrites), increasing in turn the ability of the neurons in question to make more connections, which will eventually show up on brain scans. Just as with the piano players and the taxi drivers.

Of course, the truly big question that really nags away at me is where the initial act of mental volition comes in: who/

what/where causes those initial intrinsic neurons to be 'spontaneously' active, which then leads to the 'will' to press the button, or to imagine a particular scenario like playing the piano? In the case of an experimental instruction, 'Imagine playing the piano', perhaps we can more easily trace the cause–effect: your brain is, after all, responding to an input. At a verbal stimulus, certain connections and associations will be triggered in a brain.

In the case of 'free will', however, we bump up against the stark reality that there is no separate 'you', apart from all your neurons. What starts you off, or rather activates your neurons in the first place? The only speculative suggestion I can make is that as a result of incessant, even though indirect, interactions with the environment certain patterns of connectivity are established that might appear to be 'spontaneously' active because the link between their activation and the outside world is very indirect and remote. There may be some tortuous chain of events that then leads, even in dreaming, to some neuronal groups remaining active; but it is the history of your particular brain that will have predisposed certain cells to carry on working long after the initial trigger has gone. And the more cells work, the more your brain scans will show a change.

There is clear potential here for paralysed patients. Recently, the neurosurgeon Leigh Hochberg and his colleagues implanted a 96-micro-electrode array in the primary motor cortex, the part of the outer layer of the brain most directly related to the generation of movement. Hochberg and his colleagues then showed that merely thinking about moving, namely the *intended* hand motion, can modulate electrical activity in this region as long as three years after spinal cord injury. Indeed, a patient paralysed from the neck down is now able to 'will' the opening of simulated e-mail, operate the TV, and, most useful of all, open and close a prosthetic hand, as well as performing rudimentary actions with a multi-jointed robotic arm.

But what about the other way around? Could signals be sent into the brain and simulate the 'feel' of touch, for example? The possibility is there in the future. Meanwhile, any implications for abusing this technique and directly sending in the e-mail – along with all the attendant spam – to deluge all your neurons might be fun to speculate upon in theory; but the practical prerequisite of surgery targeting appropriately the multiple, diverse and as yet unidentifiable sites in the brain must surely consign such a scenario to the realms of science fiction. But the exciting, truly central, issue is this: the brain sciences are now demonstrating that there is no distinction between mental and physical events, that every thought has a physical correlate, even if we understand poorly as yet the precise nature of that correlation, and even more remotely its causal relationship. For me personally, even just challenging the old dichotomy of mind versus brain, of mental versus physical, is one of the most important achievements of current neuroscience.

And we can go further still, at least theoretically. One seemingly far-fetched, though plausible, scenario could lead on from the now familiar and established technology of cochlear implants in the ear. Such devices are of course well established: four thousand or so in the UK and eighty thousand hearing-impaired individuals worldwide have benefited from being fitted with these devices, which enable sound waves to be converted into electrical signals directly, thus performing the job of the damaged cochlea. Interestingly enough, a complementary newer technology operates in the reverse direction: in paralysed patients who cannot use their mouth muscles to speak, a prototype device now enables the electrical signals generated in their brain when they wish to talk to be converted into sounds. This device can convert the surface brain waves detectable by electrodes on the scalp into sounds known as phonemes – the building-blocks of language.

Clearly, a lot of refinement is needed before the electrical brain signals can be transformed into words and whole sentences; but the basic concept is possible, at least hypothetically. Over coffee one morning, my colleague Martin Westwell took the idea a step further by imagining what might happen if these two technologies could be combined. Martin speculated that anyone, not simply those who are deaf, might be fitted with a cochlear implant and at the same time with the surface electrodes for turning brain waves into sounds. Such an individual would no longer need to use their cochlea *or* their mouths for, respectively, hearing and speaking; but the main point this time would be that radio controls could be attached so that the electrical signals coming in during hearing, and the electrical signals going out for speech, could be transmitted across any distance using radio signalling, and ultimately the internet: in essence, mind reading!

Meanwhile, Simone Rossi and Paolo Rossini are manipulating the very thought processes themselves, using transmagnetic stimulation (TMS). They have shown that different types of TMS can interfere with the higher brain functions that require the cooperation of different brain areas and complex neuronal networks. As yet, the effects of TMS are short-lived and the underlying mechanism isn't understood. But current evidence is suggesting that TMS induces a dynamic rearrangement of synapses in the stimulated network, with a concomitant change in cognitive performance. Here lies a clear potential application in the near future for rehabilitation of motor, perceptual and cognitive functions.

It's not just thoughts, but feelings too, that might be directly monitored and modified by direct electrical recordings and stimulation. Certain patients suffer, for whatever reason, severe, unremitting pain that appears to have no clear cause but may originally have been provoked in some part of their body. Yet even when such causes have ceased entirely, for example after shingles, the spontaneous activity of the central pain network within the brain may continue to cause agony, as it can even when there never was a peripheral cause of the pain, such as the 'phantom' limb pain that can occur following amputation.

In Oxford, neurologist John Stein and neurosurgeon Tipu Aziz have been recording electrical 'signatures' of such patients' pain through deep brain-stimulating electrodes. When they stimulate electrically through these electrodes, the patient's feelings of pain reduce greatly. But the big problem is that in order for pain to be alleviated in this way the patient needs to undergo brain surgery for the implantation of the electrodes. However, current work is suggesting that such dramatic procedures might not be necessary in the future. A similar 'signature' of pain can be obtained using magnetoencephalography (MEG). MEG works by detecting the magnetic fields generated by active brain cells, and can display very fast, sub-second events that would have been missed by the more conventional imaging techniques that only register much slower events, over several seconds.

Just as debilitating as chronic pain, and arguably much more widespread, is depression. In fact, the two often go together: in what might seem heartless yet scientifically rigorous studies where subjects are given mildly painful stimulation, depressed individuals have been shown to have a lower pain threshold – they feel pain more easily – than the non-depressed controls. According to current records, one-third of depressed patients are not helped much by prescribed drugs and are therefore trapped in a tired, numb, pointless, helpless hell. However, it turns out that, while alleviating pain, deep brain stimulation can also lighten depression. Yet few would suggest carrying out such drastic surgery for a disorder of mood alone. But now the non-invasive technique of TMS could help relieve depression where drugs fail; this surely would be a more realistic treatment, administered painlessly from the surface of the skull. The therapeutic benefit to society of such sensational advances, free of any of the side-effects inevitably associated with drugs, would be clear – especially given the alarming escalation in cases of depression.

But there remains the deeper issue with which we started this chapter. These new techniques for brain-bending that are starting to become possible – ranging, as we have seen, from gene manipulation to stem cells therapy to nanotechnology to implants to non-invasive stimulation – all have the power also to interfere directly with the thoughts and feelings of 'normal' healthy individuals. Where will future generations draw the line between alleviation of mental suffering and unremitting happiness? Thoughts and feelings are driven primarily by what has happened to you already, and the values with which you assess the world, in turn based on previous experiences and your memory of them. We have already seen how the human brain is exquisitely sensitive to any and every event and experience that impinges on it. So how might individual identity – the mind itself – arise from the biochemical banality of the exquisitely dynamic yet vulnerable physical brain?

4

DEVELOPING THE MIND, AND LOSING IT

One day I was struck by the admittedly obvious but also incredible realization that, ever since *Homo sapiens* evolved, every single member of the human race must have possessed a completely unique brain, never duplicated in over tens of thousands of years. How else could each human being have been unique? As every single one of our predecessors has lived out their particular life story, the happenstance of experiences has literally left its mark on each and every brain. And as each of our predecessors has followed their own particular narrative, so the accumulation of a morass of events has in turn acted as an ongoing frame of reference for evaluating whatever comes along next. Could this be the key to unlocking that most contentious of issues: the physical basis of the mind?

Sometimes human beings lose their minds — be they drunk, drugged, delirious, ecstatic or simply mad. All are very different conditions, but with this one crucial factor in common: something very special is missing. But what is it exactly that has vanished? Certainly not consciousness, that first-hand, subjective experience of the world. After all, in mindless moments our brains still function: all senses are present if not entirely correct, as the final perspective on what is happening around you is a little distorted compared with 'normal'. Not only that, but you can move and control your muscles, even if with a little less inhibition or with greater hesitancy. So 'loss' of mind is not the same as loss of the most basic brain functions of senses-input, movement-output. And the converse holds: a paralysed patient, or a blind or deaf individual, still has a mind comparable to that of anyone else, even if crucial brain functions for interfacing with the outside world are not operational.

What then is this 'mind', which is so bound up with the physical brain but so intuitively distinct from it? In the past philosophers, indeed most people, liked to think separately of the generic 'brain' as though it was a very different entity from 'mind' – a 'physical' thing as opposed to a 'mental' something. So while no one has ever had a problem with what and where the brain was, and with perceiving it as an obvious physical object, the very concept of oh-so-familiar yet intriguingly insubstantial 'mental' events has caused unresolved intellectual agonizing for centuries.

An immediate difficulty is that those elusive 'mental' phenomena are just that – so hard to define objectively. But we're going to see now whether perhaps that newcomer on the block, the neuroscientist, can offer a different angle on the issue, a new way of trying to understand and define the mind. First, we'll try to trace how we literally 'develop' our minds, and then see what common factors might underlie the diverse neurological and psychiatric scenarios in which someone 'loses their mind'. Whatever it may be, the crucial something that is in all cases 'lost' might be the flip-side of what could be, essentially, a physical basis for the 'mind': something arising from, but distinct from, the generic brain.

So how does our species even start to develop a mind in the first place? Although a human baby is born with a brain pretty much the same size as that of a chimp, it's the growth of the connections between the brain cells – the synapses – that accounts, in the first two years of life, for the astonishing growth of the brain that is our peculiar *Homo sapiens* birthright. It's at this time that neuronal connections are rapidly formed, matching up with the development of the different functions related to different parts of the outer layer of the brain, the cortex. This cortex, named after the Latin for 'bark', wraps around the brain like bark wraps around a tree. The primary areas are those linked directly to the processing of each of the senses and to the generation of movement, and it is these that are the first to show signs of rapid formation of neuronal connections.

The remaining (association) cortex is more loosely related to thinking (cognitive) functions. One of the first lessons in neuroscience is that the more sophisticated the species, the greater the surface area of cortex. This expansion of the cortex through evolution means that something must be done to cram it into the tight confines of a skull that in turn remains constrained in size, due to the need to pass down the birth canal. In species where the cortex is expansive, therefore, Nature has crumpled it up, rather like a large sheet of paper that must fit into a balled fist. Accordingly, the surface of the brain of animals such as rats and mice is smooth; that of the cat and dog more wrinkled; and finally the surface of the primate brain resembles nothing so much as the outer coating of a walnut.

A second phase of brain development lasts until early adolescence, and is characterized by the formation of a great number of 'exuberant' or easily forming connections. This heightened dynamism is exquisitely sensitive to the environment, the plasticity that we've been discussing: as a result, some of the very early connections remain while others disappear. Yet even if they aren't in immediate use, dormant connections remain. Just in case. The Jesuits' famous claim, 'Give me a child until he is seven, and I will give you the man', is clearly an accurate description of this time of maximal malleability.

The final phase of late adolescence is a time of more radical synaptic pruning, in which almost 50 per cent of connections will be lost as erstwhile functions that were distributed widely throughout the cortex become more localized and modular. For example, the bizarre phenomenon of synaesthesia, the ability to mix up the senses and 'see' a sound or 'hear' a colour, is more frequent in children than in adults, perhaps due to supernumerary connections between parts of the cortex that would normally be related to processing, respectively, either vision or hearing. A more mainstream example, however, is language: different aspects of linguistic skills end up 'lateralized' in the adult brain, with grammatical processing and sentence construction linked to activity in the left hemisphere, and prosody, the overall feeling and meaning behind a complete statement, associated more with the right hemisphere.

Although this sensitivity to the outside environment, this plasticity, remains a feature of all brains of all ages, there will be a time in life when they are more plastic, more readily influenced than at other times. These windows of opportunity or critical periods are a key feature of developmental biology: there are adventitious times not just for growth of neuronal connections as a result of use, of activity, but for functions as wide-ranging as glucose utilization, vulnerability and addiction. These key intervals, at a time when even underused synapses are present and have yet to be pruned, would account, for example, for that familiar phenomenon of a child learning a second language without the accent that will otherwise immediately betray the parents' native tongue. Similarly, music training needs to start before ten years of age if the child is ever likely to acquire absolute pitch.

'It is only from the sixth or seventh year onwards, in many cases only after the tenth year, that our lives can be reproduced in memory as a connected chain of events.' So wrote Sigmund Freud of the loss of memory relating to many early experiences as we grow up. It's almost as though the period of excessive plasticity in childhood is a one-way street: there is huge potential for anything and everything to leave its mark, almost literally, on the brain. As the brain matures, however, we start to evaluate the world in terms of what has gone before: now there is a two-way street between the outside and our personal memories. Many of the haphazard experiences, the deluge of disconnected events that were the hallmark of our early years, are 'forgotten' as the synapses that subserved them are pruned away in favour of a clear, connected, conceptual framework for how we see ourselves, the rest of the world and our life story as a 'connected chain': a narrative. But an increasingly prevalent tragedy is that this sequence of events can be thrown into reverse gear.

We are born, in the words of the great American psychologist William James, into a 'booming, buzzing confusion'. Accordingly, we evaluate the world in purely sensory terms: how sweet, how cold, how loud, how bright. . . . After all, we know nothing beyond what we are actually experiencing. And as we have just seen, the 'primary' sensory areas of the cortex, which process the pure sensations, are the most precocious in development.

But gradually the generic, abstract sensations will start to coalesce: the various sights and sounds and textures and smells come together in what we gradually recognize as a face or a particular object. The more cognitive areas of the cortex are starting to develop, and the brain is becoming more streamlined and modular in function. And – just as with piano playing or taxi driving – the more that face or object features in your early life the more neuronal connections (associations) it will forge; in other words, the more that face or object will 'mean' something to you personally. You can then start to navigate the world, not as the passive recipient of your senses but in an incessant dialogue between your brain and the outside world. You start to see and experience things and people in the light of previous experience. No longer will you necessarily place a premium on the brightest, the loudest or the most novel sensation, but rather on what something 'means' to you in particular. You shift emphasis from a sensory to a cognitive take on the world.

Now imagine that process in reverse. Gradually the particular things and people which had a personal significance become reduced to more generic faces and objects, and then dismantled further to become abstract sensations: the world has ceased to have a meaning. No longer can you understand what is happening, because you cannot interpret anything in the light of previous experience. You end up as confused, disorientated and frightened as a toddler: this is dementia.

We can actually see this mirror image of development and degeneration respectively in the growth and atrophy of neurons. The main part of the cell, the cell body, can remain as standard from embryo through to senile brain. The principal change is in the extent of the branches (dendrites). Remember, in Chapter 3 we saw that the surface area of these dendrites determined the amount and type of contact that other incoming neurons could make with the target cell: the greater the degree of branching, the greater the number of contacts. If, however, the dendrites die back, in a mirror image of the growth that characterizes the developing brain, it's hardly surprising that our cognitive abilities will reflect this recapitulation into childhood and on to infancy – a world of disconnected events and experiences with no overarching 'meaning', at least as I have just defined it. And if the unique *you* results from the highly personalized brain that in turn has had a unique set of experiences, it follows that a loss of mind, dementia, could effectively amount to a loss of identity. Development and degeneration, the growth of the mind and the loss of it, are important milestones on our present journey. By looking at the existing, and increasingly common, attack by Alzheimer's disease in particular on individuality, we might better grasp the consequences and implications of the other, newer threats that we're going to be thinking about shortly.

Working as I do on the cellular basis for Alzheimer's and Parkinson's diseases, I am constantly frustrated by the fact that current therapeutic strategies to halt this terrible dismantling of the mind don't tackle the root problem itself. The underlying key brain malfunction – the actual trigger setting off the process of neurodegeneration – is just not known. Instead, the best we can do at present is to combat the symptoms by dealing with the fall-out, the dwindling levels of chemical messengers caused in turn by the corresponding dwindling numbers of brain cells. The rationale of current treatment, then, is to use drugs to replace or enhance the availability of the deficient trans-mitters.

But there are problems. First, inevitably, drugs will permeate areas of the brain/body where they aren't needed, causing side-effects. For example with Parkinson's disease, a degenerative condition affecting movement, treatment with a drug (L-DOPA) that will promote the chemical messenger in the area that is degenerating (the substantia nigra), will also increase formerly normal levels of that same chemical elsewhere in the brain: but this time levels will be pushed by the drug to excessive amounts which create a risk of psychotic-type symptoms such as hallucina-tions. And even when this kind of treatment offers a temporary alleviation of the patient's basic condition, or a slowing down of the deterioration, there is no guarantee that a drug that doesn't actually cure will be available on the NHS – if anything, we should assume it won't be.

The situation is made even worse when we consider how many more of us are going to need such treatment in the future. Diseases of the more mechanical organs below the eyebrows, and their respective plumbing, are becoming easier to treat, with an increase in the ways of targeting the respective deficient mechanisms, or with a more routine approach to transplants. And the longer, healthier life that ensues means that diseases of the brain, particularly among the swelling numbers of elderly, will become more prominent. Although neurologists all agree that dementia is not a natural consequence of ageing, it *is* a disease of later life. So if in the twenty-first century more of us will live to a greater age, more of us will be susceptible to being stricken with a degenerative disease. Both for our own personal wellbeing and to be able to predict and shape the transformation of society this century, we urgently need to understand dementia and the neuronal devastation that underpins it.

At the moment, 700,000 people in the UK are suffering from Alzheimer's and 120,000 from Parkinson's, with the cost of care up to £25,000 a year per patient. Worldwide, the estimate is some 18 million. The current projections for Alzheimer's suggest that by 2050 there will be about 10 million cases in the USA, and about 1.8 million in the UK. Motor neurone disease (MND) is yet another neurodegenerative disorder: a study commissioned by the MND Association puts the cost of caring for a single patient in the final year of their life at around £170,000, and that excludes the additional costs caused by loss of earnings for patients and carers contending with all these neurodegenerative diseases. With around 1600 people dying of MND each year, the total bill to the NHS and social services is over £270 million per annum. Moreover, by 2031 provision of long-term care to older patients with cognitive impairment will be more than doubled in real terms (that is, after allowance for inflation) from about £4.6 billion to nearly £11 billion per annum.

But more insidious than economics and statistics is the human cost. While conditions such as heart disease and cancer are devastating, we all have a particular fear of the disorders that destroy our brains, and hence our minds and personality. Bear in mind that such diseases target the ability to smile, to converse and to have memories: indeed, to enjoy to the full the experience of having a unique identity. And yet the big problem remains that we still don't know why certain key brain cells embark on the pernicious cycle of self-destruction we call neurodegeneration.

The slow daily erosion of the mind is a relentless process that we cannot control, that we have seemingly done nothing to deserve and for which there is no restorative therapy. But it isn't just an increasing number of patients' lives that will be blighted. Just ask yourself this question: how many people love you or, let's just say, care about you a bit? Let's assume ten – not because it's necessarily any more realistic than any other reasonable estimate, but because it makes for easy calculations. Likewise, then, let's say that for every one person suffering from a degenerative disorder there are ten who care about that individual. If by the middle of this century the numbers of those suffering reach the expected 2 million in the UK, we could be looking at some 20 million lives devastated: roughly one in three of the population of the entire UK!

Dementia, where the Latin root means literally 'loss of mind', features at the centre of a variety of diseases: it's far more than a 'mere' loss of memory for a particular face or fact. I've often thought that perhaps it's more akin to waking up in a strange place, as most people do at one time or another, and for a few seconds not knowing where you are or why you're there or even what day it is. But with dementia that confusion and disorientation goes on and on. The clouds never lift on a clear perspective of your life, your identity, where you are going, and why.

If mind and memories are inextricably linked it's hardly surprising that dementia, a loss of the mind, inevitably involves a loss of memories. The most familiar manifestation of dementia is Alzheimer's disease, named after the physician who originally reported it, one Alois Alzheimer, in 1907: he described a fifty-one-year-old woman who showed a range of bizarre behavioural and cognitive problems, including loss of short-term memory. But it's only as medical advances and healthier lifestyles have enabled us to live longer by combating the old killers such as cancer, TB and heart disease that a condition such as Alzheimer's – more subtle in its impairment, slower in its time-course and above all presenting in older people – has become the spectre that haunts us all.

After all, even with cancer or heart disease the patient is still the person they ever were, still recognizing and loving those close to them, and still with the same habits, the same manner of speech, the same memories. But with dementia the very essence of the person, their individuality, falls away. Small wonder that the relatives and carers of Alzheimer patients frequently display all the signs of bereavement, yet society doesn't acknowledge and cater for the loss as it would in the case of real death.

With Alzheimer's disease, the problem can be monitored by measuring the shrinkage that takes place in a particular part of the brain called the medial temporal lobe, which encompasses both deep and surface regions and lies by the temples. However, an alternative form of dementia can also cause damage to the same area: Pick's disease. This condition is less well known since there is only one case of it to every fifty of Alzheimer's. Pick's disease also involves loss of memory, but of a very different type. While Alzheimer patients start to forget particular episodes, Pick's patients lose their memory for facts: for example, they might no longer be able to distinguish the identity and function of different types of brush and might consider cleaning their teeth with a clothes brush. The categories that enable the rest of us to make sense of the everyday world, and survive within it, start to blur.

Perhaps most devastating of all are the knock-on effects that this disintegration of memory for facts has on someone's outlook and personality. If you are confused and distressed because things no longer make sense, and if as a consequence people treat you differently, then surely you will behave as a different person. More basic still, if the traditional conceptual compartments according to which you live your life start to crumble, you will see the world in a very different, arguably more child-like way – and act accordingly.

By comparing these two diseases of memory perhaps we can gain some interesting insights into the processes of memory itself and therefore into the mind. In the case of Alzheimer's the problem detected eventually in the cortex, within the medial temporal lobe, has started in the deeper area of the brain called the hippocampus; the damage then spreads upwards to the overlying temporal cortex. But in the case of Pick's disease the trail of destruction goes in the reverse direction, starting with the cortex and eventually spreading to the hippocampus underneath. Since there is a big difference in the way this devastation affects memory we can conclude that memory for facts, as lost in Pick's disease, is usually linked in some way to the temporal cortex, while the memory for episodes, no longer retained in Alzheimer's, is associated with the hippocampus.

The hippocampus, as we saw with the London taxi drivers, is important for 'working memory'. But long before this study, a surgical operation performed in the mid-twentieth century had already implicated the hippocampus as a key region in the memory process. An individual known only by the initials H.M. has earned his place in neurological history as a result of a brain operation that was supposed to cure his severe and debilitating epilepsy by removal of the hippocampus. However, though it was successful in preventing further seizures, the procedure was never performed again. The removal of the hippocampus left H.M. amnesic: more specifically, he could remember nothing subsequent to his surgery, nor indeed for two years prior to that transforming event. It seems, therefore, that the hippocampus is important for the laying down of memories and for their initial consolidation for several years.

So the hippocampus is not so much 'the' or even 'a' centre for memory, but rather one of many important players in a complex process. Similarly, the overlying medial cortex is hardly a bank of memories, with individual facts neatly stored somehow in each of the neurons. We know that this scenario cannot hold thanks to pioneering neurosurgery performed in the mid-twentieth century by a Canadian named Wilder Penfield. Penfield demonstrated that if, after initial anaesthesia for the mechanics of opening the skull, he kept his patients awake during surgery – not as ghoulish as it sounds, since there are no pain sensors in the brain – then just occasionally he could observe a most bizarre phenomenon. If he placed stimulating electrodes on the surface of the exposed temporal cortex, sometimes the patient would recount a very vivid memory. The concept of a simplistic memory bank, however, doesn't work: Penfield found that he could evoke the same memory by stimulating in different sites, and conversely that stimulation in the same site often led to the recall of a different memory.

One explanation for this mismatch is that the different 'memories' weren't parcelled into different rigid neuronal compartments, but that each memory was the product of an extensive network of neurons that could overlap each other. So if by chance Penfield stimulated in another site, but still tapped into the same network, the same memory would come to the fore; or if he stimulated in the same site, but by chance tapped into an overlapping but distinct circuit, then another memory would be articulated.

A further fascinating finding that Penfield reported was that the memories themselves were like vivid dreams. How might this observation relate to the clue from Pick's disease that this area seems to be specifically linked to memory for facts? A dream is usually rather vague, indeed almost generic: the dreamer might be in a definite location, say a ship or a castle or garden, and might be engaged in a highly specific activity such as running away, climbing stairs or even flying. But it is very rare for there to be clear time- and space-frames of reference: few of us dream of an event that happened on a particular date or at a particular address. The kinds of memories related to the temporal cortex, then, are factual, but lack the time and space precision that forms the context of specific events. The best explanation of Penfield's findings is that circuits of neurons must be at work in the temporal cortex in a distributed fashion. If memory processing is distributed in this way, across many circuits and eventual regions, small wonder that in 1929 the neuropsychologist Karl Lashley failed to find the 'memory centre' in rats as he systematically removed more brain tissue: the rats merely became more and more cognitively impaired.

So what is happening in the brain of someone suffering from the loss of memory caused by neurodegeneration? Unfortunately, we still don't really know. As with the proverbial jigsaw, there are a growing number of pieces which fit consistently with each other, while others still lack an obvious place in the picture; but the underlying sequence of events – to extend the analogy to the picture itself – isn't conveniently displayed in its entirety on any biological equivalent of a jigsaw box lid.

One starting point, a corner piece of the jigsaw perhaps, is the observation that patients with Alzheimer's disease appear to benefit in the early stages of their illness from taking the drug Aricept. This works by blocking an enzyme (acetylcholinesterase) that would normally take apart, and thus inactivate, a particular transmitter (acetylcholine) once it had completed its job at the synapse; so the net effect of administering Aricept is to prolong the availability of acetylcholine. The reason that this strategy is effective in Alzheimer's is that key neurons using that particular transmitter have started to die off, to degenerate; the respective levels of acetylcholine fall accordingly. Aricept can, to a certain extent, offset this deficiency by slowing down the removal of the remaining, dwindling supplies of the all-important transmitter. But it's far from being a miracle cure, and doesn't prevent the inexorable deterioration in the patient's cognitive abilities.

Aricept has been in the British news over the last few years: the National Institute for Clinical Excellence (with the inappropriate acronym NICE) has withdrawn the drug from prescription on the National Health Service. There is vociferous and understandable opposition to this decision: many other drugs for many other diseases won't guarantee a cure, but rather improve the quality of life by alleviating suffering and prolonging a fulfilling existence, even if only temporarily. Surely, then, there is a case for continuing to prescribe Aricept. But for our discussion here, the key conclusion from this sad situation is that falling levels of acetylcholine are a symptom, not a cause, of Alzheimer's disease.

We need to know *why* the cells that use acetylcholine as a transmitter die in the first place. A further complication is that many of the vulnerable groups of neurons lost in Alzheimer's disease use as a transmitter not acetylcholine but a range of other chemical messengers. So supplementing levels of acetylcholine may be useful to a degree; but such a strategy could never be the complete treatment, never give the whole answer, never give a clue to the bigger picture on the hypothetical box lid.

Another piece of this complex puzzle, perhaps the best known since Alois Alzheimer first reported the condition, is that the brains of deceased Alzheimer's patients show clear signs of unusual deposits called plaques and tangles due to their appearance under the microscope. These pathological footprints reflect severe damage to the brain caused by a variety of otherwise normal processes that have gone wrong. More specifically, plaques are the result of the clumping of a chemical named amyloid after the Greek word for starch, and are formed when a much larger molecule (APP, amyloid precursor protein) splits up inappropriately. Tangles are just that: knots of tiny tubes within brain cells that would normally be nice and straight and transport essential materials throughout the cell. Once these essential supply lines go haywire, the brain cell dies. But what causes APP to be split aberrantly, and the tubules to tie themselves into knots? And how do these two disastrous turns of events relate to each other, and indeed to the bigger picture? One essential feature that no one has yet explained, at least to my satisfaction, is why these two markers of neuronal devastation only occur in certain brain regions but not in others; this important fact, often ignored even by some scientists, is surely offering us a vital clue. Something must be special about the brain regions vulnerable in Alzheimer's disease, above and beyond the generic functioning of brain cells. The big question, the big challenge to us neuroscientists, is to try and discover what that special something is.

So far, then, we have seen that 'loss of mind', dementia, is a kind of development thrown into reverse gear. This growth and mirror-image loss of mind appears to equate respectively with the gradual growth and loss of neuronal connections. If this vulnerable and valuable neuronal connectivity does indeed account for the mind, and with it the basis for our identity, could we explain by a similar mechanism the 'loss of mind' under other conditions, such as drug abuse or madness?

5

BLOWING THE MIND

Let's recap the story so far. We have just seen that children's brains are maximally receptive to any input; only as they start to accumulate sufficient past experiences to evaluate new events in terms of what has happened to them already does the interaction of brain and environment become a two-way street. Gradually, in each young human, the brain becomes personalized by unique experiences to become a unique entity. It is this personalization of the physical brain that, for me, is the 'mind'. And if spared the ravages of neurodegenerative disease this mind, once developed, is surely inviolate. Or is it? What we're going to look at now are other, far more frequent and sometimes only temporary, ways of losing the mind – ways that promise to be even more prevalent as the century unfolds.

Drugs can cram your world view into a singular moment, into the immediate here-and-now. As they take away pain, drugs can convert reality into a literally meaningless dream. Some substances can even make you feel 'at one' with everyone else. In any event, most can end up obliterating the omnipresent experience of your identity as an individual in favour of a sensory-laden, literally 'sensational' time. This 'losing' or 'blowing' the mind, this 'letting yourself go', is not an exclusively modern phenomenon – psychoactive drugs have kept company with humanity for centuries, if not millennia. But perhaps it is at this particular moment at the beginning of the twenty-first century, even more than in the hazy, hippy era of the 1960s, that it is becoming the cultural norm to spend more and more time in a world softened by powerful chemicals. Not surprisingly, there are a plethora of drugs that affect the brain, each with its own relevant dose range, side-effects and action. But they have one essential feature in common: all drugs that affect brain function do so by interfering with the finely tuned operations of a chemical messenger, a transmitter, at the synapse.

For example, amphetamine (speed) prolongs the availability, and therefore the action, of the transmitter dopamine and its chemical cousin noradrenaline, while cocaine slows down their removal. Meanwhile, ecstasy triggers the explosive release and subsequent depletion of a more distant molecular relative, serotonin: alternatively, heavy-duty tranquillizers block the usual chemical handshake between a transmitter and its usual target protein, known as a receptor. Then again, a drug such as heroin, a derivative of morphine, can act as an impostor and kid the brain into thinking that a naturally occurring transmitter (enkephalin) has been released.

Even from this briefest of glimpses into neuropharmacology it can be seen that different drugs interfere with different transmitters, or groups of transmitters, in different ways. But irrespective of the chemical system in question, the sophisticated biochemical symphony at the synapse – the normal, carefully tuned sequence of events which enables a transmitter to be released from one neuron and activate another – is thrown into disarray. As a result of exaggerating or blocking the normal molecular hand-shake of a transmitter with the target cell, the custom-made receptor into which the transmitter usually fits will end up either under- or overworking. What does this scenario mean in real life?

This question is important not just for a theoretical appreciation of how the mind might be 'blown' or 'lost' with drugs, but for a practical piecing together of the picture that we are trying to build up here, a picture of the mindset of future generations. One good example is the much-discussed abuse of cannabis, which remains highly controversial in terms of short- and long-term effects. Since it is eliminated only very slowly from the body, cannabis impairs driving ability, as well as perceptual motor skills, for up to five days after taking the drug, yet die-hard aficionados still claim that cannabis is not addictive and 'just like' alcohol. But surely this reassurance is misleading. Alcohol is eliminated much more rapidly from the body, at a unit per hour. And if the effects were really 'just', that is, exactly like alcohol, why not drink instead? Intake would be easier to regulate, and it would be legal! The fact that many people prefer cannabis arises precisely because the effects – the experience – of the drug are not identical but different, which has to mean that at some level, in some way, the drug works differently in the brain. Similarly, the much-vaunted analgesic effects of cannabis for multiple sclerosis patients are not seen with alcohol; so the two drugs have to be far from 'just the same'. Moreover, if cannabis is such a potent painkiller how could it achieve this effect if it were not having a concomitantly profound action on neuronal operations?

Cannabis works on specific target proteins (receptors) in the brain that enter into a molecular handshake with its active ingredient, tetrahydrocannabinol or THC; cannabis can therefore modify synapses, and hence neuronal plasticity and hence the mind. The central question at issue here is not whether cannabis is less lethal than other drugs, nor even whether it could trigger a predisposition to schizophrenia and depression, but rather that it might well change physical or mental performance without that change ever becoming apparent as a medical problem. So cannabis will probably not kill you, nor necessarily even tip the balance towards the A & E Department or the psychiatrist's clinic; but it *could* demotivate you, disrupt your memory and shorten your attention span. A user may not realize their natural intellectual potential and may arguably be a different person compared to the one they would have been if they had never puffed on a spliff.

Yet if drugs of abuse, especially cannabis, continue to be a common feature of twenty-first-century life, such might be the fate of many. We may be facing a particularly unpleasant chicken-and-egg dilemma: as pressures increase to keep up with ever faster-paced, rapidly changing technologies, and as those technologies increase our aspirations, more and more people may feel inadequate and unable to cope. How welcome the hazier world of a drug-induced wellbeing, which in turn reduces the cognitive competence and curiosity required in order to adapt to modern life.

Another but very different recreational drug that makes the world dreamier still is heroin, which locks into its target molecule instead of the real transmitter (enkephalin) and results in a much more sustained molecular handshake. The reason for this is that, while enzymes and other sophisticated biochemical mechanisms remove the naturally occurring transmitter from the site of the action once its work is done, such mechanisms are only effective for the naturally occurring substance. Drugs such as heroin might operate *like* a transmitter, but they are not chemical simulacra – they are not structurally identical. So, since the synthetic impostor cannot be removed swiftly, it sticks to the receptor for far longer. Here the handshake analogy is particularly useful. Imagine shaking someone's hand, and them not letting go. If the grip were maintained, gradually your hand would become less sensitive and eventually numb. You would need to exert a greater pressure yourself in order to feel anything at all. And so it is with certain drugs. If the receptor becomes less sensitive due to being overstimulated by the persistent drug, more will be needed for normal function – more than is usually available from the existing natural supplies in the brain. What we have here is addiction.

Heroin addiction through a desensitization of the respective target receptors is just one example of the powerful impact that drugs can have on the working of brain cell connections, and hence on the personalized configuration and status of those connections – what, as we have seen so far, could be called the mind. Neuropharmacology therefore offers a fascinating strategy for linking seemingly elusive subjective 'mental' states with the physical bump and grind of chemicals and cells within our banal brains. We can now, for example, match up the alleviation of depression by Prozac with the increased availability of serotonin, or similarly the calming effects of diazepines with the enhancement of the effects of the transmitter gamma-aminobutyric acid (GABA). By comparing in this way, by correlating biochemical processes with reports of how people feel – we can slowly start to build up a picture of the physical, chemical bases of different subjective mental states.

But such correlations don't as yet throw any light on causality: they don't explain, for example, *why* or *how* enkephalins should make you feel euphoric, or why a lack of serotonin leads to depression. Our current ineptitude is hardly surprising since neither the drugs, nor the transmitters they manipulate, have sophisticated emotions locked away in the interstices of their molecular bonds! Rather, in some as yet still utterly mysterious way, the neuronal networking that can be so heavily influenced by drugs in turn transforms the holistic landscape of the brain, and with it your subjective experience – like the well-known butterfly flapping its wings on one side of the world and, via a complex series of knock-on events, changing the climate on the other side of the planet.

Eventually, I'm sure, we neuroscientists will understand more about how drugs, working as they do at the synapse, influence the more macro-scale operations of the whole brain; but will we ever grasp how that holistic operation actually translates into the subjective feel of the moment that we call consciousness? I am fascinated by the thought that, if someone finally did make the fantastic claim that they had discovered how the objective, physical brain gives rise to the subjective experience of consciousness, we would have no idea what to expect. A performing robot? A brain scan? A telepathic rat? Some kind of shared collective experience? In fact, this issue of what kind of answer would satisfy us is as difficult as the solution itself.

But consciousness and the mind are not synonymous: of course, the latter might be a factor in determining the quality of the former, but since you can lose or blow your mind and still be conscious we can clearly separate the two phenomena. And it is the blowing of the mind that is our preoccupation for the moment. Suffice it to say, then, that drugs impair the normal process of neuronal communication: 'blowing the mind' and being 'out of one's mind' might be literally, as well as metaphorically, what is happening as the communications between brain cells become exaggerated or suppressed.

If loss of mind can occur with either dementia or drugs, and if the common factor is an impairment in neuronal networking, might the same be true for a third scenario where the checks and balances of the healthy adult human mind no longer seem to be operating? Traditionally, psychoses such as schizophrenia differ from neuroses in one basic and all-important feature: they entail a departure from reality. A philosopher might pause here to argue the toss over what 'reality' really is; but let's just think of it, for our present purposes, in a practical sense as an agreed upon set of assumptions, rules, values and perceptions. We can then appreciate just how devastating psychoses are. Although the neurotic who suffers from agoraphobia or claustrophobia or obsessive-compulsive behaviour is leading a severely compromised life, their perception of the world is normally similar to that of almost everyone else. In psychoses, however, that assumption doesn't hold. The schizophrenic is not a divided person, but a person divided from reality.

In many ways, the same could be said of young children. The strange, idiosyncratic reasoning, the strong, mercurial emotions and the easy distractability that can characterize schizophrenics also readily applies to the mentality of children, who themselves only have a shaky grasp of reality after all. I'm not suggesting for a moment that children are schizophrenic; but there *are* various features in common.

First, neither the schizophrenic nor the child can rationalize their fears, or any other emotion, by recourse to the checklist housed in the standard adult mind. The latter is a conceptual infrastructure rooted in past experiences and served by a strong and extensive network of neuronal connections slowly accumulated as we grow up.

Secondly, both children and schizophrenics exhibit bizarre or eccentric thought characterized by loose, tangential associations. Once again this observation could be interpreted as a problem with neuronal connections. The healthy adult brain exhibits robust associative learning based on synaptic strengthening through frequent use. But in the immature brain, and seemingly in that of the schizophrenic too, associations are weaker and much less well established, depending on chance: they are not sufficiently load-bearing to accommodate all the cross-referencing and internal consistency of connections that operate in the normal adult brain.

Thirdly, neither children nor schizophrenics can interpret metaphors, but take at face value a statement such as 'People in glass houses shouldn't throw stones'. Consider, for example, one patient's response to that familiar proverb: 'If you're the president of a school and you live across from the campus, as they did in Keene, Texas, and Elder

Scales was the president of the school, he lived in a glass house, so to speak, because people were always able to see him. You live right across the street from the campus and you live in a glass house, and people can see what you're doing, they can say: "That's not so." ' Clearly, this statement was based on personal, loose and above all literal associations in relation to the concept of a glass house rather than on the idea of the glass house as a more general metaphor. A metaphor is based on expressing one thing in terms of something else, so to understand it a connection has to be made. The problem here, then, can be interpreted in terms of connectivity, specifically an insufficient conceptual framework comprising only idiosyncratic, flimsy associations at best. Hence children too would perform poorly in this kind of test, having recourse only to the relatively meagre associations they have so far embedded in their brains.

Fourthly, both children and schizophrenics are very easily distracted by the sensations of the outside world. Indeed, schizophrenics often place a premium on their senses, seeing the world, for example, in glowing, bright colours. This emphasis on the outside world can also frequently give rise to the schizophrenic patient's delusion that they are in some way possessed of divine powers, that they might even be Christ come again: after all, they do see the world in an intensity and detail missed by almost everyone else. While healthy adults can often ignore the press of their senses (known as latent inhibition) while engaged in sophisticated cognitive activities such as remembering, thinking or speaking, this ability is lacking in both children and schizophrenics. Interestingly, problems in latent inhibition also occur under the influence of LSD, a hallucinogenic drug that affects the transmitter serotonin. More generally, too, intoxication with LSD can parallel schizophrenia in its overemphasis on the sensory qualities of the outside world as well as in the child-like suscept-ibility to suggestion and irrational fears. In sum, for the drug-taker, the child and the schizophrenic, the strength of the sensory and immediate experience outweighs any inter-nalized networking, even though this under-functioning is caused by different physical features in the brain in each of the three cases.

The emphasis on incoming sensations over a counter-balancing cognitive network can also explain a fifth feature common to schizophrenics and children – that they are mentally transparent. Seemingly exposed and vulnerable in their thoughts, they have no firewall between their brains and anyone else's. How plausible, then, that other people's thoughts can easily penetrate their brains and take control.

Finally, both schizophrenics and young children are incapable of appreciating that there *is* a firewall between brains, and that different people could think differently and know different things from themselves. Once again, this impairment can be attributed to a lack of the extensive working connections that enable healthy adults to differ-entiate themselves from others and to place people, events and conversations in the context of previous experience.

The crucial point, then, is that the schizophrenic, like the child, is living in the present, responding to the inputs of the moment rather than fitting them into the internalized conceptual framework that enables us to make sense of the world, along with all the benefits and losses which that facility brings. In one scenario it is a case of being 'out' of one's mind; in the other the mind has yet to develop fully.

But while all these features can be readily explained in children by pointing to the paucity of neuronal branches, and hence the connections that have yet to grow, the same cannot be said of the schizophrenic brain. Why should an adult brain, presumably replete with the standard numbers of connections, none the less behave like an immature counterpart?

There are many theories to account for schizophrenia. With the advent of the mapping of the human genome, emphasis has predictably swung to the possible genetic basis. But while it has been known for a long time that there is a family-related disposition to schizophrenia, it is clear that there is no simple, single gene 'for' this complex psychiatric disorder in the way that there is 'for' Huntington's Chorea, which even then, as we have seen, can be dramatically influenced by the environment. One idea put forward is that a malfunctioning gene can lead to an aberration in the degree to which the two hemispheres of the human brain become differentially specialized, while others have suggested the possibility of different genetic predispositions to drugs which might make some individuals more vulnerable to a schizophrenia-like mindset.

But, without doubt, a sophisticated change in mindset of the type that occurs with schizophrenia will not be explicable by a single cause like a faulty gene, nor will it be understandable at only one level of brain organization, be it at the level of (larger) macro brain regions or of the (smaller) isolated, generic synapse. So what about the mid-level of neuronal networks?

Whatever the initial trigger, one of the widely acknowledged features of the schizophrenic brain is that somehow an excess of the transmitter dopamine plays an important and immediate role in the psychotic experience, in the loss of the mind. For example, people who take the amphetamine-based drug speed often experience many of the symptoms of schizophrenia. Amphetamine, remember, increases the availability of dopamine, thereby increasing its levels beyond the norm. Similarly, patients with Parkinson's disease who take the drug l-DOPA to compensate for their dwindling levels of dopamine also often experience psychotic-like hallucinations. Unfortunately no single brain area has a monopoly on any single transmitter: when drugs change transmitter levels in one part of the brain they have the same effect in other areas as well – areas where the change isn't needed. Side-effects such as drug-induced psychosis in Parkinson's disease are the result.

But if the living-in-the-moment scenario of schizophrenia and childhood characterizes the absence of the mind, could the absence of a mind *in general* be associated in some way with an excess of dopamine in the brain? Dopamine, like its chemical cousins noradrenaline, serotonin and histamine, emanates fountain-like from a hub of cells deep down in the most basic part of the brain, the brain stem. However, unlike the rest of the family dopamine doesn't access vast tracts of the outer layer of the brain, the cortex. Yet there is one exception, one part of the cortex where dopamine does indeed play an important role. This is the prefrontal cortex, which, as its name suggests, lies at the very front of the brain.

As with other demarcated regions of the brain, the

prefrontal cortex seems to be involved in many aspects of brain function, in particular the more sophisticated higher cognitive processes that characterize our species in particular. No surprise, then, that the neuroscientist Terence Deacon has estimated that, even compared to the same organ in chimps, the brightest of the other primates, the human prefrontal cortex is twice the size it should be in an ape brain of our size. Because of its disproportionate size in humans the prefrontal cortex has, over the years, been an obvious target for attempts at localising a myriad complex and highly diverse cognitive functions. I may be exaggerating, though only slightly, if I suggest that the prefrontal cortex often seems to resemble a kind of neuroscientific kitchen sink: when researchers are trying to find a cerebral home for some sophisticated function by performing brain scans, one or another subdivision of the prefrontal cortex will always seem to oblige.

In any event, we have to be careful not to turn the prefrontal cortex into an autonomous mini-brain by ascribing to it 'functions' all on its own. Rather, the critical question is: what might dopamine do within the prefrontal cortex of a schizophrenic, that in turn enables it to intercept in some way the otherwise correct functioning of neuronal connections, that in turn revisits the situation in the very young brain?

Damage to the prefrontal cortex has resulted in a wide variety of problems from recklessness to obesity to 'irrational' emotion. Perhaps the best-known case of prefrontal damage was that of one Phineas Gage, foreman of a nineteenth-century railway gang laying tracks across America. One day while pushing explosive down a hole with a

4-foot-long iron rod there was a premature ignition and the resulting explosion drove the rod through Gage's brain – more specifically through his prefrontal cortex. Our hero earned his place in history not just because he survived, but because of the nature of his consequent impairments: subtle cognitive changes that only became apparent several months later. Gage didn't suffer from any basic problems with movement, speech or the senses, but his character changed to one of impulsiveness and little regard for his fellow workers. He has remained the prototype of the 'frontal' syndrome ever since – a syndrome characterized by recklessness and living in the moment.

Another problem that can result from prefrontal damage is source amnesia. The problem is not merely loss of memory – as it happens, memories for faces, facts and so on are just fine. Source amnesia is much more subtle: it is an inability to place a time and space reference point on a particular episode. So you might well remember going to the seaside with Auntie Mildred, but it would be an almost generic occurrence, lacking a place and time in your life narrative. It would become the kind of generic memory that perhaps animals or small children have: a vague association of something being pleasurable or dangerous, but not occurring at a specific time that can be related to other events in a clear sequential order or a specific context. After all, a rat may learn to press a bar for sugared water, or run a maze, without knowing how that experience relates to, say, the wider context of sleeping, drinking water or running in an exercise wheel. These would be precisely the type of childhood memories that, as we saw earlier, Freud described as occurring at an early stage in childhood, before past events and experiences had been incorporated into a clear narrative.

I pointed out in Chapter 5 that the best explanation of Penfield's findings is that circuits of neurons must be at work in the temporal cortex in a distributed fashion, and the same principle applies to other brain areas. Perhaps these other brain areas, such as the prefrontal cortex, operate in conjunction with the temporal cortex to add a specific time and space frame of reference that converts a generic fact into a specific one-off episode. If the prefrontal cortex, when damaged, leads to source amnesia – a loss of memory specifically of the time and place of an episode – then perhaps the generic, timeless, dream-like memories generated in the distributed neuronal circuits of the temporal cortex are unleashed they would no longer be constrained by time and space coordinates normally imposed under the direction of the prefrontal cortex.

This scenario would explain the bizarre collapse in 'reality' that characterizes schizophrenia, linked as it is to under-function of the prefrontal cortex. Moreover, were this critical region to operate in this way, it would also account for the fact that only we humans, with our exaggerated prefrontal cortex, have a specific sense of accurate time and space frames of reference, while other animals and indeed young children have memories, which are usually generic and generalized. We could go on to speculate that the consciousness of non-human animals, and indeed of small children, would be more like a generic dream compared to the precise, compartmentalized 'reality' of us human adults.

Perhaps, after all, a general theme is emerging for the

prefrontal cortex, and one that we can relate not only to damage but to schizophrenia and childhood as well. In the case of children, we have seen that it is the prefrontal cortex that grows most after birth; hence in infancy it will be the least developed part of the brain, with proportionately, the greatest lack of connections. In some cases, such as Phineas Gage's story I related earlier, mechanical damage will have massively disrupted those connections. But what of schizophrenia, where there is merely a surfeit of dopamine? How might an excess of this transmitter be the functional equivalent of an impairment in neuronal networking?

I would hazard the following explanation. By so massively inhibiting the activity of cells in the prefrontal cortex, excessive amounts of dopamine might render the region as inactive as if it had received an iron rod through it, or as though the connections had still to form. (For those who enjoy the biochemical detail, dopamine can have the net effect of driving out potassium ions from inside neurons. Because potassium is an ion that carries a positive charge, the effect is to make the inside of the neuron more negative. But for a cell to generate an electrical blip, an action potential, the reverse has to happen – the inside of the cell has to become temporarily more positive. Dopamine has therefore made this eventuality less likely: it has 'inhibited' the neuron.)

More recent evidence points not so much to dopamine as the central player but to another class of transmitters, amino acids, that operate within the local circuitry of the prefrontal cortex itself. Remember that, as with the various brain regions, no transmitter operates alone; interaction is key. The incoming dopamine would inhibit the cells in the prefrontal cortex and thus impair their normal internal networking with local amino acids. We need not trouble ourselves here with details of the intricate relations between amino acids and dopamine, but rather focus on the effect: a weakened connectivity.

This under-networking in the prefrontal cortex, though resulting in a whole range of dysfunctions, seems none the less to fit into a common theme. The obese individual living in the moment for the taste of food, and the reckless compulsive gambler high on the roll of a dice, are placing a premium on the sensation of the experience of the moment rather than considering the consequences as normally monitored by the adult mind: precisely the same pattern of behaviour seen in children and schizophrenics.

So, by looking at a range of cases where people are described as 'losing their mind', blowing their mind' and being 'out of their mind', we can draw certain conclusions as to how our minds, our identity, might develop and how it might be sustained. For a neuroscientist, the old dualism of 'mental' and 'physical', indeed of 'mind' and 'brain', is as unhelpful as it is misleading. The mind, far from being some airy-fairy philosophical alternative to the biological squalor of the physical brain, *is* the physical brain – more specifically the personalized connectivity of that otherwise generic brain. We have seen how essential it is that that connectivity, particularly in areas such as the prefrontal cortex, is able to operate properly in order for us to see one thing in terms of something else, to place ongoing experiences in the context of what has gone before.

However, we have also seen that adult human beings can recapitulate the booming, buzzing confusion of the small child: various normal, abnormal and disease conditions can, in their different ways, lead to a brain-state comparable with that of children. Drugs and schizophrenia offer ways of blocking or distorting normal access to any personalized brain connections. Another example might be fast-paced sports whose dominant feature is the raw quality of the sensations, devoid of cognitive content: the speed at which one momentary experience is superseded by the next, the rapid interaction of the body with a fast-moving environment, militates against the slower, normal accessing of idiosyncratic associations through personalized, indirect connections.

These states – childhood, drugs, sport and psychosis – obviously cover a wide spectrum. But they share a crucial characteristic: the personalized 'mind' is not fully operational, and recourse to the conceptual framework realized by personalized brain connections is suspended. In the case of the adult, then, it is not necessarily that the physical connections themselves are absent, as with the small child, but rather that the normal complement of neuronal connections themselves malfunction (drugs/psychosis). Or perhaps it could just be that the excessively strong, purely sensory stimulus of the normal external world (raves/music/wine/food) over-rides any personal 'significance' and often occurs as such a rapid succession of events (sport/sex) that there is no time for the full connectivity ('meaning') to be realized, since the emphasis is on the pace and all-consuming sensation of the immediate environment.

We can therefore go beyond drugs and madness to everyday life and find instances when, at one time or another, we have all 'let ourselves go'. In all cases, the common factors are an absence of self-consciousness, extreme emphasis on the senses *per se*, high emotion and loss of the 'reason', the checks and balances, that characterize the mature human mind. This respite from having a mind, an identity, seems – except for the extreme example of psychosis – desirable as an intermittent state. It is an interesting paradox of human beings that many of us are hugely attracted to hedonistic experiences that allow us to leave our minds behind in the here-and-now of drugs and sex and rock and roll, yet at the same time most of us would shun and disparage engaging in such (literally) 'sensational' activities all the time, in favour of retaining our self-conscious identities.

Indeed, for most of the time our adult human minds, our personalized brains, provide the appropriate constraints and checklists that enable us to make sense of the world, a world where objects and people have varying degrees of 'significance' or 'meaning' to us in accordance with the number of associations they invoke from past experience. We evaluate the world in terms of what we have experienced previously: conversely, everything that happens will change, however slightly, that personal view.

Our species is unique in the animal kingdom for interpreting the immediate experiences of daily existence in terms of an individual journey from birth to death – a life narrative predicated on the notion of a self-conscious self. It is an essential part of being human to have this unique life story and to be conscious of it; however, never so much as in modern times has the potential for a truly individual identity been so greatly acknowledged and emphasized.

i.d.

We have just seen how the individual mind can be dramatically transformed, even obliterated, by degeneration, drugs and disease, or even by sex, sport and gluttony – as it has been throughout human history. But now the twenty-first-century technologies are holding out the prospect of brand-new influences that could transform our mind, and hence our identity, in ways that previous generations could never have contemplated.

6

MANIPULATING THE MIND

By now I'm assuming that you are going along with my idea that the mind is the personalization of the brain through a unique neuronal connectivity, driven in turn by unique experiences; if so, you'll agree that if we have direct access to the brain, and change its physical configuration, we will inevitably transform the mind. But until now most incidents of mind-manipulation have either been indirect, through manipulation of the environment (say with drugs, sex and rock and roll), or the result of direct changes to the physical brain that have usually been uncontrolled and undesirable (accidents, surgery or disease). The time has come for us to take a look at the very latest technology. Now, at the beginning of the twenty-first century, it not only offers the promise of throwing new light on previously incurable brain disorders, but even has the potential to intercept directly and actually 'improve' upon what would pass as a 'healthy' mind.

Because it's the most prevalent, most greatly feared and fastest-growing group of diseases, let's start with neuro-degeneration. As we saw a while back, there is no current treatment that can stop the characteristic, inexorable cycle of cell death in its tracks. Sure, we can peer into the brain after death and see certain abnormalities, the plaques and tangles that clinch a diagnosis of Alzheimer's; but these markers could well be the result of the problem, not its cause. The dead brain of someone who has suffered from dementia for five, ten or even fifteen years is not helpful in revealing the actual sequence of cause and effect, the domino-like chain of processes that trigger a sequence of destruction where only the end result is irrefutable.

Needless to say, there are many hypotheses about the underlying problem. But this isn't a specialist textbook or learned journal, rather a glimpse of the power of future biomedical strategies and technology. So let's take just one example, albeit speculative and controversial and from my own lab, to show at least how neuroscientists try to piece together clues that may enable them to come up with an explanation for what is going on in the brain of a living patient with a neurodegenerative disease. That said, it's important to bear in mind that this exercise is no mere academic crossword puzzle: were we to work out and describe a plausible scenario in neurodegeneration, of what was going wrong and why, the next step could be to devise a novel therapeutic strategy for combating it.

Our story starts with a particularly intriguing potential clue, often overlooked by scientists but long and widely acknowledged by geriatricians and neurologists: some unfortunate patients suffer not only from Alzheimer's disease, but from Parkinson's disease as well. Parkinson's is well known as a severe disorder of movement, leading to uncontrollable tremors and muscle rigidity, as well as preventing the sufferer from moving easily. The problem here is death of brain cells in a very specific part of the brain called the substantia nigra. Although so far you might have thought there was no obvious link to Alzheimer's, the actual process of slow and progressive death of brain cells, neurodegeneration, is similar.

As it turns out, the anatomical areas that are primarily affected in both Alzheimer's and Parkinson's are adjacent to each other in the brain. Moreover, some additional neighbouring regions, the locus Coeruleus and the Raphe nuclei, are similarly affected in both conditions. In fact you can visualize a continuous hub of brain cells containing the areas affected in either of these diseases, as well as some

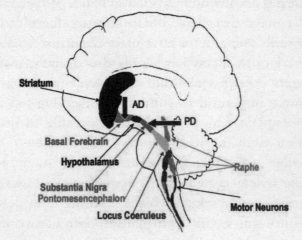

The 'hub' of brain cells primarily affected in Alzheimer's disease, Parkinson's disease and motor neurone disease

that are equally vulnerable in both. If large areas of this hub are damaged, both diseases will occur.

But the different regions use different chemical messengers; so, when certain regions die, the problems can be temporarily treated by different drugs (Aricept and l-dopa) that will boost the levels of the two different transmitters, acetylcholine and dopamine, and alleviate respectively the characteristic cognitive or movement impairments. But the frequent simultaneous occurrence of Alzheimer's and Parkinson's suggests that these two different sets of symptoms and treatments might be masking a much more fundamental common factor that triggered those diverse catastrophic outcomes in the first place.

Remember that the drugs are treating the symptoms, not the actual cause of cell death. They are merely trying to increase the availability of the appropriate transmitter, whose levels are dwindling because many of the cells that normally make them have died; the drug doesn't actually stop the cells dying in the first place. And just because the different groups of adjacent cells use different chemical messengers doesn't mean that they don't have something much more important in common, something that might perhaps explain why they are so vulnerable to neurodegeneration while most other brain cells are not.

One idea as to what this common factor might be first struck me when I read a review about ten years ago by the Californian neurobiologist Nancy Woolf. She described how all neurons in the brain fell into one of two groups. Most neurons had similar properties in terms of how they developed and matured: they all originated from a certain part of the embryo (the alar plate), were sensitive to substances that helped them grow (trophic factors), but in maturity lost that sensitivity along with more general mechanisms of plasticity of the type discussed earlier.

But, I read with mounting fascination, there was also another group of neurons deep down in the brain. This was really exciting, because I suddenly realized that this distinct group comprised the very hub of cells affected in neurodegeneration! Nancy pointed out that these hub neurons come from a completely different part of the embryo (the basal plate). The fact that this separate origin is already apparent at the very start of life in itself suggests that any differences will be very basic indeed. Even more intriguing, these hub neurons retain a sensitivity to chemical agents that are important in development. Most significant of all Nancy wrote, these hub cells, are different from other cells in the mature brain in that they have retained an ability to regenerate. These cells deep down in the hub, then, unlike those in the cortex and other evolutionary higher centres, are permanently in plasticity overdrive – just as though they were in permanent infancy!

My own opinion is that this Peter Pan ability to remain in a state of immaturity might be a key factor in the actual mechanisms of neurodegeneration. Perhaps the common problem in the entire gamut of neurodegenerative diseases is the misguided, aberrant activation of developmental mechanisms. Perhaps neurodegeneration is no more, and no less, than an aberrant form of development.

So brain damage of any type – be it a stroke, a blow to the head or the effect of toxins – outside of the critical hub may well result in serious problems. But the loss of these cells will not trigger any further loss of brain cells: in fact, the patient will often show partial or even complete recovery as compensation from undamaged neurons comes into play. By contrast, imagine comparable damage to the hub cells: this time the neurons there will bring into play their special feature, the specific ability to regenerate that they have retained. Only this time, Nature has moved the goalposts for the mature brain: the consequences of the cells in the hub trying to regenerate will prove to be, tragically, the exact opposite.

These neurons in the hub will activate their special mechanism for development, one that allows calcium ions into them. Calcium is an important trigger for a whole host of processes within neurons, not least activating genes, and is essential if the cell is to grow its branches (dendrites) and then make connections. But now the neurons are much older: they don't have the same molecular resources of their embryonic counterparts. All this excess calcium won't therefore be used as it would be during development, but will gum up the neurons' energy powerhouses (the mitochondria, which generate most of the cell's supply of the chemical adenosine triphosphate, a source of energy) so the neuron eventually dies. More cells will die, and the process of attempted compensation will start again, thus creating a vicious cycle of continuing cell death: neurodegeneration. If damage is confined to one part of the hub (the substantia nigra) the dysfunction will manifest as Parkinson's disease, if to another (the basal forebrain) as Alzheimer's, while if it is extensive both diseases will occur.

While this may be an attractive theory, it is still controversial and far from universally accepted. But if this hypothesis is correct – and it really is still very much 'if' – it might eventually open up a new way of treating Alzheimer's and related diseases. Let's just say that we could develop a medication that blocks this pernicious cycle by preventing the normal chemicals involved in development from doing their work – if we could do that, no more cells would die. A doctor would be able to say to the patient, as they do now, 'I know you're having memory problems and are a bit confused', or 'I know you're starting to have movement problems.' But the doctor would also be able to add, 'If you take this medication each day, it won't get any worse. Your condition will stabilize.' In short, the patient's identity wouldn't crumble away any further. Anyone reading these words whose life has been touched by the devastation of neurodegeneration will know what an almost miraculous advance such an outcome would represent, especially if treatment was started in the early stages of the disease.

One reason I have taken you on this occasion into my own research strategy in some detail is so that you can appreciate how neuroscientists need to think about the brain and mind. We cannot concentrate on isolated cells, but need to place them in the holistic context of how the brain might be working and to develop theories that account for *all* the known observations – such as the fact that only certain cells are affected in neurodegeneration, and that Alzheimer's and Parkinson's can occur together.

The second reason it was important to make this brief detour was so that you can appreciate what might happen to healthcare in the future. Although my own particular research may not work out, there are many other labs around the world with the same dreams. It may be no exaggeration to predict that in the next few decades, even if we have no cure for neurodegeneration, someone somewhere may have come up with new insights into early diagnosis, prevention and neuronal stabilization.

The final reason that we journeyed into more technical realms was to show how, in any event, this Peter Pan brain hub could help us understand more about the physical basis of mind more generally – at least as I've defined it in this book. The first important insight is that if these cells are in a state of continuous heightened plasticity throughout life, just as is the rest of the brain during early childhood before the 'mind' has properly formed, then surely we cannot just look at isolated neuronal connections as a generic, catch-all phenomenon for understanding the personalization of the brain. Clearly another important feature, beyond the synapses themselves, must be the particular anatomical region in the brain where those synapses are forming.

Although we saw previously that the development of 'mind' appears to be optimal when the cortex has calmed down, when the synapses have been pruned, clearly it is only within the cortex that a modular specialization matters. The evolutionarily more primitive areas of the brain, such as the hub, carry on being highly malleable. We have already seen that the cortex, so much more expansive in us humans than in other species, is directly related within the animal kingdom to sophisticated cognitive mental ability. Here, then, it is important to have efficient modules and the neuronal basis for a conceptual framework in order to navigate through life. But the more primitive areas such as the hub – even in humans, similar in layout and chemical composition to that of rats and mice – clearly has another role to play.

I cannot emphasize too strongly that it is very hard, and often downright misleading, to try to pin a specific function on a specific brain region. On the contrary, any one function is divided up among many brain regions: with vision, for example, at least thirty regions are involved. Conversely, any one brain region will be linked in some way to more than one function. So the primitive hub, although linked for a long time with 'arousal' and sleep/wake cycles, will in turn influence other functions by virtue of its interplay with other areas. An obvious example is the one we've just explored in the previous chapter, where excessive dopamine released from the hub cells on to the prefrontal cortex is a critical factor in schizophrenia. Another instance would be depression. Within the hub are a group of cells called the Raphe nuclei which are the brain's main source of the transmitter serotonin. Since drugs such as Prozac alleviate depression by enhancing those levels of serotonin, the hub must also be involved in a function as refined and sophisticated as 'mood'.

The reason the hub can have such a wide range of functions, or more precisely be involved in a wide range of functions, is that it has a global cerebral outreach – in other words, it provides a steady supply of dopamine and serotonin and a variety of chemicals throughout the higher, overlying brain regions such as the hippocampus and the cortex. These transmitters can act not only in the conventional, highly precise way at the synapse for which they are best known, but also as widespread 'modulators'. Modulation, in neuroscience lingo, is an umbrella term whereby a wide range of neurochemicals, including transmitters, act in a variety of ways to achieve a common end: not to have any action on their own, but to predispose the target neurons in question to respond more (or less) effectively to normal inputs. If a neuron is modulated, it might well end up being more sensitive to a repeated activation from a neighbouring cell, and the connection in turn would become stronger and more effective: this is the plasticity we observed earlier in piano players and taxi drivers. So these more primitive neurons down in the hub could aid and abet plasticity in the cortex to whatever extent the species of the brain in question, and its age, mandated – but without being themselves the actual 'site' of the mind.

But while few people would dispute the merit of devising drugs that intercepted modulation, and thereby arrested neurodegeneration, other drugs and sophisticated new forms of chemical intervention might have a much more ambiguous agenda. Current biotechnology is not simply about better therapy for obvious illnesses – certainly not when it comes to the brain. As this century unfolds, we will witness increasingly a blurring of the distinction between interventions in the cause of therapy and those aimed at improving lifestyle – and with it, far-reaching consequences for future life in general.

A new idea based on the concept of 'transhumanism' holds that there is room for improvement even in the healthy human brain and body. Transhumanism is the promotion of science and technology to go beyond the norm – whatever that is – for physical and mental enhancement. The concept, and indeed the term itself, go back to 1957 when the biologist Julian Huxley first coined it to describe a future point when humanity would find itself 'on the threshold of a new kind of existence'. More recently Francis Fukuyama, a professor of international politics at Johns Hopkins University in Baltimore, has described it as 'the world's most dangerous idea'. Transhumanist technology can span many types of science, and comes in a very wide range of flavours varying in their degree of credibility and feasibility.

As the technical hurdles are overcome, and as the trend for high expectations of individuals and society soar, so will the desire to be 'perfect'. For example, pharmacological strategies with growth hormones are holding out to an increasing number of us the still distant dream of at least a prolonged, if not eternal, youth. And still more immediately, 'lifestyle drugs' are attracting interest and indeed enthusiastic acceptance by many: Prozac and Ritalin, for example, are already household names for tackling the problems of depression and attention disorders respectively. But what do these drugs actually *do* to the brain?

Danielle Turner and her colleagues at the University of Cambridge's Department of Psychiatry have studied the effects of Modafinil, a drug with a similar clinical profile to Ritalin but with a novel mode of action at the level of the brain cells, which is used in cases of attention deficit disorder (ADHD). A one-off dose to healthy young men significantly enhances their performance on certain specific tasks – visual pattern recognition, spatial planning and reaction time. The subjects report that they feel more alert, attentive and energetic, but with a tendency to reduce any impulsive responses. As such, a drug like Modafinil might prove the treatment of choice for ADHD. There's also a benefit for those who aren't hyperactive: the drug could actually improve mental performance in normal, healthy people and achieve so-called cognitive enhancement.

These cognitive enhancers are currently much debated in relation to their prescription for ADHD. But the underlying issue with drugs such as Modafinil is that they don't target a single trait such as mood or concentration or wakefulness. Nor could they – not least because we don't yet understand how such functions are generated as a cohesive operation in the brain. The same problem applies to drug action as it did earlier to gene function, only this time we're dealing with transmitters. Any one transmitter whose availability will be changed by drugs will, as with the proteins triggered by genes, have many functions throughout the brain. It would be impossible for a single transmitter to have a complex mental trait trapped inside it, any more than, as we have seen, it would be possible for a 'function' or trait to be trapped inside DNA or the protein that ensues. For example, a transmitter may change arousal levels very generally, or operate throughout many different circuits; therefore it will have many actions and no single one-to-one exclusive 'function' with a trait or behaviour. Always keep in mind that drugs work within a very broad bandwidth.

But as well as taking Prozac to combat depression, some people, undeterred, are already turning to related drugs such as Paxil as an antidote for shyness, and Sarafem to control moodiness: these drugs, like Ritalin, all target the hub neurons and elevate levels of the chemical cousins dopamine and noradrenaline. Meanwhile the plant-based product gingko biloba is claimed to improve and maintain one's memory: it works by combating those molecular Rambos the free radicals, which become increasingly hard to control as one gets older. But while such drugs might combat existing impairments in mental function or prevent future ones, how might they make a healthy individual even 'better'? If someone was super-outgoing, had perfect recall and was monotonously and unconditionally jolly, would that really be an ideal?

In any event, transhumanism is an umbrella term covering many different technologies beyond pharmacology. In recent years we have seen an increase in non-drug interventions such as cosmetic surgery and pre-implantation genetic diagnosis – in IVF, screening the embryo for hereditary diseases before implantation in the womb. Meanwhile gene therapy, brain implants and other nano-technological devices are already in development. But surely the idea of 'enhancement' is sinister in whichever way it might be applied? In the unlikely event that absolutely everyone was regarded as 'improved' to the same extent, we would end up in a predictably homogenous world predicated on the assumption that each of us was otherwise naturally inadequate. Worse still, and more likely, would be the scenario where only a minority were so favoured: a sector of society consisting of techno-haves increasingly divergent from the techno-have-nots. Needless to say, there are equal numbers of supporters and critics of transhumanism.

The bioethicist Arthur Caplin, for example, points out that we have always striven to improve ourselves physically and mentally. And if we have external assistance from computers and the like, surely now we are merely internalizing those aids: the new technologies simply offer a powerful way of achieving that goal. Moreover, if a body part wears out, surely the obvious strategy is simply to fix it. And as for the argument that inequality is bad, inequality has been with us for millennia and attempting to improve our status is by no means the monopoly of the latest high-tech.

Another vexed issue, as with drug treatments, is when exactly the same level of enhancement procedure would be viewed as appropriate for therapy but inappropriate for a healthy individual. What if the two were at the same level of ability, but only one as a result of an illness? Would treating early cognitive impairment be 'enhancing'? In general, there is no clear distinction between therapy and enhancement. Transhumanism technologies don't automatically imply that you are passing beyond the normal functioning of your species, but rather could simply be seen as improving on what is normal for any particular individual.

The counter-arguments, those against transhumanism, are perhaps easier and more obvious to articulate: global inequality, diversion of valuable medical expertise and the usurpation of precious time from saving lives and alleviating suffering. But perhaps the most important question of all is this: what would be the implications for a society, and indeed for each individual, in which physical and mental perfection were the expected norm? Although it might be possible to imagine a world in which everyone was healthy, would that mean they were all within the same weight range and the same height? That none would wear spectacles, or be bald, or have grey hair or big noses? That we would therefore all look much more similar to each other?

More importantly still, what would our enhanced minds be like? Would it mean we all thought the same? In any case, just as there is no 'perfect' body – different cultures and societies have different norms – it is even harder to imagine the 'perfect' mind. How would this 'perfection' manifest itself? Here once again is a mismatch: as we saw with the example for neurodegeneration, we might be able to trace a link between an aberrant neuronal process and a respective brain disorder and, theoretically at least, fix the problem with a drug. But because the link is most often necessary rather than sufficient, we cannot simply assume that by increasing or decreasing that process even more, we will have a super-whatever mental trait. And even if we could, who is to say whether a perfect-recall memory is ideal, or a greater or lesser degree of arousal, or a longer attention span? Moreover, tweaking one mental trait might have an unexpected, adverse affect on other inter-related abilities within the individual's mental portfolio.

We cannot deconstruct 'intelligence', 'ingenuity' or any other mental characteristic so readily, nor indeed specify how emotional make-up would fit into this much-changed inventory of mental abilities. There is no such thing as an idealized super-brain. Just think about Einstein or Mozart or Picasso or Shakespeare as examples of 'perfect brains' – surely the 'perfection' was in the uniqueness of each, not in some simple, shared desiderata!

Even more so than for bodies, the whole point of minds is surely that they are diverse and individual. And in any case, what actually would be the point of having a better memory, or IQ? Would that give you more insight into the world and its problems? Or enable you to be more creative? It's difficult to see how qualities such as kindness or wit could be fostered in any direct way. And anyway, such appealing attributes are already there for us to develop using our ordinary old minds just as they are; because the whole point, the main point, is that the phenomena of seeing, changing, developing and adapting are the prime characteristics of brains – talents already brilliantly realized in humans.

Yet beyond transforming oneself into physical and mental perfection, perhaps the most extreme application of transhumanism is living way beyond the human lifespan. The more developed the society, the more do hereditary factors hold sway over environmental and nutritional factors; yet even though some of us live longer than others, the age limit of 120 years or so has never been significantly exceeded. None the less, attempts to stretch the lifespan continue apace. For example, the longevity-enhancing effects of calorie restriction seen in rats might be caused simply by the fact that eating less food greatly increases the levels of enzymes that destroy free radicals, those naturally occurring chemical terminators of cells. (Note: anyone tempted to embark on a rigorous diet after reading this should note that such severe calorie restriction, at least in rats, appears to inhibit copulation!)

Another approach is based on the idea that dysfunctional ageing cells release a killer substance, so perhaps a terminator gene to finish off such cells quickly might cut off the otherwise prolonged release of the killer substance. A comparable molecular biology strategy is to target chromosomes, the molecular coathangers for genes, the ends of which normally deteriorate with age. The most famous sheep in the world, Dolly, turned out to have shorter chromosome ends than might have been expected thanks to her cloning from cells not in their prime. However, certain chromosome ends do remain in mint condition – those in sperm, egg, stem and cancer cells; this is because they contain an enzyme called telomerase that isn't present in any other cells in the body. So another good strategy might be to preserve the ends of chromosomes: if telomerase could be introduced into all body cells they would all remain pristine!

A third genetic strategy aims not so much at anti-ageing but at the promotion of longevity itself, in the search for a possible 'Methuselah' gene. Apparently, some fruit flies with a certain gene can live a third longer than their normal counterparts; but in humans it is more probable that ageing will turn out to be, like 'intelligence', a complex trait – a catch-all term for many processes.

Coming full circle, perhaps the most immediate impact of biotechnology on our outlook, our minds, concerns reproduction. Your reproductive status is a powerful factor in how you see yourself, and how you relate to others. A dramatic change in your reproductive abilities over your lifetime would inevitably transform how you see that life. Already the technology is close not just for freezing human eggs, but for thawing them. Once perfected, this advance could make almost as much difference to a woman's (and hence a man's) life story as did the advent of the Pill a half a century or so ago. If eggs were harvested in peak condition, when a woman was at her optimum reproductive age in her late teens or early twenties, then she would pursue whatever career she wished without the all-too-familiar biological timebomb ticking. If and when she wished to reproduce, even when post-menopausal, it would then be possible to have a child with the breeding partner of her choice, if needs be with IVF.

Further into the future, there is the prospect of that partner being of the same gender and even of circumventing the issue of sperm and eggs altogether as the source of the particular sought-after DNA. One distant technology could be to extract the genetic material from any cell in your body, and combine it with that from anyone else, even someone of the same sex. As a result the current tight constraints on who is fertile, and when, would be removed. Anyone could reproduce at any time: not only could same-sex couples have their own biological offspring, but a grandmother or grandfather could be parents again, and even a child could have a child. Just because it might be *possible* to have a very old or a very young parent doesn't of course mean that it would be desirable. It is arguable that the natural constraints on our reproductive timeframe exist to ensure that a child has the most mature yet at the same time longest surviving parents possible; but if, in the future, both maturity and longevity could be changed by technology, then such constraints would be less compelling. In short, one of the most fundamental forms of classification of people, both in terms of how others see you and of how you see yourself – one of the biggest milestones in your life story – would be removed. The generational divide would no longer exist.

Inextricably bound up with health and reproductive status is appearance. Your appearance tells the world how healthy you are, but the reverse is also true: your appearance can affect your health. For example, a wonderful programme called *Look Good, Feel Better* aims to help women regain their confidence and restore a positive sense of wellbeing after their appearance has been changed dramatically by anti-cancer treatments such as radio- and chemotherapy. And, more generally, appearance plays a non-trivial part in how we see ourselves, and certainly how we are perceived by others. Here too is a further arena in which biotechnology is set to make a massive change. Already one programme of stem cell research aims at combating baldness, while new and more powerful approaches to weight loss, in the form of a pill, are still a dream for many people who aren't necessarily morbidly obese – but a dream that is coming closer.

Yet perhaps the most complex and powerful connection between appearance and identity is associated with the face. In 2006 a French woman, Isabelle Dinoire, was paraded before the world's media with the lower half of her formerly dog-ravaged face restored with a transplant from a dead donor. The technology for full transplants of the face is already viable; but the ensuing and essential ethical debate is centred on the big question of how greatly we see our identity as being bound up in that particular configuration of eyes-nose-mouth. Inevitably, the issue of how important your face is to you for your own sense of identity varies from person to person. In the case of identical twins there is presumably a gamut of attitudes. Some might exhibit an exaggerated disregard for the outward appearance of identity in favour of the 'real' inner person that they know is truly different from their twin; while perhaps for other identical twins, the similarity of what is seen in the mirror to a completely separate person who features daily in their life might dilute their sense of individuality in favour of a more collective dual entity.

But these intriguing alternatives might soon become not just a riddle regarding twins but a more widespread issue.

As with the body generally, might increasingly easy technologies for 'improving' the face render it more standardized, moving towards a more uniform 'ideal'? If so, there would be an uncoupling of the erstwhile equation, captured even in the purpose of the name of the website Facebook, of the face as the outward sign of your identity.

Two options would logically follow: either looking so similar to others might lead to the sense of a more collective identity, or alternatively the face would no longer be the outward mark of the individual. Would the individual then atrophy, or be outwardly manifest in different ways – perhaps by more eccentric behaviours or unusual clothing? The possibilities are impossible to predict, so intimate and unconditional, until now, has been the connection between 'you' and your face, bearing as it does the full brunt of your particular life story.

But beyond the face value of faces – whatever that may be – the human mind has for millennia developed into a truly unique entity, one for every single person that has ever walked the planet. And, as we have seen in previous chapters, for almost as long, these minds have been vulnerable to diseases and drugs. But we have also just seen how the normal generational distinctions – health, appearance, reproductive status – might all become blurred or even disappear. Be it through changes as 'superficial' as a change in appearance, as immediate as a lifestyle drug, or as desirable as an extended lifespan, biotechnology will bend the mind in ways we have never thought possible and with implications that test our imaginations to the limit. In addition, we could well be living in a society where inequality is without precedent or parallel, where some people have exceptional, enhanced physical and mental prowess, and where in any event, for everyone, the idea of perfection is paramount – and a reality. But as individuals, could we, would we, really be *that* different?

BEING SOMEONE

How could you possibly be the same person you were ten years ago, one year ago, a month ago or even a minute ago? Having deconstructed the human mind down to molecules and cells, we're now in a good position to put it back together. You'll be very familiar by now with the idea that inside your head there is endless upheaval: circuits of neurons ceaselessly shifting their allegiances and their balance of power with their neuronal neighbours, both near by and more distantly throughout your nervous system. Since drugs and disease, and now the newer technologies, all intervene at the level of this neuronal networking, it is hardly surprising that the resultant 'mind' is so vulnerable. Or have the preceding chapters been talking of exceptions rather than rules?

Throughout each normal day the world, and living in it, is leaving its mark on the effectiveness of your synapses, the levels of neurotransmitters, the activated and silenced genes, new neurons and newly dead ones. Yet despite the endless and spectacular dynamism of your brain – one that we have just seen may be increasingly and dramatically manipulated and accelerated in the future – there is none the less usually a reassuringly consistent theme that is *you*: your identity.

This identity is the most basic assumption for going through life and interacting with others. It can be reflected directly in the perspective of 'mind', or much more indirectly in the perspective of 'personality'. But surely they are really two sides of the same coin? The 'mind' is the first-person perspective of your identity – how you see yourself; 'personality' is the third-person perspective, how others see you as a result of what you say and do to them. Of course, how you see yourself may differ from how others see you, and you may not 'reveal' elements of yourself to everyone; but that's the whole point of different first- and third-party perspectives.

People may vary in their 'personalities' according to the context of the moment, given that most of us like to be admired and respected – but above all accepted. Within a group, our behaviour will most usually adapt to a norm that varies from one group to the next, be it with work colleagues in a meeting, a family gathering or friends having a night out; in each case different mores, standards and modes of speech will prevail. The important point is that you don't function in isolation. Those around you and the happenstance of the moment may bring out different behaviours, some of them quite surprising in retrospect even to you yourself. And as we have seen already, from moment to moment events will subtly change your brain and, with it, your mind. So we cannot think of an individual as an isolated entity, but rather as a provisional product of what has happened in that person's brain to date, combined with what is happening to change that brain right now.

This chapter, and most of the rest of the book, will be all about how the human brain can generate a sense of unique individual identity, and the different future scenarios that could jeopardize it. For the moment, your identity lasts a lifetime: it will encompass all those transformations to your neuronal landscape as your mind correspondingly broadens, or arguably narrows, as the result of living a life. But the enduring theme is somehow always the same: an irrefutable sense that you are a unique and continuous first-person consciousness. And others acknowledge you as such, just as you in turn view them as unique individuals. But although each of us is unique, our identity as twenty-first-century individuals is in crisis, or at least more open to change than ever before. As I see it, three broad options are in play, and we'll be looking at each in turn in the chapters that follow.

Let's start first with the type of identity which is the most familiar to us in modern Western culture: the 'Someone' scenario. To be 'someone' is to have a clear identity, the limits of which have been defined by the extent of your physical body in time and space. In this most basic sense, all of us since the dawn of time have most probably enjoyed a sense of self. Without question, our physical bodies play a part in our sense of identity. In fact, the neurologist Antonio Damasio has introduced the concept of a 'somatic' identity – from 'soma', the Greek for body. The idea is that our sense of self is based on neuronal mappings in the brain of bodily experiences as we interact with the outside world. And, indeed, cases of stroke in certain brain regions can lead to 'neglect' of certain limbs, or even half a face. In this scenario the patient will attempt the most elaborate of confabulations to explain why, for example, the hand that has been disowned is wearing a ring they admit is theirs: the patient will insist that it is in fact the doctor's hand, and that the doctor has stolen the ring!

But surely the most important aspect of this body awareness is the self-consciousness that accompanies it, not the feedback or lack of it from the body itself. An animal with comparable brain damage might not groom a neglected limb, but in so doing they wouldn't be displaying a distorted sense of identity. Feedback from your body may be necessary for a first-hand sense of identity, but it isn't sufficient. There must be something more essential and basic still, something that not all animals would have or do.

Although all animals also have distinct, independent bodies with which they navigate their own trajectories in the world, only the more sophisticated species seem to have any sort of claim to 'individuality'. And even then they would not necessarily have a first-person identity – a sense of self, a mind. Remember the dead goldfish back in Chapter 2? Only when members of a certain species have individual experiences, and those experiences can drive individualized changes in their brains, would we say that any kind of 'individuality' could be attributed to the organism in question. But even then – as in the case of pet cats and dogs, say – would that uniqueness derive from just the third-person perspective? We could and would talk about the 'personality' of a cat or dog, but that wouldn't mean to say that the cat or dog itself had any sense of a cohesive and enduring identity – that it viewed the world and itself from the first-person perspective of an individual 'mind'.

For brain scientists who are interested in identity, one tempting strategy – in fact the one that we've been adopting here – is to try to extrapolate how a sense of self might be normally, as well as abnormally, generated in the human brain. The neurologist Todd Feinberg suggests that 'disorders of self' relate to aberrant connections with other people: you can either cease to recognize certain family members or friends as significant to you, or conversely perceive distant strangers, perhaps work colleagues or medical carers, as close relatives. Feinberg traces these aberrations to impairments in the right frontal lobe; but does that mean that this particular brain region is the 'centre for' identity?

Of course not. One of my favourite mantras, repeated throughout these pages, is that we should abandon the concept of a 'centre for' different functions housed in autonomous brain regions. That is not to say that the all-important associations underlying the abandoned or invented relatives are not linked in some way to the right frontal lobe. But that is a far cry from trying to find a neuroscientific basis for a sense of self. Once again, as already seen with stroke patients and those suffering bodily 'neglect', such phenomena may relate to a sense of self but are not the essence of it. Although we certainly define ourselves in relation to others – be they family or carers – I would argue that the issue is not so much who those others are, and the family history or otherwise that you might share, but rather how all the people you encounter, be they close and meaningful relations or the receptionist whom you have never met before, treat you and react to you.

The psychiatrist Chris Frith has studied the sense of self from this angle by exploring the fragile identity of schizo-phrenics, who are often convinced that they are under the control of others. He has come up with the ingenious explanation that schizophrenics are under the delusion that their active movements are in fact passive, driven by others. And once you move in a certain way, you can 'internalize' the action as part of your thought processes. For example, rats and monkeys trained to 'will' a robotic arm to move a joystick have the same activity patterns in their brain as their counterparts which are engaged manually in the task. Perhaps schizophrenics have similarly internalized the movements they make to perpetuate the delusion that everything to do with them, even thought regardless of movement, is under external control.

Fascinating though this idea is, it is hard at the moment to express it in terms of physical brain processes. More importantly, the concept still doesn't really capture the essence of how we define ourselves. A fragile identity under the control by others is not the polar opposite of identity; surely the loss of mind altogether, through drugs or dementia, would be nearer the mark. We have seen that the mind, which I have now equated with a first-person perspective, and indeed with self-consciousness, is realized through highly extensive connections developed gradually in early human life. The resulting sense of identity, the 'Someone' scenario, is best summed up, in my view, by the anthropologist Clifford Geertz as 'A bounded, unique, more or less integrated motivational and cognitive universe, a dynamic centre of awareness, emotion, judgement, and action, organized into a distinctive whole and set contrastively against other such wholes.' Geertz adds that it is 'A rather peculiar idea within the context of the world's cultures.'

So let's think about the 'world's cultures'. Until relatively recently, up to the mid-eighteenth century, the social position into which you were born defined your identity, and broadly determined how you would live your life: there would have been little chance of a transformational inner perspective. You were a son, a daughter, a wife or a husband: you most probably spent much of your time in physical labour, spinning, weaving and cooking, or out in the fields. It would have been a life story that was predictable and that offered little deviation from a predicted course. You were a cog in the machine of a feudal society. Not only would you have had much less time than nowadays for introspection, but the very notion of 'individuality' in our modern sense of being truly and completely unique may have been a lot less obvious.

Then the Industrial Revolution came along to change everything. Just as a twenty-first-century revolution in technology is currently transforming not only our lifestyles but how we might actually think and feel, so it must have been almost three centuries ago. Imagine writing about the future back then. Our prophetic predecessor might have just started to realize that the manufacturing industries would create a new middle class with not simply more leisure as a result of manual labour becoming increasingly mechanized, but the potential to escape the stranglehold of feudalism and caste.

Now, for virtually the first time – and disregarding the fact that there have always been exceptional cases throughout history, upward social mobility could depend on your personal ambition and initiative: it would be up to the individual to act on their own ingenuity, with the new manufacturing age desperate to draw on diverse types of individual talents. For the first time, Someone could be defined not just by their place and function in society, but by what happened to them in particular, and, most importantly, by the much wider repertoire of potential actions open to them. The emphasis would shift from the birthright role you played in different communities and groups to the kind of individual person you were. An individual's life story could be determined more by their thoughts, their own mind, than by the external world – the treatment and attitudes of others. In brief, our ancestors would have reached a real milestone: a shift from the reactive to the proactive. You would be able if not to control, then at least to shape, in part, your own life story according to the dictates of your own mind – your unique consciousness.

Probably it is no coincidence that it was at this time of huge social change and shift to an individual agenda that the novel first appeared as a literary genre. In eighteenth-century novels, ideas of identity start to be linked to a narrative, a life story such as that of Henry Fielding's *Tom Jones*. The writer David Lodge has linked this new form of writing closely with that biggest mystery of all, consciousness – that private inner world that no one else can share and which we recognize as the vehicle for our modern identity. Lodge points out that, although humans have of course been conscious for far longer than the last few centuries, we have only explicitly labelled the phenomenon as such for some 350 years – interestingly enough, since about the same time that the novel first came on to the scene as a new form of literary expression.

The coincidental appearance of these seemingly unrelated indices of identity could be just that – different routes into the mysterious 'self'. Perhaps the novel and the actual concept of consciousness appeared as recognizable cultural entities simultaneously because the time was ripe for an important step forward in the human psyche that transcended any specific arts or science label such as, respectively, 'new kind of writing' or 'property of the brain'. From both directions, the important new step was towards the same end: personal privacy.

The essential feature common to both the novel and consciousness is one of a private state – an inner world, therefore, that differs from that of all other individuals. An obvious question for a neuroscientist investigating consciousness to ask would be, 'How is it done? What are the mechanisms, the tools of each respective trade?' So, similarly, we might ask such a question when we look up from our absorption in a good read, where we have been living out the second-hand but subjective experience of some fictional character: just as the neuroscientist tries to discover what brain mechanisms are at work, so we attempt to understand the impact of a novel in portraying consciousness by trying to dissect the literary mechanisms and ploys that enable the reader to share, at first hand, an alternative identity.

Clearly the tools at the respective disposal of scientist and novelist are very different, yet in order to answer the same big question about how to get inside someone else's head, how to see the world as they do, we have to address three important issues common to the wannabe novelist and the neuroscientist. The most obvious problem is the discrepancy between first- and third-person accounts of the world; the second is the notion of life as a narrative; the third is the distinction between consciousness and self-consciousness.

First, let's look at the difference between subjective and objective views of the world. Apparently, the earliest of the eighteenth-century novels struggled between conveying what was real 'out there' and what the fictional characters actually felt. The subsequent history of the novel actually reflects a growing trend towards a first-person, subjective view. Jane Austen was a pioneer in bridging the gap by writing in an objective author's voice as well as in the subjective voice of her characters. David Lodge illustrates this idea by quoting from *Emma*: 'The hair was curled, and the maid sent away, and Emma sat down to think and . . .'. Now there is a shift from objective to subjective perspective: '. . . be miserable.' And now even more directly into the heroine's consciousness: 'It was a wretched business indeed!'

Gradually this approach led into that of the 'modern' novel, in which the inner subjective state started to hold increasing sway over the objective narration of events, leading inevitably to a greater preoccupation with the idea of an individual human entity. The extreme form of utter subjectivity eclipsing any 'reality' or storyline is found in the works of James Joyce, with not so much a flood as a tsunami of consciousness that masterfully conveys the subjective feel of someone else's private, inner world; the most obvious example is Molly Bloom's famous mono-logue at the end of *Ulysses*.

Yet even Joyce still only had the tools of words, arranged one after the other into quasi-grammatical strings. Herein lies the big difficulty for writers, David Lodge maintains: they are obliged to use prescribed sequences of words, but strive to describe a phenomenon that does *not* follow a plodding linear sequence. The 'solution' was for the post-modernists to stop trying to describe feelings altogether, and to revert instead to what could after all be described in a linear sequence: objective, external events. Readers could then extrapolate for themselves the 'feel' of the conscious-ness of the character. In this latest strategy, there are certain clear parallels with the way a scientist might start to approach the phenomenon of the first-hand experience we call consciousness.

The brain sciences can also cite examples of doing a lot with a little, of extrapolation from minimal input. Visual illusions are just that because they rely on spaces being 'filled in' by the brain with illusory lines and so forth. On a more sophisticated level, we know that we humans are capable of 'change blindness' – seeing something or someone as having remained the same as they were because the most plausible scenario to us is that it, or they, *should* be there in a constant and unchanging world. Yet this type of demonstration is really not the same as the smoke and mirrors of the novelist. By conceding the subjectivity of each individual, by reaching the 'scientific' conclusion that we 'see with our brains not with our eyes', we aren't cracking the big problem of the physical basis of that subjective private world at all – merely acknowledging and respecting it. By contrast, the successful novelist would do better than the scientist here, since they would at least have conveyed a *sense* of someone else's subjectivity for readers to share, even if its physical, neuronal provenance were unknown and unknowable.

The second issue is this notion of life-narrative as a clue for insights into a first-person perspective. I can appreciate that a series of events would be a useful means for conveying the shadowy framework for a life, for the gradual growth of an individual mindset. Similarly, in the human brain, we have seen that the bump and grind of daily existence literally leaves its mark on the brain as the physical connections between neurons become personalized to reflect experience.

But this account of the 'mind' is too localized, too slow to form and too long-lasting to account convincingly for a flash-flood moment of consciousness, which is clearly distinct from 'mind'. The personalization of brain circuitry by experience is arguably the 'mind', but, as we have seen, you can 'lose your mind', 'let yourself go', and still remain conscious. The unfolding events of a novel may well be conveying the shaping of a first-person view, yet in so doing they are conflating these two separate terms, 'mind' and 'consciousness', that are actually discernible scientifically.

The third key factor is the important distinction between 'self-consciousness' and plain old 'consciousness'. While any animal with a nervous system has the potential for some kind of inner state, a subjective experience, only we humans and perhaps the more sophisticated of our primate cousins can enjoy self-consciousness. Even then, this self-consciousness is not a phenomenon that we are born with but one that emerges as our brains develop beyond infancy. Moreover, you can lose your self-consciousness from time to time, with drugs and sex and rock and roll, or skiing, or even fine food – any experience in which where the emphasis shifts from a rarefied cognition to a rawer and more communal, common sensation. Science can surely add value by providing the kind of description we've already seen, of how crossing such a Rubicon into the distinctly human experience – contemplating one's own demise, for example – might be achieved in the gradually personalized physical brain.

My own particular suggestion is that consciousness is variable, like a dimmer switch. I speculate that you can have more or less of it: consciousness will grow as brains grow. And this 'depth' of consciousness would not just depend on your status either in terms of phylogeny (evolution) or ontogeny (individual development), but on what was actually happening in your brain at any one moment. This personal neuroscientific model, inevitably controversial and still highly speculative, hypothesizes that highly transient coalitions, sub-second 'assemblies' of tens or hundreds of millions of neurons lasting a fraction of a second, will determine the 'depth' of consciousness at any one time. In turn many chemical, internal factors, combined with external features in the outside world, will determine the size of the assembly itself from one moment to the next.

The corresponding degree of consciousness could range from the reactive, purely sensory experience of many/most animals and very small infants, to more 'cognitive' states where the personalized brain makes a contribution only in more sophisticated species. The more extensive the neuronal assembly, the more tens of millions of neurons are involved, the greater the possibility for self-consciousness.

If the brain in question is small, as with non-human animals, or if extensive networking in humans is prevented by drugs, for example, then only the more basic inner state of sensations without personalized significance will be possible: 'blowing the mind', an abrogation of a sense of self, of individual identity.

That said, all I'm suggesting here is a correlation, a matching up of phenomena in the physical brain and subjective sensations. No one should be under any illusion that we scientists, and least of all me, are anywhere nearer to solving what the Australian philosopher David Chalmers has dubbed the 'Hard Problem' of how the realization of subjective thoughts and feelings occurs by means of the spaghetti junctions of neurons and squirts of chemicals.

Luckily for them, novelists don't have to contend with a Hard Problem. Novels vary in the extent to which they offer a vicarious experience of a character's consciousness, as with Joyce, or let us see the world through their values, their mindset, as with Austen. For novels, in contrast to brain research, the distinction is not critical: the important issue is that, unlike literary forms developed earlier, such as plays, poems, epics and legends, the novel encapsulates a sequence of events seen primarily, essentially, through someone's *personal* perspective: the defining characteristic is the preoccupation of a self in interaction with others, a recognizable, realistic social model.

The development of the novel has reflected the changing mood of the times in real life, as Progress swept away the old order: as the nineteenth century led into the twentieth, so objective narrative, mere action, led instead into the diversity of subjective attitudes, the individuality and sense of identity that today gives most of us the basic reference point for our lives. So when that sense of self is threatened our very worst fears are ignited, which is why two of the greatest novels of the twentieth century had such impact. Aldous Huxley's *Brave New World* struck at individuality by turning the clock back to a society reverting to feudalism, albeit through high tech: in it, detailed genetic and environmental manipulation stratifies each member of that society into a predetermined hierarchy ranging from sassy alphas through to the lift-operating gammas. Meanwhile George Orwell's *1984* undermined individual identity by breaching the firewall between the outside world and the inner self, as the original Big Brother read everyone's every thought.

Writing as they were in the mid-twentieth century, Huxley and Orwell were remarkably prophetic in anticipating how the bio- and information technologies could jeopardize the inner privacy that we regard as the very essence of who we are. Because those of us born in Western cultures in the twentieth century have taken our personal inner world of secret thoughts and personal views so much for granted, the very idea that it could be violated makes for riveting reading. More recently, it has also made for alarm at the way a technology driven by fears for national security could now be depriving us of our most treasured possession.

The very notion of identity cards already worries many people in the UK: even if one has nothing to hide, it doesn't necessarily follow that all should be revealed. Most of us would want to keep even our most anodyne secrets and views away from automatic and indiscriminate scrutiny by others, in favour of selective sharing at our own discretion. The identity card is perhaps sinister, not because it has any intrinsic high-tech power to read your thoughts, but simply because it has deprived you of the option of anonymity.

But lurking behind the modern-day identity card *is* a vast hinterland of electronic chicanery. At the time of writing, the British government are contemplating the value of 'joined up' information bases, whereby diverse facts from various public departments could be interlinked to provide a more quickly accessible and more comprehensive source of personal information on the state of your health and finances, as well as what you have been doing. At the same time the private sector is developing the power to 'profile' each of us, according to our consumer activity, with ever greater precision; we are just going to have to get used to the idea that we may well be targeted for marketing goods and services for which our retail track record has flagged us out as likely punters. Simple shopping cards, for example Tesco's Clubcard and Sainsbury's Nectar, are already monitoring our spending habits. And Google have recently been in the news with the confession that they were eventually aspiring to advise their users on everything from career moves to use of leisure time – all deduced from each user's particular history of queries. So strong already is this electronic footprint that it has led to an alarming escalation in 'identity theft' – a term that would have been unfamiliar to most of us only a few years ago.

Further into the future, but not that far, is the prospect of an identity chip below the skin, perhaps implanted at birth. Such chips already exist in prototype and are already in use, for example, to gain admission to a club where one is a

member, without the tedium of having to carry and produce a membership card. For membership card, read
identity card. At the moment the VIP club card only holds
information concerning the owner's membership, but
clearly much, much more could be added. So, rather than
carrying a card, you would simply have with you, for the
whole of your life, an electronic identity that was updated
every time you did anything or anything happened to you.
Accordingly, your consumer profile and your records spanning government departments would all be cross-referenced
and available at the brush of your arm against a scanner. In
fact, even such a voluntary gesture would not be necessary
for monitoring what you were doing from one moment to
the next. Imagine a GPS-type device in your identity chip,
rather as some offenders on probation currently carry
externally on their ankle. Now, literally, every move you
make could be on record every minute of the day. Meanwhile, another current news item is the debate over the
introduction of loudspeakers linked to surveillance cam-
eras, so that a voice shouted at you to pick up the litter
you'd just dropped.

This powerful combination of constant monitoring and
profiling must surely already be impacting on how you are
thinking and how you think about yourself. Identity is
likely to become an increasingly transparent, fragile and
questionable entity as this century unfolds. And, although
our society is not yet at the extreme of *1984*-type invasive
reading of actual thoughts, succeeding generations may
well feel that the consequences of their intentions being
so precisely monitored was pretty much as though their
thoughts were being revealed directly, and online. Just as

with Facebook, and the fears of the sixteen-year-old intern in our lab, Amy.

This erosion of the firewall between your inner privacy, your 'real' identity, and the outside world would perhaps be a little like an indefinite prolongation of childhood. Infants have none of this sense of self until well into their third year. The insight that they are separate entities only really takes hold at roughly the same time as they start to use the personal pronouns 'I' and 'me'. Moreover, it is not until they are about four years old that children realize that not everyone has the same thoughts and knowledge as they do themselves.

A now much-repeated and well-known experiment demonstrates this transition beautifully. Child A is shown an object such as a pencil case and asked what is inside, to which the response is, invariably, 'Pencils'. The experimenter then shows the child that something unexpected, say chocolates, is actually in the case. Now comes the critical part, as the chocolates are zipped back up again away from view. The experimenter now asks, 'If your friend B were now to come into the room, what would he/she say was in the case?' Younger children under the age of four, and indeed those with autism, cannot conceive that different people know different things and have different thoughts: their answer therefore will be, 'Chocolates.' Meanwhile if the same questions are put to an older child C, say, aged four or more, they will now be aware that different people have different thoughts depending on their different experiences, and will reply, 'Pencils.'

As the neuronal connections are configuring in the young brain, so gradually the inner private world assembles. The child realizes that they can lie and have secrets, that they can choose what they tell and to whom. This mental inner sanctum that is so vital to our sense of distinct identity is under threat in modern-day culture because technology and fear-driven legislation are taking us back to the world of our infancy, where mother had eyes in the back of her head, where she or any grown-up seemed to know exactly what you were planning and wanting, and where the adult in question was able to over-ride your own wishes and determine how and what you should be doing at any time.

The question as to whether the most sophisticated of non-humans, the primates, can also be self-conscious is one that is much debated. One famous observation inevitably brought forward in support of the idea is based on the painting of a red blob on the forehead of a chimp. When the chimp looks in a mirror he touches his forehead, demonstrating that he recognizes his reflection.

But recognizing yourself in a mirror is a far cry from having a sense of a unique life story, of being conscious of being conscious, and being able to contemplate your own demise. Recognizing yourself in a mirror is only the start of having an identity, and a progression arguably only made by maturing humans. Since even human infants are incapable of self-consciousness, it is perhaps not surprising that our primate relatives may never progress to full recognition of themselves as unique beings.

But although we all feel we know 'who we are', it is less obvious what criteria we might be using to define ourselves. For the last few centuries in Western society, but more obviously in recent decades, we have been using a host of subtle and not-so-subtle checks and balances: the 'Some-one' scenario. And, as we're about to see, it is this striving to be a highly individual Someone that arguably underpins the notion of 'human nature' stretched to its conceptual limit.

8

BEING HUMAN

'Being human' is actually a very tricky concept. What do we actually *mean* when we speak so readily of 'human nature'? After all, 'human' disenfranchises all other species in the animal kingdom, while 'nature' suggests a homogeneity and ubiquity in time and space. Throughout history, it has been a fairly straightforward matter to recognize exclusively the behaviours of our species that we call 'human nature', even though the context of that behaviour has been historically, geographically, and culturally disparate. The behaviours and thinking that we would describe as 'envy', for example, are immediately identifiable in Ancient Greek history and literature, even though the object of that envy and the underlying cultural context would have been so different from our own. Yet I for one have really struggled to put my finger on the all-important, definitive key feature.

The question has been asked many times, but let's ask it again: how *do* humans differ from other primates? Some might say by using language: after all, well-established studies have shown that chimps, when taught sign language or manipulation of symbolic plastic objects, can eventually learn to conduct a basic kind of silent conversation. But there are some critical issues to address here. First, chimps in the wild don't have access to sets of plastic objects, nor do they normally have these types of dialogue. Rather, such interactions are the result of painstaking training with humans. Secondly, even when acquired, their use of this artificial language is different: a chimp will rarely volunteer information, as does a human infant, by pointing out planes and cars and birds just for the sheer sake of it. Perhaps the young human is already trying to make connections, to see one thing in terms of something else, with a verbal label. The motive behind the now well-documented human–chimp conversations, however, is usually acquisitive: the chimp requests an apple or, in one enchanting film clip I once saw, to hug a (very unwilling) cat.

The archaeologist Steven Mithen has argued that these lab-driven skills in primates are not quite the same as the naturally occurring language skills of the young human. In his view, the ability of a chimp to learn to associate signs or plastic symbols with objects reflects the species' very impressive learning ability, but a *generalized* intellectual ability and one that doesn't make the extra leap that characterizes human cognition. That transformational extra step is one that Mithen refers to as a 'breaking down' of separate mental compartments; and this 'breaking down' from a rigid classification of the world has enabled humans, and only humans, to think 'metaphorically' – to see one thing in terms of something else. So although chimps live in complex hierarchies, and although they are highly dextrous, they would never express their status in an external symbol, such as a necklace.

According to Mithen, language could be regarded as an example, rather than the single all-defining criterion, of what makes us human: words stand for other things – but then so does cave art. Yet it is with words that we can best transmit information, and so bootstrap up from one generation of our species to the next, by passing on technologies rather than starting from the here-and-now. We can also escape the here-and-now by contemplating our past and future, and with it our life stories. And once you have a unique life story, you have the glimmer of a unique identity. But how might this identity establish itself? Clearly, the whole point will be to find ways in which you can distinguish yourself as much as possible from everyone else: your status relative to others.

But just a minute! Many other animals too recognize status, perhaps exhibited by being the first to eat in a pack, or by exercising exclusive copulation rights with the females. So what could it be that humans do *exclusively* to realize identity, the status of being an individual 'Someone'?

A good place to start might be to think about when we use the term 'human nature' in the first place. Whatever it might be, we often fall back on this concept of human nature as an ultimate excuse when logic and reason fail. So what behaviours are there exclusively in the human repertoire that are ubiquitous in time and space, and that also account for our species-specific frailty of actions?

'Of course he'd be jealous of Bob's new car. . . . It's human nature' . . . 'And human nature being what it is, she just lost it – exploded into a rage' . . . 'So they fell madly in love: human nature, after all' . . . 'Do you *really* need to ask if I want more cake? I'm only human!'

It dawned on me one day on holiday, when I had the time to let this problem just float around in my thinking, that when we invoke human nature as an excuse we are often describing one or more of the Seven Deadly Sins – which seem to be shorthand labels for particular behaviours arising from particular thoughts, feelings and contexts. I warmed still more to this theme as I reflected that a fascinating feature of the Seven Deadly Sins, leaving aside any theological considerations, is that they do seem to be exclusively human: animals eat and copulate, but do neither in excess just for the sake of it; and animals don't amass money, nor stare at themselves in a mirror. And yet, irrespective of era or place, we humans have done and do all these things all the time. So, weird strategy though it may be, might we be able to use the Seven Deadly Sins as unexpected clues to understanding the essence of human nature?

The Sins could indeed be viewed as exclusively human strategies for establishing individual status: they have transcended their original biological functions to symbolize something essential about us as individuals. For example, although all animals will display aggression when there is a clear survival issue, only humans show unwarranted aggression in situations that don't endanger physical wellbeing in any way. This is the Sin of Anger. Obvious examples include road rage, drunken brawls and domestic violence. So anger can often occur when not so much life itself, but rather status, is perceived as threatened. You feel the need to display how important or powerful you are in situations where you consider that your status isn't being appropriately recognized or acknowledged. This can have terrible consequences, with for example, the alarming rise in gun crime among teenagers, which frequently relates to status and represents a terrible over-reaction to a perceived social slight.

Might each of the remaining six Deadly Sins also be specifically interpreted as a behaviour for establishing individual status, and hence as a means for establishing an individual identity, being Someone, in our current society? If it works, this approach will be particularly valuable to our overall exploration of the neuroscience of identity, as the Sins themselves are actually phenomena that can now be described from a neurobiological perspective.

Let's continue with one of the most basic biological functions of all: eating, and the Sin of Gluttony. All non-human animals, leaving aside the special and arguably artificial case of over-indulged pets, consume just the right quantity of food to balance their energy expenditure. But food consumption in humans can send out signals about a diverse range of issues in our lives, way beyond the need for calories. The most obvious example is that under- or over-eating may be an important factor in the status that others attach to you and that you attach to yourself. The symbolism of eating and the significance of its consequences are most obviously apparent in the Western obsession with dieting: the serious escalation in incidences of bulimia and anorexia testify to the low status of the obese in the USA and UK. The all-important issue is that a biological necessity has become distorted, although the manner of that distortion is incidental and will vary from one culture to the next; for example, in certain Afro-Caribbean cultures fatness in women elicits admiration.

Food itself can also symbolize the comfort of childhood,

with sweets as an immediate reward that produces a warm psychological glow: chocolate in particular remains possibly the one permissible vice that can be indulged in by any human worldwide, irrespective of gender, age or religion. More generally, comfort eating has nothing to do with being hungry or needing calories, but everything to do with regressing perhaps to a secure time in childhood when you were being rewarded or praised, and above all loved – the bar of chocolate symbolizing how special you were.

'Food is the sensuality of old age': the lifelong appeal of abandoning oneself to the direct experience of the sense of taste also symbolizes something perhaps dangerously unfettered. The pure sensory indulgence that food offers will mean in more religious contexts that the rejection of food, for example in Ramadan or Lent, can symbolize the practice of devotion, showing that you have control over your baser urges.

Meanwhile the consumption of food with others is also freighted with the symbolism of status. Seating below or above the position of the salt cellar on the table in medieval times was a clear sign of rank, just as even today the raised High Table of Oxbridge colleges and at formal banquets, and even the carefully planned private dinner party, all reflect your apparent status in the eyes of others. And in extreme cases in certain cultures, it would still be unthinkable for those of inferior status such as servants or women or or lower-caste Hindus to sit at the same table as their perceived social superiors.

Eating together is an affirmation of equality (even if that equality is modified by one's position at the table), and the most basic sign of friendship is to share a meal: the very word 'companion' derives from the Latin *com*, with, and *panis*, bread – literally 'a sharer of bread'. But why might eating together bond friendships and be so special? Perhaps sharing a strong, dominant sensory experience at the same time is the best way of feeling *almost* 'at one' with others. Moreover, by sharing a strong, sensual experience you would be able to bond with a much larger constituency of individuals than you would for the still more intimate, and much more intense, bonding experience of sex.

And when it comes to the Sin of Lust, the circumstance that ideally accompany copulation, an orgasm, temporarily obliterates a sense of self altogether as one 'drowns' in a sea of strong sensations and 'let's oneself go'. The French even refer to orgasm as a 'little death'. However, it is the preludes to the sex act that have been hi-jacked for other, less obviously biological and more symbolic purposes relating to status: the rock star surrounded by the bevy of female fans, and the pride that many men take in being seen with an attractive companion, are blatant signs of status.

In Western society at least, 'romance' in its broadest sense is one of the most popular ways of asserting a sense of self, of self-fulfilment and of status. It strikes me that romantic love, whether or not it remains unrequited, could be inter-preted as an extreme example of expression of the individual – your unique needs, your values, your hopes and hence your personal life narrative, that can only be met by this unique Other. Moreover, irrespective of whether other species exhibit pair bonding, to the best of my knowledge there is no evidence, and it's most notably absent in chimps, of anything resembling our idea of romance – a sustained courtship, often with an unfulfilled outcome.

Love comes in many forms: a Yale psychologist, Robert Sternberg, has actually proposed that there are as many as seven types. The ideal is 'consummate love', combining intimacy with commitment; but if you have only one of those two qualities, then things are different. For example, commitment alone is 'empty', whereas intimacy alone amounts merely to 'liking'; but combine the two, intimacy and commitment, and you have 'companionate love'. Then again there's the romance that eludes chimps, that passion of infatuation celebrated on 14 February: being 'in' love captures the essence of the Sin of Lust that I'm arguing will say something about you, will signal your status both to yourself and others.

As a society we are enslaved by, thrilled by, scared by and addicted to this romantic state of being 'in' love. After all, it's the subject of most pop songs and many conversations and, as most of us know, it can turn your world upside down in a very short period of time. Just think of Marlene Dietrich singing 'Falling in love again, never wanted to . . . can't help it', and you can identify immediately with the inevitability and utter takeover of one's mind and body. Small wonder that romantic love is enough to justify, as it has done, endless thought and wonderment even on the part of scientists.

Frank Tallis, a clinical psychologist, suggests that the uncontrollable drive of infatuation is actually an illness, more particularly a mental disorder: love-sickness, indeed. Obsessive thoughts, mood swings, insomnia, loss of appetite, recurrent and persistent images, impulses to phone or text, superstitious and ritualistic compulsions, and inability to concentrate are all too recognizable as a description of the behaviour of someone in love. But this list could just as easily be a repertoire of behaviour that would be diagnosed as a major clinically depressive episode.

The idea that love is like a mental illness is not new, but stretches back from the Ancient Greeks and Arabs through to the Middle Ages. But Tallis has analyzed this illness from a more scientific perspective. The first question might be: why has being in love such power to take over all aspects of your life? The answer appears to lie in evolution. Reproduction is so important from an evolutionary point of view that it cannot be left to the caprice of humans to hum and ha over whether or not they want to procreate. Hence the obsessional thoughts and the despair on separation, all comparable to the symptoms of a real mental illness, yet here serving to ensure that you prioritize being with the loved one above all else. So, how do you get someone to fall in love with you? For women, at least, Tallis's answer is as disappointing as it is predictable as it is physiologically logical: be beautiful. Beauty, after all, is associated with good health, and health with fertility.

But is there a scientific basis to the phenomenon of love at first sight? Some people, or 'types', will clearly trigger love more than others, in the light of previous experiences that may not be overtly remembered but will none the less have left their subconscious mark on your neuronal connections. But once again, the critical issue is that the choices themselves will vary according to cultural context: it is the exaggeration of behaviour that is all-important. So, although varied experiences will clearly lead to different types of attraction, what will *not* vary so much are the effects, the most obvious and most problematic of which is obsession.

i.d.

We now know that, when prospective lovers meet, certain chemicals are released within the body. Phenylethylamine is like a naturally occurring amphetamine in that it energizes and arouses. Combined with this in-dwelling stimulant, other chemicals present in the body such as adrenaline and noradrenaline – also unleashed when danger or stress puts us in fight-or-flight mode – present a potent cocktail of huge excitement: the rush. And as with drugs, withdrawal – when the love wanes and the chemicals subside – is devastating. The abandoned lover can become depressed and agitated, similar to the withdrawal symptoms experienced by drug-takers.

In fact, being in love is not unlike being on drugs. However, with love it isn't a sledgehammer blow from a single chemical but rather a subtle combination comprising, as well as the substances that arouse you, airborne molecules called pheromones which work through your nose into the subconscious. These sneaky molecules can then enhance attraction along with the endorphins – the morphine-like chemicals that create a feeling of dream-like euphoria. If all proceeds to plan, this chemical deluge is followed by a further wave, including a surge in oxytocin, a hormone essential to the birth process and which increases, most significantly, with orgasm and potential attachment. During orgasm, a man produces three to five times more oxytocin than normal, and a woman generates higher levels still. (As an aside, perhaps this is why young women are slightly more prone than their male counterparts to form dependent relationships.)

Despite the power and complementary functions of this sequential barrage of subtle substances, it would be silly to think that love was trapped inside a molecule. What would fascinate me would be to find out how these different chemical arrows find their specific targets within the brain and, indeed, precisely how they work together to change the holistic configurations of brain cells in such a way to give you that simultaneously exquisite and scary state of mind called being in love.

Love, or at least being 'in' love, must be ultimately all in the mind, in your personalized brain – your unique patterns of neurons. So what happens when you are 'out of your mind' with love? In some way, during a strong emotion such as lust, those carefully evolved brain connections, our minds, are not as operational as usual; just as we saw with illness and drugs, the personalized neuronal networking is impaired. Although the brain connections are physically present, the various hormones and other chemicals that are suddenly activated could well gang up to tamper significantly with their normal working.

At such moments, when we were actually with the loved one, we wouldn't have access to all the covert, unique associations that we have built up over our lives: we would lose, for the moment, the ability to see people in terms of the sobering checks and balances that we have learnt from daily life. We would no longer evaluate what was going on around us in terms of what it meant to us personally, but revert to seeing everything at face value: how bright, how loud, how fast, how hot, how beautiful. In the words of the 1930s' song, love would be the sweetest thing, a '*vie en rose*'. We would be back in the primal world of the ongoing raw sensation of having a 'sensational' time.

A while ago, we unpacked the possible neuroscientific

basis of a world with less cognitive content. We saw how in children the brain connections haven't yet grown fully, so raw feelings dominate. Similarly, when we dream, the personalized brain connections may not be working at full tilt, because they aren't being activated by the usual strong inputs from our eyes or ears. And, again, there are instances when the chemical messengers, those same transmitters that can be activated by being 'in love', will malfunction and trigger conditions such as schizophrenia, a condition characterized by strong emotion, a lack of adult-like logic and a tendency to see the world with the eyes of the dreamer or the child: a place where one is out of control. Of course, I'm not saying that lovers are *exactly* the same as children, dreamers, or, as Tallis suggests, the mentally ill. But there are strong parallels. The common factor in all cases could lie in the underuse, albeit for different reasons, of the usual, otherwise extensive configurations of brain connections that characterize the adult mind.

Of course, such states would be counter-productive for living out one's life in the longer term, so it's important that this intoxicating machinery only operates for the timespan within which there would be a reasonable chance of conceiving a child, say one to two years. But if it was simply a question of the hormones rendering us mindless in all other pursuits, why bother with the fairytale courtship and wooing? Again, Tallis has an interesting answer: that in Western civilization at least, for most of us romance is the closest thing to a religious faith in a predominantly secular society. The rapture and ecstasy of being with the loved one is the nearest we will ever get to the intense experiences that many other cultures, particularly those in the East, associate with religion and worship. It is telling, surely, that the notion of romantic love features far less in more fundamentalist societies, where, as we shall see later, identity can be realized in very different ways.

But here's a completely different scenario, one that we shall also examine in more detail in the next few chapters. In Western culture too, our society is driven increasingly not by religion but by technology, which might be about to weaken the current importance of romantic love as an exprssion of identity. Already, allegedly, some three-year-olds in the UK are needing lessons in conversational skills, since so much time is nowadays spent instead in communication with and via a screen either in play or with the screen acting as a stand in, electronic babysitter. Perhaps it would not be too extreme to imagine a time, not so far off, when the whole idea of messy, face-to-face interaction, with its pheromones, body language, immediacy and above all unpredictability, may have become an unpalatable alternative to a remote, online, sanitized and far more onanistic cyber-persona and life. But for the time being, status in much of Western society can be raised or lowered by the person you are seen to be in love with and, most importantly, whether or not that emotion is reciprocated – while, paradoxically, the desired end-point of lust, the orgasm, will abrogate, even though transiently, any sense of self.

A far easier way of putting your identity on hold is simply to do, say or think nothing. The Sin of Sloth offers an obvious antidote to the current obsession with 'stress' and 'work–life balance'. Interestingly enough, the act of 'relaxing' is an almost exclusively adult behaviour: the need to 'chill out' is often a response to one's status being strained and challenged, for example by overwork precipitated in turn perhaps by a perception of underperformance. In a similar vein, having the time to refrain from working and indulge in conspicuous leisure once again sends out a strong signal of status in contemporary society, where rich and therefore high-status individuals have time to relax while comparable inactivity is seen as laziness in low-status individuals.

The behaviour, the lack of activity itself, is not really the issue; but, rather as we saw with obesity, the status, or lack of it, that in this case sloth symbolizes will depend on the cultural and social framework in which it is expressed. Within the workforce, at different times or in different contexts, either overwork or conspicuous time out can be regarded as denoting power and high status. Surely the most common opening conversational gambit in social gatherings must be, 'So what do you do?' We in the West live in a society where work, above all, usually defines identity.

I'm suggesting, then, that human nature is all about establishing and maintaining an individual status expressed through certain symbols and symbolic behaviours removed beyond a biological context: if so, then the more materialistic the society the more this Someone scenario will be nurtured. In such societies the Sin of Avarice will be central to the sense of self in providing opportunities through the accumulation of money. Money is the ultimate symbol, since it is actually nothing *but* symbolic: it has no direct biological function and is intrinsically worthless. The avaricious accumulation of money for its own sake is the most removed of all the sins from direct biological roots, but at the same time, is the most obvious route to the hi-jacking of all of them – sex, food, leisure – to increase personal status. In a similar vein, the Sin of Envy is related indirectly yet widely to the misuse of biological functions to promote a fulfilled sense of being Someone. If an individual identity is based on sustaining competitive differences between individuals, then those of lower status will inevitably act in ways that reflect a wish to redress the imbalance.

The Sin of Vanity can be interpreted in several ways. We have already discussed how the self is realized and expressed particularly in the individual face, and in physical terms generally. Since beauty is universally rooted in health and youth, it is a direct biological symbol of readiness and ability to reproduce. But in terms of symbolizing status, vanity is not simply skin-deep. More profoundly, and more than any other sin, vanity is predicated on a strong sense of a cohesive package, a conviction that you are not just a distinct Someone, but a Someone with superior attributes to most other people. Just as with the other sins – emphasizing as they do the status of the individual – the more fundamentalist the ideology the more will vanity be reviled: modesty will be at a premium, along with the promotion of loose clothing, hiding or shaving the hair, and perhaps even hiding the face.

So what might be the consequences of high technological advances in the beauty industry that increasingly democratize beauty and inevitably standardize appearances? We have already looked at how the new technologies such as the use of stem cells could also be applied beyond therapy, for conditions such as baldness. And soon we might not even have to resort to these measures. If we are communicating behind a screen for most of the time, adopting artificial cyber-personas as in *Second Life*, where might that leave an identity derived from physical appearance? Perhaps the Sin of Vanity will feature less and less in our human nature portfolio as we sit in front of a screen rather than a mirror.

Perhaps, then, the essence of human nature, that primary and ubiquitous feature that distinguishes our species from all other animals, could be no more and no less than the quest for an individual identity, the need to be Someone. And being an individual Someone might be explained, surprisingly, by reference to the Seven Deadly Sins. But if human nature is a constant factor in *all* our societies, surely this suggestion is in direct contradiction to the main conclusion of Chapter 7, that the relevance of being Someone can vary from one culture to the next, and has reached its most prominent position in modern Western society of the last few centuries?

The answer is that the two concepts, 'human nature' and 'being Someone', differ in quantity, not quality: individual identity, being Someone, is an extreme example of human nature taken to its limits, and realized in the increasingly frequent and unfettered expression of status through the Seven Deadly Sins. The Sins in turn are, for our current non-theological purposes, behaviours exaggerated beyond their original biological context to become exclusively human status symbols.

The Someone scenario comprises a life narrative that enforces the notion of a private individual, and as such it is surely very attractive. Most people would wish to retain the underlying assumption of current society that your particular lifestyle and views should be respected and, even more, that your unique personality, agenda and achievements are of value. In an ideal world, the development of you, the individual Someone, should be intensely rewarding as you set yourself goals and attain them. But as we become more bound up in the arms race to own more, achieve more, be more, so the stress and frustration at the inevitable lack of permanent fulfilment lead to an increase in depression and anxiety. The psychologist Oliver James encapsulates the extreme Someone scenario in the metaphor of a virus in his book of the same name, *Affluenza*, which he defines as 'a contagious middle class virus causing depression, anxiety, addiction and ennui'. Those afflicted with this sickness, James argues, have neglected their basic needs in the frenetic pursuit of their wants. These basic needs – to feel secure, part of a group, competent and autonomous – have been eclipsed by desires engendered in turn by a ruthlessly capitalist economy, based on particular products that have the prime purpose of enhancing your status.

In *Status Anxiety* the philosopher Alain de Botton argues that status is important because it inevitably brings attention – a kind of widespread love. The higher your status, the more those round about will defer to you; meanwhile those of low status are ignored as, literally, mere 'nobodies'. Apparently, one of the worst features of a low-paid job – be it driving, cleaning or serving at table – is not necessarily the low pay but rather that you are treated as though you were a machine rather than a person. You are ignored.

In a Western society predicated on the Someone scenario, you define yourself by the way others treat you. Inevitably, a dominant feature of your everyday life will be to strive for, and maintain, an ever-higher status: this is 'status anxiety'. For a long time, scientists have known that primates in the lower ranks of a troop produce lower levels of the transmitter serotonin, a lack of which is associated with depression in humans; an elevation in status will increase serotonin levels concomitantly. The epidemiologist Michael Marmot in his classic *Status Syndrome* has shown that status has a direct impact on health: blue-collar workers are more prone to stress-related diseases such as hypertension than are their arguably more stressed bosses. The critical issue is not status itself, but the extent to which, in the particular society in which you happen to be living, low status deprives you of social participation and autonomy – two of the basic human needs.

From another angle, in *Toxic Childhood* teacher Sue Palmer has introduced the notion of a 'toxic' lifestyle characterized by early twenty-first-century society: it has a self-centred perspective driven by values pushing us to be better in order to achieve higher status. She points the finger at no one in particular, but suggests that an unfortunate concatenation of factors in our society – screen culture, diet, security fears and work–life balance, to name but a few – have all conspired to make us, especially our children, unhappy and unwell.

De Botton, James, Marmot and Palmer all come from very different areas of expertise and in their highly diverse books the approach that each takes is inevitably very different. However, there is a clear consensus that is hard to ignore: the Someone scenario taken to extremes – the promotion of the self against others – leads to a far from desirable outcome. This form of identity is private, but not fulfilled.

So what are the alternatives? If the Seven Deadly Sins are the behaviours through which we each establish our unique identity, it follows that in contemporary societies, where the individual identity is encouraged, the significance and dread of sin are greatly diminished. Conversely, such behaviours would have been, and sometimes still are, perceived as undesirable, 'deadly' indeed, in societies where, and in times when, the significance and nurturing of individual identity were, or are, not paramount, as in fundamentalist societies. We shall explore this scenario a little later.

But first, let's take the current 'toxic' world to an extreme. Just imagine a possible future society where status, being Someone in the real world, need no longer matter because it's offset by living most of the time in the cyber-world. Could it be that, for the first time, the ideal is, after all, to be a Nobody?

9

TWENTY-FIRST-CENTURY THINKING

Surely we're now getting into the realms of far-fetched science fiction! How could it be the case that, for the first time ever, perhaps your great-grandchildren won't see themselves as individuals at all: a bleak, ultimately Nobody scenario. In this and the next two chapters we shall be looking at the evidence and trends that might lead to the realization of this literally incredible concept.

'Screen culture is a world of constant flux, of endless sound bites, quick cuts and half-baked ideas. It is a flow of gossip tidbits, news headlines and floating first impressions. Notions don't stand alone, but are massively interlinked to everything else; truth is not delivered by authors and authorities but is assembled by the audience.' So writes the journalist Kevin Kelly, drawing key differences between people 'of the screen' and those 'of the book'. Until now, at least in twentieth-century Western society, humans have been living out their lives with a fuzzy sense of some kind of identity, of being Someone. But the twenty-first-century technologies could be challenging this most basic of tenets, as we live increasingly through a screen.

According to one recent survey of eight- to eighteen-year-olds, children are now spending on average 6.5 hours a day using electronic media: moreover, the trend towards multi-tasking – using one or more devices in parallel – stretches that daily timeframe to an effective 8.5 hours. No surprise, then, that 25 per cent of all seven-year-olds and 89 per cent of children aged eleven–twelve own their own mobile, and that 92 per cent of nine- to nineteen-year-olds access the internet from a computer at home or school. More worrying, however, is that 30 per cent of such children have received no lessons at all on using the internet, and only 33 per cent of regular users of the internet have been taught how to judge the reliability of online information.

The 2007 annual report from Ofcom, the independent regulator and competition authority for the communications industries in the United Kingdom, has described a growing general trend: the latest technologies, such as MP3 players, mobile phones and television on demand, are leading, perhaps not surprisingly, to a decrease in more traditional forms of entertainment such as listening to the radio, watching regular TV broadcasts – and, presumably, socializing in face-to-face encounters. In fact, a particularly interesting finding is the growing popularity of social networking sites such as Myspace and Facebook. What might this increasingly dominant screen socializing mean for the way future generations interact in relationships?

The Family Education Trust, established in 1973 as an independent think-tank, conducts research into the causes and effects of family breakdown. Norman Wells, its Director, is convinced that the new technology could destroy family life: 'Technology is a very good tool, but a very poor master. There is a real risk that it can take over children's lives to the detriment of family life. . . . Dependence on electronic gadgets and technology may be one factor behind the marked decline in the verbal communication skills of children and young people that has been noted in recent studies. . . . Since children are particularly impressionable, it is vital that parents seek to control their exposure to violent and sexual language and images. Allowing children to have a television or unsupervised internet access in their own rooms is particularly fraught with danger.'

No one would deny that children are indeed living in looser family 'networks', as the adults in their lives divorce, remarry or cohabit with others who themselves have children from previous relationships. But on top of that, the current way of life is opening up previously unpredictable scenarios, such as the possible negligence of erstwhile high-achieving, professional parents now frustrated by the slow pace of a home life that is the inevitable consequence of supervising the very young. Meanwhile at school, pupils are becoming increasingly self-obsessed and easily bored, and consequently harder to teach. The situation is worsened by education audits and demotivated teachers, bedevilled as they are by the current political obsession with a test-and-targets culture. No wonder that children themselves, a new generation of consumers – nascent Someones – seek refuge in the hyper-stimulation of the cyber-world, where brands are the currency of love and identity, where what they look like and own is more important than what they are. Fashion and early sexualization for girls, 'domination' and 'mastery' for boys, are the theme of many products.

This is the black picture painted by Sue Palmer in her controversial book *Toxic Childhood*. Palmer's main proposition is that a wide range of nevertheless inter-related factors in modern society are causing our culture to change very quickly, too quickly for our biology – more specifically for our very human needs. Palmer is clear to stress that this 'toxicity' is no one's fault, and lists the numerous potential contributors to this frightening and uncharted new landscape: poor diet, lack of exercise, too much time indoors, insufficient sleep, parent paranoia over stranger-danger, less parental attachment in infancy, the amount that adults talk to children and the manner in which they do so, the reduction in childhood first-hand experiences such as climbing trees, inconsistency of childcare, inappropriate role models, a lowered level of emotional security, reduced social interaction with the family, weakening parental confidence and the demise of the previous tacit understanding that adults in general would take collective responsibility for the next generation.

And Palmer's concern seems justified. One British research survey has shown that behavioural problems in the young have doubled over the last thirty years, with emotional problems increasing by 70 per cent. Moreover, the American Psychological Association report that one in five young people are suffering from mental health problems, while the World Health Organization predicts that by 2020 disorders such as depression and schizophrenia leading to suicide, drug abuse and self-harm in children will increase by 50 per cent, placing them among the five main causes of disability and death. Of particular relevance to what we are looking at here is the rise in what are known as autistic spectrum disorders, problems of relating to the outside world and communicating with others.

However, not everyone shares this doom-and-gloom scenario. In the optimists' corner is Steven Johnson, author of *Everything That Is Bad Is Good for You*, in which he describes how the cognitive abilities of the screen generation are indeed changing – but in many ways for the better. This suggestion inspired a recent survey, *Their Space*, conducted by the think-tank Demos: the results of interviews, group discussions and informal conversations with young people around the UK, plus the polling of 600 parents of four–sixteen year olds, were in general upbeat. The children in question, born in the 1990s, are the first generation who cannot remember when they first used a computer. For them, the digital technology was 'completely ingrained' in their lives: they used it for maintaining existing networks, searching for homework on Google and playing games.

Demos concluded that the new technologies could actually nurture the learning experience, defined in their report as, first, finding information and knowledge; secondly, doing something about it; thirdly, sharing it with an audience; and fourthly, reflecting on it. However, the learning in question was far less formal and demarcated than would traditionally have been the case. The young people were as likely to seek help from peers and strangers as from teachers and parents, so that the boundary blurred between expert, amateur, friend and mentor. Similarly, work and leisure, entertainment and information were also far less distinct than for earlier generations. Teachers, parents and the children themselves all agreed that they were learning a whole host of transferable and wide-ranging skills including social/personal communication, general knowledge, risk-taking, multi-tasking, problem-solving and hand–eye coordination.

However, one enduring problem was highlighted in the Demos report: schools are failing to recognize that there is more involved in this kind of learning than merely providing the appropriate hardware: the issue is *how* children access information and thereby gain knowledge. Screen activities result in 'accidental' learning – learning by doing. The main worry of the report was that none of these 'soft' skills is as yet actually taught in school, even though we are living in a world in which 'personalized' learning is now the ideal and in which, if anything, the screen experience is encouraging what is called metacognition, defined as 'the capacity to monitor, evaluate, control and change how one thinks and learns'.

For optimists and pessimists alike, therefore, the crucial issue boils down to the brain and how it adapts to screen technology. Familiar as I am with the malleability of the human brain, I predict that spending so much time in cyberspace will inevitably lead to minds very different from any others in human history. And if that sounds over-dramatic, better that than a misplaced complacency. We just cannot afford to assume that our brains are inviolate, and then end up with a world in which our key values are lost for ever. But what *are* these key values? What do we want future generations to learn? This question could not be more urgent, as it amounts to asking what kind of people we want our grandchildren to be.

As a first step, we need to determine what effects the singularly twenty-first-century experiences of the screen might actually be having on the mind, particularly on the highly impressionable minds of young people and how they are thinking. But then, what do we actually mean by 'thinking'? Just as we saw with the seemingly obvious concept of 'human nature', which proved to be anything but obvious to define, so again here: the more you think about thinking, the more slippery the term becomes. After all, we tend to take this most basic of activities for granted, as something that human beings in particular do almost by default. All right, it may be easy to list different types, such as problem-solving, remembering, imagining and analyzing: but, good examples though these activities may be, a common factor is far from self-evident.

So let's try a different ploy. What about cases of *not* thinking? Arguably, road rage would be one example, along with a whole gamut of other, milder situations where passions of one sort or another sweep everything else aside in favour of the feel, the experience of the moment. We saw in Chapter 5 how drugs, sex and rock-and-roll are clearly effective strategies for 'losing' your mind, and with it access to all the usual cognitive checks and balances that constrain the adult repertoire of behaviour. But we cannot define thinking as merely the default mental condition that occurs in the absence of strong emotion.

Let's look at another interesting instance of experience outweighing thought processes: poetry. 'Poetry is the spontaneous overflow of powerful feelings,' wrote Wordsworth. Or, according to Wikipedia, it's 'an art form in which human language is used for its aesthetic qualities in addition to, or instead of, its notional and semantic content'. My own favourite definition of poetry is 'The right words in the right place'.

All these different attempts at definition would none the less be consistent with the idea that poetry doesn't depend on a logical set of steps, or even on a correct sequence of words: by tapping into our half-formed, pre-existing associations it gives us sometimes an insight, but always a powerful here-and-now experience. A good poem makes the hairs stand up on the back of the neck, puts a lump in your throat, makes you sigh. With poetry you are not travelling through a sequence of serial steps – you have already arrived somewhere.

Surprisingly, in many ways ordinary conversation and poetry have much in common: the disconnected phrases, the lack of emphasis on logic and the whole point being more than the words themselves. Rather, poetry and conversation share with sex, drugs etc. the emphasis on immediate feeling. Perhaps 'thinking' differs from all these very different yet comparable activities in that there is a kind of journey, a narrative, a sequence, in the actual structure of the sentences, via the logical order of those sentences, through to the correct sequencing of the propositions they contain.

Not all thinking need be as lofty as this operational description sounds. We are 'thinking' when we conjure up a fantasy event, or, in best revisionist fashion, rearrange past events to redress a grievance. So it could be that the all-defining hallmark of 'thinking' as opposed to just being awake is the placing of people/objects/facts/words into a serial sequence: a temporal narrative of some sort. Just as our own lives have been stories – unique journeys through time and place, at least until now – might it even be that our brains work in the same way over momentary epochs? 'Thinking' could be the generation of endless narratives in which we also view other people, world events, everyday objects, even the weather, in the context of that eternal storyline of yesterday-today-tomorrow, albeit highly condensed.

This idea is not completely left-field. The psychologist William Calvin has already suggested that we humans are distinct from all other animals in that we are always, inevitably, 'stringing things together in structured ways, ones that go far beyond the sequences produced by other animals. Besides words into sentences, we combine notes into melodies, steps into dances, and elaborate narratives into games with procedural rules.' These 'structured strings' might therefore be a core facility of the human brain. Calvin goes on to describe thought as 'movements that haven't happened yet, and maybe never will'.

And even earlier, the pioneering neurologist Oleh Hornykiewicz – who developed the drug treatment for Parkinson's disease that has been used for the past forty or so years – once commented that 'thinking is movement confined to the brain'. The issue here is not that there is something special about movement, but that a similar kind of sequence is involved for both thought and movement, in particular the type of movement impaired in Parkinson's disease.

Interestingly enough, Parkinson's patients are able to move normally so long as they have ongoing visual feedback, such as paper footprints on the floor. The reason is that when we make movements under ongoing visual guidance, a different part of the brain (the cerebellum) is engaged, instead of the region ravaged by neurodeneration (the substantia nigra). However, most of the movements we make are 'ballistic', a term coined from the fate of cannon-balls once fired – and which in our context refers to a movement that, once initiated, cannot be adjusted moment by moment by ongoing inputs from the eyes. The ballistic movement, be it standing up, reaching for the door handle or simply walking, is a preordained sequence of muscle contractions. So what Hornkiewiz meant by his somewhat enigmatic statement is that, as far as the brain is concerned, thinking and moving are one and the same – except that the former happens not to involve recruitment of muscles. Moreover, while the latter is common to all animals, prolonged, internal brain sequencing not realized as muscle movement seems much more the exclusive preserve of humans, and maturing humans at that.

So now we can add prolonged temporal sequencing to the other special human talent we established earlier – that of seeing one thing in terms of something else, thinking 'metaphorically'. Where does this combination of skills get us? Cave art, language itself and use of tools are all examples of our ability to think metaphorically: symbols, as we saw just now with the Deadly Sins, are the pivot of what we do from thought processes through to our quintessentially human behaviours. Now the really exciting issue is that in ancient Greek *logos*, literally meaning 'word', also has implications of organization and order – logic, no less. That most familiar of openings, 'In the beginning was the Word', also implies not just the word of God but a still more general sense of the initiation of some sort of systematic organization. Similarly, language doesn't just enable us to communicate more efficiently and effectively – it gives order, in both senses of the word, to thought itself. Once we have language, a word symbol for an object or person, then we can make the most of our already present natural propensity for temporal sequencing: we can relate one thing or person to another in a sentence.

With these two special talents, use of symbols and sequential ordering, we can start our journey into the past or future, freed up from the press of the moment. And, beyond the impact on our own thinking process, let's not underestimate the power of communication. As we escape the present moment we can take others with us, just by talking. Even more far-reaching, we can embark on journeys with those long dead, or living on the other side of the planet, just by reading.

When those of us who were born in the twentieth-century read a book, usually the author takes the reader by the hand and you travel from the beginning to the middle to the end, in a continuous narrative series of interconnected steps. It may not be a journey with which you agree, or that you enjoy: but none the less, as you turn the pages, one train of thought succeeds the last in a logical fashion. We can then, of course, compare one narrative with another and, in so doing, start to build up a conceptual framework that enables us to evaluate further journeys which, in turn, will modify the conceptual framework anew.

Surely this is one of the cornerstones of education as we last-century folk would recognize it: the building up of a personalized conceptual framework through which we can relate incoming information to what we 'know' already. We can place an isolated fact in a context that gives our perceptions a 'significance' – that is, we can see one thing in terms of something else, or more usually in terms of many things. Now, in addition, we can make use of symbols called words that remove us from the press of the moment and take us not only into the past and future, and on journeys with others, but also into our own inner world where the senses are shut out completely. As a neuroscientist, I have always been fascinated by what happens in the brain when reading a good novel. By 'good' I don't mean necessarily a work of great literary merit, but one so gripping that the reader can shut out the real world in favour of the shadowy personas that aren't necessarily describable in photographic terms, but who none the less are so vivid as to have an all-consuming importance.

One of the biggest questions we as a society now face, surely, is whether the competition of the screen against the book means that young people are starting to acquire different skills. According to the Literacy Trust, there is currently no conclusive evidence that reading standards are deteriorating, although there is a growing concern that standards are slipping in the UK compared to those in other countries, and that many British schoolchildren are not reaching literacy targets. Moreover, there is some evidence that the enjoyment of reading has declined in the last five or ten years, and also that children perhaps have more interests competing for their time: they may be spending a lot less of their day just playing or 'doing nothing'. Of course, 'doing nothing' would presumably include thinking and letting your imagination roam free. The Literacy Trust points out that reading from the screen is just as legitimate as reading from a book; but given the ever more icon-laden, text-light multimedia pyrotechnics, we might wonder just how long this situation of treaing a screen like a book, could last.

But why should we worry? Perhaps we have too much nostalgia for reading – maybe we are too ready to accept that it is a Good Thing, never to be challenged. In this spirit of pure intellectual honesty, Steven Johnson makes a fair point in *Everything That Is Bad Is Good for You*: we tend to regard reading as the gold standard since it has been ingrained for so long in human history, but compared to the screen, books do have some disadvantages. For example, reading follows a fixed, linear path, and as such it is not an active, participatory activity but a passive one. Then again, the passive following of a linear path may be precisely the way an individual can eventually construct their own conceptual framework to make sense of the world: the narrative, the linear sequence of related steps, may be the all-important building-block of the thought process itself. The straight, undeviating line of one supposition following from the previous one is perhaps just what is needed. The fact that such thought is directed by someone else, the author, is surely a prerequisite for anyone, but especially for the young, to arrive at intellectual destinations that would have been impossible alone and unguided. True, such journeys are indeed passive; but they do allow us to make an eventual comparison, to see one journey in terms of another, and hence to reach an ever-wider 'understanding', a multifaceted context within which everything that one encounters and experiences is then evaluated, has 'significance'. And as we've seen, we can view 'understanding' as seeing one thing in terms of another; 'significance' would occur when something could be linked to something else. The more connections, the deeper the significance and the greater the understanding.

Of course, our predecessors didn't necessarily read books; but they heard stories recited, or went to see plays. Their imagination and attention spans would have been stretched to the full. However, even more powerful than reading, hearing or watching stories, is writing them; how often do we hear people claim that they 'think with their fingers', that they need to write things down in order to understand them, or to write diaries and letters to set out their thoughts clearly to themselves as well as to others? There is an interesting correlation, surely beyond coincidence, between the great civilizations and the use of written language.

The American writer Neil Postman suggests that writing actually 'slows down' the mind. Why would this seemingly repressive phenomenon be either desirable or effective? I suggested just now that, with the exception of poetry, writing is very different from ordinary conversation because it's more rigidly structured, from the preordained ordering of grammar through to the clear, sequential, 'logical' or at least associated steps by which one statement succeeds another. By having these requirements routinely imposed on it, the brain will in turn adapt to functioning more readily in this way. If the brain is indeed personalized through a unique and ceaselessly changing configuration of neuronal connections, then the key factor underlying thinking will be the efficacy of the formation and re-formation of connections between brain cells. And as we've seen, such 'plasticity' takes time and an unambiguous, uncontested input (or 'signal'). Both these requirements would be met by a time-consuming and exclusive activity such as writing.

Another important factor for the strengthening of neuronal connections is repetition: just as with taxi driving or, perhaps more appropriately, piano playing, so reciting and singing nursery rhymes, especially with the added reinforcement of the musical beat, will enable certain appropriate connections to be made and sustained. Even more effective might be dancing: once again there is a set sequence of steps, and this time the involvement of the whole body in a way that would amount to even stronger stimulation, precluding rival inputs and allowing the new neuronal configurations to be as unambiguous and unopposed as possible.

Indeed, any form of physical exercise seems to be a positive factor in learning. Charles Hillman, at the University of Illinois, noticed recently that the local women's cross-country team did particularly well in exams compared to their peers. Hillman has now gone on to demonstrate that the introduction of classic PE routines to eight- and ten-year-olds had a significantly beneficial effect on maths and reading skills. The basic trigger for this remarkable effect appears to be the enhanced blood flow that deluges the brain as a result of exercise. And in a astonishing study, the neurobiologist Rusty Gage and his colleagues at the Salk Institute have just shown that the actual generation of new brain cells (neurogenesis) is coupled with enhanced blood flow in an area of the brain related to memory.

Gage's group studied a brain area related to memory, the hippocampus – the area which was found to be enlarged when the taxi drivers we encountered a while ago had to memorize the street configurations of London. It is here in the hippocampus that, amazingly, physical exercise in young animals increases neurogenesis and improves learning. But the research group were particularly interested in the well-known effects of ageing in relation to cognitive decline. The idea was to investigate whether exercise, in this case voluntary wheel running, would benefit mice that had led sedentary lives until they were, in mouse terms, geriatric: nineteen months old. Young and aged mice alike were housed with or without a running wheel and injected with a chemical marker that would label any newborn cells. After one month, the elderly runners showed faster acquisition and better retention of the optimal maze-running route than their age-matched counterparts. Just by running, the older animals had increased the rate of new neuron production to some 50 per cent of the levels seen in the normal young brain! What's more, the actual shape and state of the new neurons did not differ between young and aged runners: so ageing was not an issue in the initial maturation of newborn neurons.

The exciting conclusion to all this is that physical exercise appears able, at least partially, to turn the clock back for the production of new neurons and for resultant cognitive skills linked to the hippocampus. In addition, in other brain areas exercise causes the growth of more blood vessels (angiogenesis), which would lead to more effective delivery of oxygen and hence more effective synaptic operations in mice *and* humans. More specifically, exercise raises levels of a powerful substance called Brain Derived Neurotrophic Factor (BDNF), which, as its name suggests, triggers the growth of neurons. Add to that the observations that people who take exercise seem less prone to Alzheimer's disease, and that there is an apparent increase in the volume of the frontal lobes following exercise, and we can appreciate how and why young children are biologically designed to be constantly on the move.

Just to recap: 'thinking' has so far in the history of our species differed from other forms of mental phenomena, such as feeling a strong emotion, because it involves a connected sequence, be it of words, logic, symbols, sounds or scenes, that stretch beyond the immediate here-and-now. Non-humans can think to varying degrees but, in the absence of symbols for objects or people that are not in their immediate vicinity, 'thought' for animals would most likely be limited to the sequencing of whatever happens to be immediate in time and place: the chain reaction of stimulus–response–stimulus.

But the use of symbols, most notably words, that take us into the past, the future or a fantasy requires the extensive neuronal networking that characterizes the human brain. Moreover, our thinking is at its best when the brain is aided and abetted by large quantities of oxygen delivered as a result of physical exercise, by repetition of the same inputs, and by focusing inputs so that they are unambiguous and uncontested – through activities such as reading and writing. But might this all-defining human predisposition for 'thinking' and the lifestyle that has nurtured it now be under threat? If interacting with a screen is preferable to exercise, reading and writing, what will happen to the thought processes of the next generation?

LIFE IN TWO DIMENSIONS

'**B**y the early years of the millennium, approximately half of all one year olds will be unable to listen satisfactorily to the sound of their mothers' voices against the TV.' So warns Sally Ward, who studies attention skills in babies. In 1984, apparently, 20 per cent of nine-month-olds were unable to listen selectively; but just fifteen years later, in 1999, that proportion had doubled. And, equally depressing, the psychologist Dimitri Christakis has estimated that for each additional hour of TV per day that a child watches before the age of four, the risk of attention problems by the age of seven increases by 9 per cent.

A plausible explanation for this worrying state of affairs could be that the longer a child experiences the fast pace of the TV world, the more they might expect a higher level of stimulation than was available in real life. In line with this idea, the neuroscientist Daphne Bavelier has observed that video gamers possess increased visual attention, and can handle more complex visual attention-switching tasks. But the news isn't entirely good: this talent in the cyber-world could actually lead to increased distractibility in visually weak environments of the type that arguably constitute the 'real' world. Might it just be the case that constant, fast-paced and noisy thrills and spills, with one screen image tumbling in after the other, could well militate against the long spans of attention that we of the twentieth century have taken so much for granted, from the time we first listened to stories and then escaped into a magic world by reading on our own?

The capacity to sustain only shorter attention spans might itself drive the need for more stimulation within short periods of time. And, along with shorter attention spans, the ability to 'lose' yourself in a good book might also be in jeopardy. Just as reasoning and thinking skills may be stymied by a fast, screen-based and therefore visual experience, so also might that mysterious and very special cognitive achievement be threatened that, until now, has always made the book so much better than the film: imagination.

From birth and for the first year or so of its life a baby is locked into the here-and-now, at the mercy of the external environment. But as the memories of past adventures accumulate, so the infant increasingly evaluates what is happening, or about to happen, in terms of previous experience. And as the toddler learns symbols, words in particular, and how they can stand for things, so they can escape the press of the moment altogether as their mother tells them what excitement might be about to happen tomorrow.

Or perhaps it won't be what will happen tomorrow at all, but the fantasy of a story read aloud, which enables the young mind gradually to conjure up a special inner world. The passport into this world is language; but if you want to travel on your own, the additional entry requirement is literacy. As practice enables you to become more adept at creating this powerful and secret inner place, as yet inexplicable in neuroscientific terms, so the flat pictures in your story books start to atrophy: compared to the reality of your own first-hand imagination they are now unneeded, second-rate and second-hand.

But hang on: surely a screen-based life, rather than a literary-based one, has been with us for quite a while. For the last fifty years or so, the flickering external images of the TV screen would surely always have competed with books, and would already have placed the development of sustained attention spans and imagination at risk? Not quite: just think of the enormous differences between daily life then and now, and you'll realize that these differences are probably crucial. One of the most basic points is that the hours when TV was broadcasting were much shorter, so there would have been less opportunity for the waking hours of the pre-school child to be as saturated by the screen as they are today.

Secondly, since back in the mid-twentieth century there was only one TV to a household, watching would have been a communal, family activity. Programmes would be discussed on sofas and across coffee tables as they were broadcast on a schedule that you either caught or missed; to varying degrees the screen input would be diluted and offset by real conversations and human interactions. How different things are now! By 2005, 80 per cent of five–sixteen-year-olds had a TV set in their bedrooms – and broadcasting 24/7 at that. TV watching has now become a solitary activity, a substitute or competitor for family-based activities rather than a backdrop for them.

Sue Palmer has pointed out that, in addition, wall-to-wall TV might pose a serious issue for very young children if used as an electronic babysitter that replaces real conversations. In the same spirit, Peter Hobson in his *Cradle of Thought* maintains that for language learning there must be a 'triangle' consisting of parent in one corner, child in the second and outside world in the third. Only then can a child develop a notion of himself or herself as a separate being, one that can then communicate with others. In order to speak, and then to read, an infant needs an awareness of phonemes (the smallest unit in language that distinguishes meaning, roughly equivalent to sounds, such as 'a' as in 'cat' or 'ae' as in 'gate'), for which early exposure to language and talking is essential. Hence a hearing infant of deaf parents who was exposed to TV in an attempt to encourage him to talk persisted in using sign language until he was exposed to real, interactive conversations at school. It was the act of speaking and evoking a reply that mattered. The electronic babysitter might therefore be a serious impediment to eventual ability for learning to read.

But perhaps the most generalized drawback of TV, however, one just as valid for the sitting room of the fifties, is quite simply that watching TV is not living life to its fullest. The experiences are second-hand. Hence the conceptual framework, which is so important for thinking, might not be as extensive nor composed of such diverse elements when TV-derived as one generated by a combination of reading books and setting out into the happenstance of the outside world in order to have real-life 'everyday adventures'.

While the value of escapism, relaxation, information access and entertainment should never be undervalued, the stark reality is that TV does little for the inner imagination, nor is it an outer real life. However, real life, even of somewhat distanced, is moving in. Steven Johnson in *Everything That Is Bad Is Good for You* attributes the rise and rise of reality TV to the fact that it offers the nearest thing yet to your own 'real' emotions. Because the contestants in these shows are not paid actors but ordinary people, experiencing the all-too-familiar vicissitudes of domestic arguments/makeovers/new business ventures/wife swaps/house purchasing, it is easier to identify and empathise or indulge in *schadenfreude*, all from the safety of the armchair. And then we come to the third and biggest difference between twentieth- and twenty-first-century TV: instant interaction.

This safe involvement with a sanitized reality can be simulated further thanks to interactive TV, and the opportunity to have a hand in deciding an individual's fate with a vote. A plethora of channels and round-the-clock broadcasting are mushrooming, yet even now the relatively cumbersome and slow mass participation which the TV screen offers means that it will never be as pervasive as the computer the defining feature of which, after all, is interaction.

Both the social scientists Dimitri Williams and Sherry Turkle independently suggest that the internet will amplify whatever tendencies an individual might have – the highly social will become generally more so, while those who are shy will retreat even more from real human contact. While the TV in the bedroom might encourage solitary tendencies in the young, the interactive game-playing and web-based socializing offered by the computer can, it seems, take the scenario of the poorly socialized nerd to worrying extremes. In Japan, one estimate is that currently more than one million individuals, predominantly young adult males, are locking themselves away in their rooms to live a screen life. There is even a new term for this withdrawal from all real human contact: *hikikomori*.

But for the sociable and anti-social alike, a still bigger issue is what is happening in their brain, how they are thinking. The whole point of a screen is that it rarely contains mere text. Were it to do so, then the printed page would still have an advantage in terms of portability, power needs and general ease of access. But the great appeal of the screen is that you actually see something on it, an ever-changing visual image. And usually it's an image that's arresting and fast-paced and that invites you to interact. And if you are spending on average some six hours a day literally taking the world at face value, might you not start *only* to see the world literally?

For us People of the Book, an icon on the screen can be a symbol for many other things. But without a pre-existing conceptual framework, there can be no metaphor: the icon is there for and of itself, in its own right. For example, how many of those born in the 1990s, for whom screen living is embedded as a way of life, would actually recognize and understand the significance of that most-used icon, the egg-timer?

An intellectual skill that comes as we develop and read books is the process of generalization of an abstract concept from a multitude of different examples and scenarios. Might succeeding generations be less automatically inclined to savour ideas without icons? Perhaps we should no longer take for granted the ability of young people to 'understand' concepts such as democracy or honour or the soul. How would such concepts be described and displayed using icons or visual images in multi-media? Of course, once you have framed your question about an abstract concept, once you know you want to find out about democracy, or different notions of love, or what poetry might be, then you can turn to Google or Wikipedia. But my real, deep concern is that such open-ended questions just won't occur to those brought up in a here-and-now world of screen experiences, nor will the concepts be introduced amidst the pace and sensation of a screen life.

Another basic and novel feature of screen-based interaction is the directory tree. If you are always working with directory trees – where menus are offered with fixed numbers of options, where in order to get to another action you have to plod up and down through various branch lines of thinking – might that pattern not impose itself on the way you think in general? Perhaps such fixed and systematic thinking could, on the one hand, give a certain rigour and logic to your thought processes; but on the other hand, surely it would be highly restrictive? Fixed options might exclude, especially in the developing mind, the possibility of thinking laterally, of defying the up-and-down iterations. Might it be harder to innovate, if you are so used to all options being limited and laid before you? As the Nobel prizewinning physicist Nils Bohr once admonished a student: 'You are not thinking, you are just being logical!'

Beyond our reasoning ability, and even more basic, is our ability to appreciate, 'understand', what is happening around us. The computer, even more so than the TV, may be initiating a fundamental change in the development of a robust conceptual framework based on a wealth of different narratives. Imagine you are sitting in front of a multi-media presentation where, because you haven't had the experience of many different journeys led by an author or authority, you're unable to evaluate what's flashing up on the screen. The most immediate reaction would be to place a premium on the most obvious feature, the immediate sensory content: the 'yuk' and 'wow' factor. As the sounds and sights of a fast-paced, fast-moving, multi-media presentation grabbed any time you might have had for reflection, and hence for the forging of any sequential steps in your brain, you would be having an experience rather than thinking.

In *Toxic Childhood*, Sue Palmer expresses concern that such a lifestyle for the young will compromise the normal pattern of learning which has stood most of us in good stead so far: first, focusing on other people's choices rather than what grabs your attention; secondly, being able to defer gratification; and thirdly, becoming able to balance your own needs against those of others. Perhaps future generations will live instead, in the fast-paced, immediate world of screen experience: a world arguably trapped in early childhood, where the infant doesn't yet think metaphorically. It's a world, remember, that lacks the checks and balances of the adult mind: reality can blur easily with fantasy, since there is no read-off against past conversations, thoughts or events. It is consequently a frightening, exciting, unpredictable and above all emotionally charged world – a world of immediate response rather than one of reflective initiative.

A further issue of relevance to future education is plagiarism from the net. We don't need here to discuss the ethics, technology or regulations of downloading answers and essays, but rather the basic question of 'understanding'. In fact, the concern here is not plagiarism *per se*: after all, cutting and pasting from search engines and learning valuable facts from Wikipedia, as many of us do nowadays, are arguably at different ends of the same continuum. The key issue is, rather, how much use of search engines aids and abets 'understanding' – the placing of facts in a context that enables them to be evaluated in terms of other facts or events.

In the twentieth-century classroom, when it was just not possible to import information in macro chunks, the ability to précis textbooks was a key talent and one we were made to practise: it enabled us to see the wood for the trees. The copying of paragraphs wholesale from much-used and familiar textbooks was pointless because they were rarely succinct enough, in such short extracts, for wholesale plagiarism. In any event such slavish, unmodified reproduction would have been immediately spotted!

But now précised, predigested paragraphs are readily on offer; the BBC in their promotional trailers even at one stage referred to the availability of 'bite-sized' chunks of revision. No, the danger is not the trend for downloading *per se*: but rather, again, the lack of an ensuing guarantee of any real understanding, of placing one thing in the context of something else, of seeing one thing in terms of another. Surely we should not be reducing information, but doing quite the opposite – expanding it into a much wider context. If the context is shrivelled to bite-size, if facts are stripped bare and left on their own, what will the student 'understand'? Already, a simple augury of what might be to come is the inability of many of today's younger generation to 'understand', say, grammar or long division: after all, you just have to press the appropriate keys. Given that the current education system, in the UK at least, still requires good old twentieth-century homework, the application of twenty-first-century delivery to meet an arguably old-fashioned need means that students in school could well be passive go-betweens, passing on messages as though in a code that they themselves didn't know but that would be comprehensible at the point of delivery – the teacher.

Another arguable impediment to 'understanding' would be the discouraging of precisely those activities that we listed earlier as favouring the formation of neuronal connections: physical exercise to ensure the greatest amount of oxygen reaches the brain and repetition to strengthen the respective synapses that make the associations required for seeing something in terms of something else. In a traditional game, be it football, or Cowboys and Indians, or just climbing inside a box that becomes a castle or a car, the use of symbols, of something 'standing for' something else, is inescapable. But with the advent of toys that are computer games, or that link TV shows to console games, the emphasis has shifted towards taking the world at face value with little need to question or understand it, let alone create it for yourself.

A final factor that would distinguish computer games from movies or conventional card-playing is whether or not the latest generation of punters really does regard the screen world as 'reality'. Sherry Turkle gives a good example of this phenomenon in *The Second Self*, where she looks at the computer not as a 'tool', but as part of our social and psychological lives: on a holiday in the Mediterranean, her eight-year-old daughter saw a jellyfish and said, with amazement, 'Isn't it realistic!' This world can readily intermingle science fiction with everyday objects, can have plants and animals and weapons that are almost like their counterparts in the real world, but intriguingly not quite. This eerie similarity to, but lack of total congruence with, reality is all the more captivating as it is more readily believable: a version of our banal everyday lives that is more exotic but at the same time not so wildly different as to disorientate and confuse.

And if future generations end up being far more dominated by sensory, particularly visual, inputs in a way that requires more ongoing external stimulation, what knock-on effects might there be? One particular tendency that could well be modified, and in a way that is potentially both good and bad, is risk-taking. The degree to which we do or don't take risks, how we perceive risk under different conditions, and how the degree of risk shapes not just our overt decisions but our general attitudes to goods, services and other people, are all of obvious relevance to present and future society. If the cyber-world is one where it's all a game, where no one feels pain when shot, or actually dies for ever, might the long-term consequences of actions in the real world be harder to grasp?

A neuroscientist's approach to understanding more about risk could consist of examining different brain conditions in which attitude to risk is abnormal – most usually where it is excessive enough to be regarded as recklessness – and see what each of these different conditions might have in common. Earlier we met Phineas Gage, an individual for whom much was changed by the iron rod driven through his prefrontal cortex; one big transformation was that he suddenly became reckless. His physician at the time, a Dr Harlow, reported:

> His [Gage's] contractors, who regarded him as the most efficient and capable foreman in their employ previous to his injury, considered the change in his mind so marked that they could not give him his place again. He is fitful, irreverent, indulging at times in the grossest profanity (which was not previously his custom), manifesting but little deference for his fellows, impatient of restraint of advice when it conflicts with his desires, at times pertinaciously obstinent, yet capricious and vacillating, devising many plans of future operation, which are no sooner arranged than they are abandoned in turn for others appearing more feasible. In this regard, his mind was radically changed, so decidedly that his friends and acquaintances said he was 'no longer Gage'.

Recklessness does indeed seem to be generally symptomatic of damage to the prefrontal cortex. Sadly, there have been some twentieth-century Gages with the same problem. Michael was a soldier in the US army in Vietnam, where one day an explosion drove a piece of shrapnel through his prefrontal cortex. As a result of the severe change that the injury made to his overall outlook, Michael was discharged prematurely from the army to lead the more limited life of a hospital janitor. Of the many tests that neurologists and neuropsychologists have asked Michael to undergo, one is a gambling task. Michael has to gamble chips on whether a card is high, in which case he wins, or low, when he loses. The cards are deliberately stacked to give him a winning streak followed by a steady run of losses. Most people would quit while they were ahead; Michael, characteristic of those with prefrontal damage, will play on until he is completely out of chips.

And yet radical mechanical damage to the brain tissue of the prefrontal cortex is not by any means necessary to make someone reckless. An imbalance of neurochemicals, such as dopamine in excess, can have the same effects: an under-working of the brains cells in that area, leading to less neuronal networking. Such a situation underlies schizo-phrenia, where one of the symptoms is recklessness. The parallels we drew in Chapter 5 between schizophrenics and children would hold here as well: children too take more risks, not least because they are simply, through lack of experience, unaware of the consequences. The connections are just not there.

Perhaps not surprisingly, risk-taking could be linked to a scenario where the checks and balances of the normal adult mind simply don't exist, or, for whatever reason, cannot be accessed, or are offset disproportionately by the sensory thrill of the moment. We have already talked about how children and schizophrenics are not so adept at seeing or expressing one thing in terms of something else – inter-preting proverbs, for example. So it may not be surprising that metaphorical thinking, 'understanding a situation', seems to develop with age, whereas the first and most basic tendency of humans is not to rely on the personalized associations of neuronal connectivity but to take the world at face value, as do schizophrenics.

Another entirely different group of people characterized by the taking of excessive risks are the sleep-deprived: this is not unreasonable when you consider that sleep deprivation leads to a chemical imbalance in the brain that in turn gives rise to abnormal perceptions, such as hallucinations, that are hard to distinguish from real psychoses. However, a less predictable set of individuals characterized by recklessness are the obese. In a recent study in Italy, for example, clinicians compared the performance on a gambling task of twenty obese versus twenty normal-weight subjects. The number of 'good' choices made by the two groups differed significantly: the obese group didn't learn to maximize advantageous choices compared to their normal-weight counterparts – behaviour that could be consistent with a prefrontal cortex defect.

Why should the obese have this flaw? What might these individuals have in common with schizophrenics? The issue in either case is not that the prefrontal cortex is malfunctioning in isolation, but rather that the functional balance with other brain areas is thrown out of kilter. Perhaps normally there are two opposing forces at work: on the one hand the strong sensationalist present, where you are the passive recipient of strong stimulation, and on the other the checks and balances of the personalized mind. One intriguing possibility in the case of obesity is that again the emphasis is skewed disproportionately in favour of the here-and-now: the strong sensation of the moment, this time of the experience of taste and smell.

In the normal situation, this here-and-now thrill would be balanced by the 'mind' that takes you beyond the present into a past and a future: the ability to see one thing in terms of something else, the ability to be conscious of yourself as a distinct entity in an unfolding narrative. This ability to place the present in a wider context will be reflected in the degree of activity in the prefrontal cortex, and its relative dominance.

But if, for whatever reason, the 'mind' is suppressed, or if the sensations are stronger, a here-and-now mentality will dominate. The obese individual 'knows' the consequences of overeating, but lets the sensation trump them. And similarly with Michael. Compulsive gamblers, for example, might well 'know' the consequences of what they are doing; but such thoughts are as nothing compared to the thrill of the moment, the adrenaline rush of excitement as the cards are revealed, the wheel is spun, the starter's gun cracks, the flag comes down at the finishing line.

So the underfunction of the prefrontal cortex can be linked to excessive risk-taking. In turn, underfunction of the prefrontal cortex characterizes a variety of conditions and life situations beyond Phineas Gage-type damage, namely schizophrenia, obesity, sleep deprivation and childhood. All are very different scenarios in themselves, but they share an unusual weighting of the here-and-now sensations over the checklist of the standard adult mind. If the screen world constantly encourages here-and-now sensations, perhaps in the future the malleable human brain will respond accordingly and we could shift the balance more generally. It's not difficult to see how perhaps future generations will be more predisposed to a mindset characterized by less prefrontal function, and so with a tendency to take more risks.

Would a less risk-averse society actually be desirable?

Clearly, much would depend on just how reckless twenty-first-century citizens became, and what they were doing at the time. From my own perspective, a risk-averse attitude to scientific research, where people were less afraid to be wrong, would be very welcome. On the other hand, such a tendency wouldn't be encouraged in an airline pilot. Attitudes to risk, and how they might change, can only be evaluated in the broader context of the agenda and abilities of future society and the various sectors that will constitute that society. So many scenarios are possible that all we can say is this: less risk aversion may well be a feature of twenty-first-century society, and, as with technology itself, may have the potential to be both very good and very bad in its knock-on effects.

But we need to address an even more immediate issue. Screen culture is set to dominate for quite a while yet: but in the not too distant future we might also have to take on board another key transformation in how we think. As we have discussed already, the screen by definition emphasizes visual inputs and so could impose a literal, face-value outlook on the world. But soon computing will become increasingly 'embedded': technology will be so sophisticated that a screen and keyboard will be obsolete. Instead, devices within your clothing, jewellery and spectacles will respond by voice interface command: the eyes will give way to the ears. From an icon-dominated world, we shall move on to a world of sounds.

Who knows – such a transition might herald a return of the imagination, just like that developed by our ancestors when they listened round the campfire to the recitation of sagas. But then again, the big difference is that embedded computing will offer not the chance to dream, to retreat into your imagination following the narrative 'structured string' of a story, but instead a fast-paced interchange of action–reaction. With embedded computing and the demise of the need to balance a keyboard on your knees you will be able to wander about in a wrap-around Google. Already the 2007 Ofcom report has pointed to a predilection for those technologies, such as iPods and multifunctional mobiles, which maximize mobility. As you speak and move, the outside world will respond to you: inert objects will no longer be that different from people. Just as screen culture could eventually favour and foster a blurring of reality with fantasy, so a world dominated by the spoken word – and one of mainly warnings and statements, of question and answer rather than protracted conversation – could radically change the way upcoming generations see the world, and themselves in it.

The critical issue facing us will be how we make a transition from the old question-rich, answer-poor environment of the twentieth-century classroom to making sense of – indeed, surviving in – the current question-poor, answer-rich environment delivered by a fast-paced technology. We, or our children, will need to remember not facts *per se*. If search engines can and do deliver up-to-the-minute information, why does it now need to be internalized, imperfectly, into our highly unstable brain memory banks?

But it will still be essential to ensure the presence of over-arching conceptual frameworks, a context into which those facts can be placed and related to each other, can be given 'meaning'. Just as the invention of the printing press freed humanity from a huge burden on their working memory, and gave people a wider and more flexible means of finding things out, so search engines have the potential to free up more of us for asking questions and 'thinking' than we could ever have imagined possible. But how will we think? What we will think about? What questions might we ask? The answers might lie in the current obsession of both adults and children for computer-based games and alternative cyber-lives.

11

BEING NOBODY

Adults have always played games, but in the past they were different. Let's leave aside the issue of sport and keeping fit as activities with clear physical, social, even political benefit. What we're going to talk about is games for their own sake – games that have been literally pas- times, a way of whiling away the hours. Such games might involve cards or boards, or, as with charades or hide-and- seek or treasure hunts, merely a handful of other people and some space; but, with the exception of Solitaire and Patience, most games have always been part of a group activity. The whole point of playing games in the twentieth century and before was surely social. For most of us, most of the time, playing games was something that was fun to do with friends or family, just like going to the pub or going for a walk; the game itself was usually secondary to the company – until now.

Where computer games are so radically different is that the priority has reversed. Now the game itself is the most important factor; in fact it's often the only factor, since as likely as not you are playing with only yourself. Screen-based games are often much more solitary and much more part of the fabric of life than the drawing-room games of wet afternoons, the bloated Christmas or jaded dinner parties. So why do human beings now want to spend so much time

191

each day with these screen-based activities that have no obvious benefit or outcome, when instead they could be thinking and talking or simply having fun just being with friends? An immediate explanation might be this: one aspect of most computer games is that they plug into the thrill of the moment, an immediate sensory stimulation that is emotionally compelling. But then so are running or walking in the fresh air; and yet parents often complain that their offspring shun the great outdoors, even when the sunshine beckons, in favour of sitting in front of a screen.

Steven Johnson in *Everything Bad Is Good for You* would probably contest that computer games are much more than empty pastimes. He enthusiastically claims that the basic skills involved – probing, hypothesis formation, re-probing – all become more proficient through game-playing. Covertly, then, perhaps without realizing it, the player is honing their general thinking skills. And Johnson goes on to suggest that working with computers might be developing certain skills better than did the books on which previous generations were reared. Indeed, there has been a steady rise in IQ over the last few decades, known as the Flynn Effect after the political scientist James Flynn who first reported it.

Such a change, Johnson suggests, may be due to the ever-increasing interaction with the screen. This idea is certainly persuasive if you compare the kinds of skills needed to perform well in IQ tests with those required for computer games. Both call for an ability to recognize connections, anomalies and above all rules which, Johnson himself does not hesitate to point out, are independent of content – the latter can be as implausible and irrelevant as rescuing a princess or slaying a dragon.

It's not surprising that we don't necessarily see a link between avid game players and conspicuous intellectual achievement, either in education or beyond in professional life. When the all-important issue of appreciating, questioning or manipulating *content* is considered as a factor, the Flynn Effect disappears. Although IQ scores have risen, vocabulary and mathematical abilities have remained constant: for example, a study carried out at Munich University in the early 2000s concluded that computers did not substantially contribute to maths and reading ability. Moreover, there seems to be no corresponding increase in the number of brilliant scientific breakthroughs or artistic creations. The reason is probably that the Flynn Effect is seen mainly in the middle range of ability, among the vast majority of us who don't win Nobel prizes or compose symphonies. As Johnson himself admits: 'Game players are not soaking up moral counsel, life lessons, or rich psychological portraits.'

But the central credo of *Everything Bad Is Good for You* is that we should discard the simplistic notion that screen culture is dumbing us down. Rather, intimacy with the screen is developing minds that are, in terms of mental agility and processing, adapted to greater complexity, multi-tasking and attention than previously. This issue of content versus process is surely of crucial importance.

But your time is finite. The more you play games, however much you are improving your cerebral agility, there will be less time for learning specific facts and working out how those facts relate to each other; in other words, building your own highly personalized and individual conceptual framework. Until now, at least as I see it, such has arguably been the purpose of education: to enable an individual in both their professional and personal life to place the events of each day into context, to assign them a 'meaning' , and thereby to evaluate them and act accordingly. This ever-evolving framework of meaning has, until now, come from books. But with the screen the emphasis is shifting away from *content* towards a much faster-paced and all-consuming *process* – and it is this process that has an appeal all in itself.

Now it's the excitement of attaining a goal that counts, and that feeds back to give that goal a significance: the imprisoned cyber-princess herself means nothing, and rescuing her would be irrelevant. But the *process* of rescuing the princess is everything. How much more attractive this must seem than the real world with its shifting caprices and irrational, varying values, a world of unrewarded and unappreciated effort, of complicated issues of body language, sneaky pheromones and, above all, other people with different, inaccessible minds and agendas. Yet computer games are more than merely attractive, more than just the next sanitized step on from reality TV. Perhaps the journalist Caitlin Moran speaks for many, and perhaps we could generalize her view and broaden it to cover a whole range of screen activities, when she says that 'it would simply be a statement of a fact to say that *World of Warcraft* is as addictive as methadone'.

This idea that computer games might be as potentially addictive as drugs would explain why a healthy child might prefer to stay inside on the computer rather than running out to play in the garden. And if the compulsion really is comparable to drug addiction, there may be some critical issues for the future of society. More immediately still, we can gain valuable insights into what might actually be happening in the player's brain. The pivotal issue is that the compulsion appears to come from the process of the playing experience itself. This process could be characterized as one in which the rules are fixed, the chances of random events intervening and distracting are reduced, and the goals are clear. Once again, the content of the game is far less relevant than, in Johnson's words, 'the cocktail of reward and exploration'.

And let's be under no illusion that the exploration is easy: the player may not even know what rules there are at the outset, but has to discover them as the game unfolds. So the endpoint, well defined though it may be, is often very hard to attain. But the player is kept going by the desire to see what happens next, to reach the very distant goal. Unlike real life, however, this screen world is not cluttered by messy and unnecessary details, by content. Moreover, the chances of being rewarded as a result of your actions are much, much higher. After all, life may not be fair but most games certainly are. Steven Johnson suggests that computer games will be seen as preferable to normal human endeavour because they offer a reliability and certainty that are lacking in the more hazardous way of achieving the same experience in real life. And your likelihood of sticking at the game is enhanced by the very nature of the subroutines. As Caitlin Moran continues: '. . . already the addictive side of *World of Warcraft* was becoming apparent – through a cunning combination of small, quick tasks and longer, more complex ones that can be chipped away at over time: there's always something you could "pop in" and do, or just spend "ten minutes more" knocking off.'

But why exactly should a process, the playing of a computer game, be so compulsive? In the search for an answer, we need to make an excursion into the world of neurons and the chemical messengers, the transmitters, which enable the neuronal networking which is at the core of brain function. Let's start by looking at how 'pleasure' and 'reward' are realized in general in the brain.

'Pure' pleasure is a direct hit, an immediate here-and-now feeling: the all-encompassing experience of the fine wine, the beat of the music, the orgasm, the sun on your face. Such sensory-laden raw feelings of euphoria are linked to the actions of the natural occurring opiates called endorphins, which serve as transmitters in certain parts of the nervous system, surge in 'jogger's high' and offset pain. Of course, the endorphins don't have 'pleasure' magically trapped inside their molecular structure; but somehow this family of transmitters configures the holistic, functional landscape of the brain into one that correlates with an experience of pure euphoria.

And that's as far as neuroscience can currently go. There is no inner little man – or, heaven forfend, any little woman – in the brain, who then 'feels' the pleasure. It is one of the greatest mysteries, if not *the* greatest, how a certain objective neuronal landscape translates into a subjective sensation, realizes your particular consciousness. But this conceptual issue of the 'hard problem' – of how the water of brain events is turned into the wine of subjective conscious experience – need not delay us right now. So long as we are careful not to talk about transmitters 'for' or 'of' pleasure we can concentrate on what might be happening in the brain, correlating different types of experiences such as reward.

Reward isn't synonymous with pleasure, though it can of course bring about pleasure. Pleasure is a direct, visceral sensation: its whole essence, as suggested in Chapter 5, is the abrogation of a sense of self in favour of being the passive recipient of the here-and-now experience of the moment. With pure pleasure you are having, literally, a sensational time. The endorphins are able to induce in the brain a configuration of some sort whereby the neuronal connections that normally personalize your brain into a 'mind' are temporarily suspended: you 'lose' or 'blow' or are 'out of' your mind.

My own view is that the endorphins, most probably in common and in conjunction with other neurochemicals, play a part in modulating the neuronal connections so that they don't work as normal. And if neuronal connections aren't operating properly, the highly transient, subsecond coalitions they can form, the 'neuronal assemblies', mentioned earlier, will be reduced in size. It is these neuronal assemblies that, I have already suggested, correlate with conscious states: the more extensive an assembly at any one moment, the 'deeper' your state of consciousness. So if an assembly is unusually small, due to the depressant action of morphine or the endorphins on neuronal activity, then the degree of consciousness will be reduced to a dream-like state. But how would such a 'pleasure' situation differ, in brain terms, from 'reward', in particular the reward of screen games?

There are two big differences between pleasure and

reward. The first is timing. Pleasure is immediate, while reward is a delayed process that ends in that pleasure. Reward is a consequence of your actions, so that reward-seeking is, almost by definition, sequential – a narrative series of steps – and thus has a strong component of 'thinking', as defined a little while ago. The second major difference is that, unlike the final pleasure experience itself, reward is predicated on a pre-existing set of values: throughout life we are seeking rewards, be they in the shape of a smile, a pay-rise, an exam success or whatever. In all cases, however, the reward that is significant to me may well not be meaningful, understandable, to you. Rewards and the significance you attach to them therefore depend on your pre-existing individualized brain circuitry, your individual mind, as we saw it, composed of restless circuits of neuronal connections that would be suspended during raw, 'pure' pleasure.

The euphoria of pure pleasure, unless it is heroin-induced to unusual levels, rarely brings with it a risk of dependence. In any event, there is a crucial distinction between physical dependence and addiction. Addiction is characterized by a craving, and one that, unlike dependence, can recur even after prolonged abstinence. It is this type of craving that can occur not just with drugs, but also when you are seeking a reward – as with computer games.

Yet we are seeking rewards all the time as we live out our everyday lives: so why should a computer game, as opposed to most other aspects of our daily lives, be more likely to enslave us as addicts? A critical issue is that the connectivity required to assign significance to the 'reward' in a computer game – say, rescuing a princess – could well be more modest than the more personalized and complex rewards of job promotions or a new baby. The *process* itself would thus dominate the *content*, and wouldn't be eclipsed by the unremarkable, unsophisticated, standardized cyber-prin-cess. And it is conceivably this difference in balance, this differential dominance of the process itself, that could be all-critical and lead to addiction. So let's look at what happens in the brain in addiction.

No matter what has caused the addiction, from gambling to drug-taking, a raised level of the transmitter dopamine is implicated as a critical intermediary: all addictive drugs of all types are associated with increased levels of dopamine in a particular area of the brain, the nucleus accumbens. We know that these levels of dopamine are important in contributing to the feeling of wellbeing when you finally attain a goal, when long-deferred gratification is delivered at last. Plummeting levels of dopamine conversely appear to accompany the opposite type of situations, when gratifica-tion is anticipated but doesn't arrive – for example, waiting for the phone to ring or expecting an e-mail that doesn't appear. So unbearable is this experience of 'non-reward' that some psychologists claim it to be as aversive and unpleasant as pain itself. And, if possible, we take immediate action to remedy the situation and to boost our levels of dopamine again.

No one yet knows precisely how elevated levels of dopamine actually plays a role in addiction, though most experts would agree that isn't essential for the experience of pleasure itself, nor for the subsequent learning of the significance of rewards, their 'content'. So what might be happening? The area of the brain that seems to be pivotal here, the nucleus accumbens, is connected directly to the area at the front of the brain where, as we saw in Chapter 10, under-functioning because of schizophrenia, childhood or obesity leads to recklessness: the prefrontal cortex.

By unleashing excessive amounts of dopamine into the prefrontal cortex, addictive drugs could dampen down the activity of the neurons there; this partial shutting down of the prefrontal cortex would lead to a shift, as we saw in Chapter 10, to greater focus on the experience of the here-and-now. Instead of placing the here-and-now into a more 'significant', albeit personalized, context that reaches into the past and future, the very experience of the ongoing process would be an end in itself.

But why should such a shut-down of the prefrontal cortex by an addictive drug be so rewarding? If an under-active prefrontal cortex causes an exclusion of the past and future, the resultant immediacy of the present moment will make you place more attention on whatever you are doing, and the immediate result of your action, than if it was diluted by the much broader context of the past and future of your entire mind, as realized in a fully operational prefrontal cortex. Perhaps making the here-and-now link between the current action and the immediate result is the all-important step; perhaps this linking is correlated with a very subjective positive feeling, just as the actions of endorphins correlate with pure subjective euphoria. But once again we run into the 'hard problem' of subjective consciousness of how the water turns into wine; but the crucial point here is that, in any case, this link between action and result/response is one that you want to repeat, and will even crave. And dopamine makes it all possible. Excessive amounts of dopamine might reduce the influence of the prefrontal cortex, and in so doing tip the balance away from the 'significance' of an action to the action itself, the link between a stimulus and response: the very *process* that is rewarding and therefore addictive.

Throughout this chapter, I've italicized for emphasis the crude distinction between 'content' and 'process', the building of a slow, logical conceptual framework over fast, idiosyncratic connections leading to the 'feel' of gratification in the process of attaining a goal. In the presence of an addictive drug, this feel of gratification is perhaps much less contested and acquired far more easily than when, without excessive, suppressive dopamine, the more conditional and stringent checks and balances of the full, fussy mind are at work.

For the mind to operate fully, the prefrontal cortex must be active and *content* will be the highest priority: the world will be experienced as redolent with 'meaning'. The development of the mind – actions based on, and causing the growth of, *content* – would require exercise, slow processing, repetition, low arousal and use of symbols with little intrinsic sensory distraction: indeed, the world of iterative focused conversation, nursery rhyme repetition and, later, recitation and rote learning, of reading and writing interspersed with bouts of physical activity in the real world where there are first-hand, unique adventures to provide a personal narrative, personalized neuronal connections. Education as we know it.

Meanwhile, the facilitation of *process* would depend on strong sensation with literal icons and fast, interactive sequences where rewards are attained so that a sensation of frustration and disappointment can be avoided, and where the *feel* of winning is everything. While addictive drugs will supply the dopamine that enables this phenomenon to occur within the brain, computer games could have a similar effect. This time, the game is facilitating the very features just listed as involving the prefrontal cortex less, whilst overworking the dopamine production in the nucleus accumbens.

While drugs have a direct biochemical action, with the screen activities dopamine would be released naturally, but in higher than normal amounts, driven by the particular, unprecedented type of sensory inputs that specifically characterize computer games. You would end up addicted to the behaviour, in this case the stimulus–response chain, the *process* driven by the screen, simply because the screen is a process-heavy/content-light activity. And the brain will reflect in the activity of its neuronal circuitry whatever dominant activity you engage in, be it piano playing, taxi driving or computer games. By practising computer games, the brain may become configured in a way that favours excessive dopamine release, which in turn can be addictive, leading to still more computer games . . .

A brief health warning: I'm *not* claiming that the nucleus accumbens is the 'centre for' reward, nor that the prefrontal cortex is the 'centre for' the mind. What I'm saying is that the activity of these two areas may be in a dynamic relationship, a delicate balance that can be shifted by addictive drugs or computer games. The question of why this shift, arguably in favour of an immediate, here-and-now chain of stimulus–response–stimulus, should be so 'rewarding' impacts again on the great riddle of the subjectivity of the 'hard problem'. Suffice it to say, for our purposes here, that the essential feature of 'reward' might be the very linking of an action with an anticipated response; and such a linking is delivered more reliably by a hyper-real, very strong and unambiguous screen stimulus.

I have been trying fairly persistently to persuade you that the personalization of the brain, through a plasticity that builds up a personalized conceptual framework, is a helpful way of defining the 'mind' – your unique identity. This 'mind' would be 'lost' by anything that impaired the connections – dementia, drugs or indeed a fast-paced environment with strong sensory inputs. So, if the old world of the book aided and abetted the development of a 'mind', the world of the screen, taken to extremes, might threaten that mind altogether, and with it the essence of you the individual. This would be the ultimate triumph of process over content, the ultimate 'Nobody' scenario.

Remember the idea that the Someone scenario was human nature taken to its conceptual extreme? Here, the extreme situation – purely hypothetical, of course – would be the possibility that for the first time human nature, viewed in this way, could be obliterated in favour of a passive state reacting to a flood of incoming sensations – a 'yuk-and-wow' mentality characterized by a premium on the raw senses and momentary experience as the landscape of the brain shifts into one where personalized brain connectivity is either not functional or absent altogether.

Although this option offers the excitement of sensational experience, and the thrill of attaining an immediate and unambiguous goal, it has obliterated that valuable narrative of personal identity and with it the type of thinking that has a *content*, a real meaning. In its place we could be facing a hypothetical society in which status, being Someone, no longer matters because we define ourselves no longer as separate entities but as passive recipients having reactions and feelings to strong sensory inputs. Instead we will revert to being permanently in the sensationalist here-and-now. If the Someone scenario was private but not fulfilled, then this form of identity, Nobody, is neither private nor fulfilled.

However, before we arrive at the literally mindless thinking that characterizes such an extreme scenario, let me introduce two variants. In both cases there would be more content than merely chasing along a pure chain-reaction process of trying–failing–trying–winning: hence in both cases there would be an identity of sorts. These two alternatives would be a false identity and a collective one.

First, the false, the avatar – so named after the Sanskrit word for 'incarnation'. Avatars flourish in screen-based lifestyles such as *Second Life*. Although those living this parallel cyber-existence claim that they are not simply playing a game, much of the appeal of screen-based games must surely apply here too: the hyperstimulation of the strongly sensory-laden screen, as well as the rules that, even though fuzzy and far from obvious, are still more reliable than the real world for delivering goals.

Once again let me quote the journalist Caitlin Moran, writing in *The Times* on her introduction into a new cyber-life as a ginger-bearded dwarf:

So here I am, a thirty-one-year-old mother of two, at 2 a.m., in bed in my Bliss Spa Socks, and having polymorphous cybersexual frisson with a fifteen-year-old gnome called Flopsy, who really lives in Antwerp.

But when it's for an inconsequential internet diversion and you have almost infinite choice of what you will become – good, evil, male, female, human, weird minotaur thing with problem hair – it brings to the fore several profound self-realisations.

Among them are the hints that another avatar has passed on: 'Find a trainer who will teach me new smiting skills, earn money skinning boars, spend the money on armour, and don't chat to people too much – they find it weird.'

Or consider the *Entropia Universe*: a brief visit to their website will show how you can acquire a completely different identity in terms of appearance, age and all the outward signs that we explored in Chapter 10. Moreover, you can purchase virtual clothes for yourself with special *Entropia* currency.

Eerily similar though the world of the avatar might be to the world in which you perform your three-dimensional bodily functions there are obviously crucial differences. The first is that avatars as yet don't pick up on body language or pheromones – hence communication is more overt and less chancy. It's no coincidence, probably, that those with autistic tendencies, and thus impairments in sensitivity to subliminal interpersonal signs, feel very comfortable in screen life.

On the other hand, such caricature interactions do call into question for the rest of us how satisfying such relationships might be compared to the real thing. The avatar world is one of immediate action, of behaviour and work and achievements similar to those offered in more conventional computer games. *Second Life* would surely be less helpful in dealing with reflection and introspection, and complex relationships where different sides of your character come to the fore as you interact with different people and, as a result, are constantly modified. The insights into individual consciousness that for over two hundred years have been afforded by the novel are not so readily available here.

Then again, we could well be entering a phase when, even for those without communication problems, offline, spontaneous 'real' communication will be as messy and distasteful as would be, say, hunting and skinning an animal to the average couch-potato meat-eater of today. Even though our ancestors regularly hunted and butchered their quarry, most of us would prefer to pluck the clingfilm-wrapped end-product from the supermarket shelf. Who's to say that a similar transition, with the similar appeal of safety, simplicity and distance, might not in the near future apply to human interaction?

Another appeal of the avatar life is that, as with computer games, you are never ignored. Being noticed is one of the most gratifying things that can happen to a human being: we have already noted how people in low-status jobs, for example, complain that their unhappiness stems not necessarily from poor pay but from simply being ignored. Whereas on the screen, everything you do is guaranteed to elicit a reaction.

However, if we define our own identity in relation to the reaction of others, the question arises as to whether overuse of the avatar life will cause the real-life individual to atrophy. As yet, no one has really explored the long-tem consequences on human personality, or on its first-person equivalent, the individual mind, of prolonged existence as an avatar.

Now the second option: the cyber alternative to no identity at all, or the false identity of the avatar, is a *collective* identity. This idea of a single, thinking collective has more recently found some purchase in the craze for 'flash-mobbing', contributing to *Wikipedia*, and open source software. In fact one Charles Leadbeater has started to write a book on this subject, where, appropriately enough, everyone is invited to be an author: *We-Think: The Power of Mass Creativity*.

Yet this notion, highly futuristic though it might sound, actually has its origins in the first half of the twentieth century with a Jesuit visionary, Pierre Teilhard de Chardin, who introduced the concept of a 'noosphere' as the ultimate collective consciousness. This term was coined originally by the nineteenth-century Russian scientist Vladimir Vernadsky as the final stage of evolution following that of inanimate matter, the 'geosphere'; the geosphere would have been transformed by biological life, the 'biosphere', which in turn would finally be changed by human cognition to develop the 'noosphere'.

In this scenario, then, the individual would not be passively reacting and interacting with the screen in isolation, rising on dopamine highs like a glider skimming on to the next thermal. Nor would they be a bearded dwarf living out a complex, though simplified, existence. Rather, they would be one small, single node in a much wider network of thought, where individuality was subsumed not just in favour of process, nor necessarily in favour of a fake world, but rather in favour of an existence in which, quite simply, individual expression and contribution were not now the priority.

Caricatures though these three possibilities for a new identity – passive processing, false world or collective effort – might be, it's possible that screen life today combines elements of all. Playing games as a collective and socializing as an avatar, as well as reward-seeking passively on your own, might well modify your true identity: certainly such activities appear to be taking up much of the time of the current generation of young people. Is this Nobody scenario a happier alternative to the previous Someone prospect, with its aspirational solution in thrall to status anxiety? Neither seems ideal.

If your life story is to be unique, if you are to be truly individual, then you will need to see yourself as different from everyone else. The strategy by which you can evaluate just how special you are is that of comparison to others in a variety of ways – literally, your status. Difference relative to others, status, is important for defining our individuality: for the private, individual identity that has been so strongly developed in Western culture in the twentieth century as an extreme realization of human nature. But an increasing number of Someones are suffering from clinical depression.

We've just seen that a new prospect could be beckoning. Taken to its extreme conclusion, screen life could bend human nature towards a passive state, reacting to a flood of incoming sensations, a 'yuk-and-wow' mentality characterized by a premium on the raw senses and momentary experience, as the chemical landscape of the brain is transformed into one where personalized brain connectivity is far less operational: the persona of a Nobody. Although this option has the pay-off of the thrill and sensuality of sensational experience, it obliterates that valuable narrative of personal identity, of being Someone.

The choice so far is stark. Few would view the ideal way forward as either the consumerist Someone scenario of definition through ownership, or the Nobody passivity of hedonistic experiences. Yet there is a third option which has always been available to us ever since the time of Neanderthal Man, and which we shall now investigate.

THE BELIEVING BRAIN

So just imagine a third option: one that arguably avoids both the arms race of unfettered consumerism and the depersonalized hedonism of screen technology. By contrast, this scenario would deliver all the appeal of the noosphere – the comfort and security of aligning with many others, along with the stimulation of interacting with them. But the *collective* identity currently being celebrated through, say, Wikipedia is nothing new. Surely you can easily remember occasions when you have been part of a group where the collective identity subsumes and over-rides you as an individual: you are just part of the whole, thinking and acting like everyone else. You suppress your uniqueness. You could be Anyone.

Being Anyone is, to a certain extent, second nature: human beings have always defined themselves, somewhat paradoxically, not just as individuals but simultaneously by what they have in common and how similar they are to certain others. And defining yourself by groups to which you belong – be it by birth or by choice – is a straightforward and obvious way of telling someone about yourself in the shortest possible time. Journalists invariably include the age of the subjects of their stories since, with just two digits occupying minimal space, a maximal amount of assumptions can be drawn about the attitudes, tastes and priorities of that person: it is apparently the most space-efficient description. Of course, if we're going to define anything – from, say, a table to love – we usually refer to the more general group or 'set', here for example as a form of furniture or an emotion respectively. So I'm British, female, a scientist, and so on.

Most of us dart back and forth along a continuum spanning these two concepts of identity: individual and collective. At one extreme, the individual trumps everything – nationality, age and gender are in a sense irrelevant in the face of true eccentricity. At the other extreme, a collective persona – say, being German as the 1930s unfolded – would have increasingly been the *only* factor that really counted in how you saw yourself. But most of the time, most of us vary in the degree to which being part of a group affects our sense of identity.

For example, as I'm writing these words I feel aligned to no one else, writing (I hope) what no one else has yet written; and yet tomorrow, were I to be waiting on Oxford station platform with a load of other commuters, my own individual identity might be subsumed under the more collective feeling of frustration and anger if the London train were badly delayed. And you only have to look at the jingoistic behaviour of otherwise highly individual Brits on the last night of the Proms, or the behaviour at sports events or hen nights, to accept that most of us can have both private and public identities to suit different occasions. But what we shall be exploring here are cases when such flexibility no longer occurs – the extreme end of the spectrum where collective identity is everything and prevails for most of the time.

The most obvious classifications determined by birth – race, gender, age – tend not to be sufficiently engaging in themselves to over-ride an individual sense of identity. I know plenty of British women of my generation with whom I feel no affinity whatsoever! No, in order for a collective identity to take a real hold something more is needed: a shared belief system. If I were to feel an affinity with a group of women, it would be because we had the same values and outlook, however implicit and under-stated. And although the chances might be higher that another British woman of my age felt as I did on some issue – as opposed to, say, a teenage boy in Nebraska – it would only be a probability. A common belief system is not only necessary but actually sufficient all on its own; mere chance issues of gender, race and age may make it more likely that certain individuals will share views, but in themselves are usually irrelevant to admission to a group – for example, a political party or most mainstream religions. So let's look at collective identity, the Anyone scenario, as a product primarily of belief systems: does it offer an attractive option for how to define yourself in the twenty-first century?

Let me stress here that we aren't going to be talking about subsuming your individuality by singing in a choir, or even marching in a demonstration. We all experience times when we are part of the crowd – as commuters, at rock concerts, or in anything else we do where we are 'The Public.' The question we're going to tackle here concerns the scenario taken to its extreme: the scenario when, for most of your daily life, your collective identity trumps everything else. Above all, Anyone subscribes to an extreme ideology, and as such has featured more and more in the events, ideas and policies that are shaping the world today. What is going on in these people's minds – literally?

Not surprisingly, given the broadness of the concept, scientific exploration of belief systems presents a formidable challenge. Theology and philosophy can provide a conceptual framework for thinking about belief systems, and for identifying conceptually fruitful ways of relating the relevant notion of belief to different levels of scientific description. Meanwhile, anthropology identifies general patterns of belief acquisition and maintenance that hold universally, as well as distinguishing features of belief systems that are culture-specific. Psychology offers an array of measurement tools that allow us both to quantify various dimensions of belief and to correlate these with broad personality characteristics, such as spirituality, that are likely to echo stable neural properties. The combined results of these disciplines thus prepare the ground for neuroscience to attempt to identify the physico-chemical mechanisms that subserve systems in the brain and elsewhere in the body.

As a broad-brush simplification, we have seen so far that Someone's brain would require the neuronal infrastructure to accommodate the meaning of symbols and symbolic behaviours – complex neuronal circuitry formed as cultural influences incessantly shape the brain from birth onwards. Meanwhile, Nobody's brain would be adapted more to immediate sensory processing and an abrogation of a personalized narrative as normally afforded by a hard-working prefrontal cortex. Would the stereotyped Anyone's brain be working differently yet again?

Back in the mid-twentieth century, the psychologist Paul MacLean was fascinated by the mindset behind the seemingly mindless behaviour of the Nazis' Nuremberg rallies of the 1930s. The mass chanting, the rhythmic and uniform movements are, of course, all too familiar today in football stadia and indeed in certain forms of mass worship. Some people may take exception to my lumping together sacred acts of worship which are 'good' with potential acts of football violence which are 'bad'. But we are focusing here just on the mass behaviour of a crowd, irrespective of the underlying belief and what might happen subsequently.

MacLean championed the idea that crowd behaviour was an example of a recapitulation of evolution. First there was the 'reptilian brain', the most primitive part of the brain that wrapped around the top of the spinal cord. Next came an additional layer, the limbic system, which MacLean dubbed the 'mammalian brain'. As its name suggests, the brain regions in this layer had evolved as a speciality of mammals and enabled these more sophisticated species to channel and adapt the otherwise basic 'reptilian' urges to meet the demands and constraints of whatever environment they had to navigate. Finally there was the outermost layer, the newest in evolutionary terms: the 'neomammalian brain'. As we saw back in Chapter 2, this layer, the cortex, is most pronounced, in that it has the greatest surface area, in the most sophisticated species – ourselves. In order to accommodate the increased surface area in the restricted confines of the skull, nature has scrunched up the cortex rather as you might scrumple up a sheet of paper to accommodate it in your balled fist. Accordingly, the surface of the human brain looks like that of a shelled walnut.

While MacLean was correct in terms of evolution and neuroanatomy, he then made the rather extravagant and thought-provoking claim that the three brains were poorly integrated. Although, through the prism of modern neuroscience, his grasp of actual brain functioning seems naïve, MacLean's suggestion is still interesting if we regard it more as a metaphor than as a hard physiological situation. As a consequence of the poor integration, MacLean argued, there might be times when the reptilian brain could be unleashed, breaking free of the moral constraints of the neomammalian brain, and even of the adapted behaviour of the mammalian counterpart. As a result, occasions such as the Nuremburg rallies betokened unfettered, unchannelled, 'mindless' aggression.

But surely the mass aggression witnessed at Nuremberg, or on the football terraces, is not the same as some atavistic, purposeless reptilian urge? Rather, this type of behaviour is part of a meaningful narrative for a group of people unified by an all-pervasive ideology, albeit a collective one. In fact, there are clear parallels between the storyline of the aspiring *individual* Someone of current Western society and the *collective* someone, the Anyone, of fundamentalist ideology. Occasions such as road rage might be more accurate examples of loss of one's 'mind' in favour of a strong emotion, where one is no longer 'self' conscious. Someone who has lost their temper, in extreme cases and under certain conditions, is indeed often deemed no longer to be accountable for what they do: this is the *crime passionelle* recognized in French law. Such people are aggressive as an animal might be, lashing out in primeval defence.

By contrast football hooligans, just as participants at the Nuremburg rallies, are not merely aggressive but also angry. Their behaviour is saying something about them, standing 'for' something – the 'human nature' we discussed earlier. The Nuremberg rallies of the 1930s and the football hooliganism that still bedevils us today are therefore different from road rage. The man (or woman) in the crowd raising or waving their arm knows very well what is happening: if they are aggressive, it is selectively directed at well-defined targets such as the opposing team or other beings perceived as subordinate. Rather than having a purely sensory experience the participants are acting out a storyline, albeit a collective one: a common belief system where the script presumably reads that they are the superior humans or the better side. In order to have a collective identity, the individual participants must have a common base; the stronger and more homogenous the thought processes and outlook (the belief system) the more robust and inviolate it is, and the less prominent is personal individuality. So, just as belief systems are not synonymous with religion, neither are they comparable with reptilian brains: beliefs, even seemingly 'mindless' ones, are the products of highly sophisticated human brains.

The Anyone scenario, then, differs from that of the Nobody in that it offers a strong sense of identity, yet, unlike the Someone option, one that is not personal but public. The last hundred years has witnessed a growth in the Anyone option – aggressive movements based on various belief systems from the political ideologies of Communism and the Nazis to cults such as that led by Charles Manson and, most conspicuously in current times, the Taleban and Al-Qaeda. All these systems, whether based on religion or on political ideology, impose clear and unquestionable rules concerning every aspect of your life, from what you eat, wear, say and do each day right through to how you think and what values you adopt.

If we are to define the Anyone scenario by belief systems, and if we are trying to see how the mind of Anyone might be characterized in neuronal terms, we'll first need to define 'belief' in order to know what we are looking for when we venture into the physical brain. Although for some people belief is often synonymous with religion, it's important to differentiate the two: many belief systems have nothing to do with religion, and religion need not imply the extreme ideologies – the strong, collective, fundamentalist identity we are exploring here.

It's worth noting, as an aside, that religion in any case touches on the other two scenarios at which we've been looking. In the Someone case of a strong sense of personal identity, a religious individual will place greatest emphasis on their own inner feelings and the particular relationship that they may have with God through prayer. However, just as Elizabeth I famously did not desire a 'window to see into men's souls', we need not investigate here the type of personal relationship an individual believer has with their God or higher being – their feelings and inner experiences – any more than their more corporeal personal relationships with those close to them would be of relevance to our current discussion. In the Nobody scenario the key feature is a sensory-laden experience of the moment, the abrogation of the sense of self in a mindless, sublime present. Religion could offer one route to this endpoint in the delirium and abandonment of extreme forms of worship – the celebrations of Dionysius in ancient Greece that are documented so vividly in Euripides' *Bacchae*, the speaking in tongues (glossolalia) in certain Christian communities, and the whirling Dervishes of Sufism are all examples of rituals where a sense of self is abandoned.

What then can we say about belief that is independent of any of these religious associations? Although everyone would have some idea what a belief system might be, just pause for a moment to reflect on how strange and conceptually tricky a phenomenon it actually is. In one sense – the technical/philosophical – virtually any thought process, any assertion such as 'The sky is blue' or 'Jane is standing in front of me', is a 'belief'. Such beliefs are formed by experience, by deductive reasoning or by indirect verbal report. But when we speak in everyday terminology, as we shall be doing here, then a 'belief' is usually an assertion that persists if deductive reasoning and/or the results of experiences are suspended or absent. In fact many beliefs, for example sexist ones, curiously persist even in the presence of strong evidence to the contrary!

Moreover, while there might well be a consensus that the sky is blue, and that Jane is standing in front of you or me, the same could not be said about the existence of God or the presence of ghosts or the supremacy of the working class. One way of defining beliefs, then, might be as responses that vary from one individual to another following input of the same data and/or sensory experience.

Another means of definition could be basically linguistic. Perhaps the best way of immediately differentiating a 'belief', in the sense that we are using it here, would be to check whether we are using the verb 'to believe' as opposed to 'to believe *in*'. Think of the difference between 'I believe Jane is standing in front of me' and 'I believe *in* Jane standing in front of me.' This simple little preposition 'in' transforms the whole meaning from an uncontroversial fact over which you would change your view as evidence or experience accrues to a statement that isn't necessarily based on evidence or deductive logic and that isn't therefore unequivocally adopted by everyone.

But while scientists such as Richard Dawkins rail against a disregard for evidence, particularly with regard to religion, the more penetrating and interesting question is how belief systems *in* various things seem to be so very much part of the human mentality. A 'belief in God' is just one example, according to the two definitions above. Secular beliefs 'in' fairies or Father Christmas or a sugar pill would fall into the same cognitive category – as Dawkins is often at pains to point out.

Because beliefs can be so varied in both breadth of contents and depth of values that they embody, it's hardly surprising that a vast range of attempts has been made to develop a system for categorizing them. We can of course compartmentalize beliefs, as we have just done, according to content, such as religious versus secular. Within the secular box we can then differentiate further into, say, political ideologies versus metaphysical beliefs (ghosts, fairies, superstitions) versus personal (such as 'believing in' your hero, role model or prodigy, believing that this figure is basically worthy; or even believing 'in' an object, a pill that will make you better).

When you believe 'in' something, first, it 'exists' – not necessarily in four fleshy dimensions in physical spacetime, but nevertheless in some way; secondly, it does something that, thirdly, is good or bad or desirable or undesirable in some way. Beliefs can be, and usually are, triple-layered in this fashion – although these increasingly detailed layers are simultaneous. A small child who has arrived at the stage of believing in Father Christmas will from the outset also 'know' that Father Christmas does things – delivers presents – and that this behaviour every 24 December is to be welcomed. Whatever you believe in, therefore, has some kind of consequence which is intrinsically positive or negative.

Another type of classification for belief systems is based not so much on content but rather on the specificity of belief. This alternative classification system would distinguish between clear groups of believers in an unambiguous ideology, such as the Masons; and much vaguer groupings around much broader sets of beliefs but unified none the less under single words or short phrases such as 'brotherhood of man', or even 'Christianity' or 'Islam'. In this case, the unifying term can mean very different things to those who subscribe – yet there is a common sense of identity, referred to by the Scottish anthropologist Victor Turner as '*communitas*'.

But whatever system of classification we might favour, and irrespective of what exactly we might be believing 'in', and whether or not those beliefs are general common labels or truly shared, specific propositions, the question is always the same. Might buying into a strongly held belief system change your brain, and hence your mind, and hence your identity?

i.d.

In attempting to answer this question, we have to acknowledge a problem: if belief systems are the products of sophisticated human brains, any enquiry is inevitably going to be restricted to humans. Since neuroscience is about the inner workings of the brain, the different processes and mechanisms by which neurons operate, a neuroscientist is going to be severely restricted in the amount of experimentation that is possible. Opportunities for direct examination and monitoring of brain tissue in a living, ideally awake, human occurs for instance in some kinds of neurosurgery. Otherwise the only way to observe the human brain at work is non-invasively, through scans.

Brain scans show different parts of the brain being active under different conditions, and have revolutionized our study and understanding of the brain. In all cases, they are used painlessly on conscious human subjects by means of 'imaging' techniques known as Positron Emission Tomography (PET), functional Magnetic Resonance Imaging (fMRI) and Magnetoencephalography (MEG). Each of these techniques exploits a different property of the brain at work: PET uses radioactive oxygen or glucose that will give off a signal (gamma rays) in the areas of the brain that are most active and therefore consuming the most oxygen and glucose. Although fMRI is like PET in that it depends on levels of blood oxygen, it is related instead to the haemoglobin that carries the oxygen. Meanwhile, MEG measures the magnetic field generated by differential activity of the various regions in the brain. Not surprisingly, each of these imaging techniques has its strengths and weaknesses: for example, fMRI gives a more accurate spatial read-out, while MEG offers a better temporal

222

one that more accurately reflects the real-time frame of neuronal operations; then again, PET offers the best indication as to what transmitter systems are operating in any given situation. But in all cases, no brain scans can tell you more than that certain brain areas are more active than others under certain conditions. And as I've stressed repeatedly, we cannot treat isolated brain regions as though they were autonomous brains; nor can we localize highly sophisticated and complex functions to any single brain area. All that said, brain scans are none the less a good place, probably the only place, to start if we are to search for possible differences in the believing brain from that of the non-believing counterpart.

The anthropologist Harvey Whitehouse has catalogued the various brain areas that are under- or overworking in different aspects of belief. For example, the visual aspects of religious imagination can be distinguished from the visual experiences of dreams because they are quantitatively rather than qualitatively different from 'normal' vision. Meanwhile, hyperactivation of certain brain systems (the temporal- and frontal-limbic) accompanies feelings of salience and realism in imagistic rituals, while hyperactivity of yet a third area (the anterior paracingulate cortex) matches up with sensations of mystical personal presence that typically accompany imagistic practices.

Interesting though these studies might be, we cannot generalize too much from them in our attempts to understand how the basic and general features of belief systems are selectively developed in the brain. Moreover, the 'functions' that we have looked at, while being part of the overall profile of belief systems, are far from being the key feature that would selectively distinguish a belief state from others. Rather, they constitute behaviours that may well be different from 'normal', but are shared with other mental states such as epilepsy and are far from being exclusive to belief. A believer's brain, then, would, from the evidence of brain scans, be hard to distinguish and identify as such from that of a non-believer. Certain areas might well be more active than normal for certain aspects of the practice of that belief; but it would be too much to conclude that such brain differences are specific indicators of believing, *and nothing else*. But brain scans might prove very helpful in a different type of study, where the strategy goes in reverse. Rather than selecting a feature of belief and attempting to localize it in the brain, let's see if a specific act of believing might make a difference to the brains scans.

Katja Wiech, Irene Tracey and Miguel Farias in Oxford have made the fascinating discovery that a particular religious belief *can* show up in a brain scan. Self-confessed Catholics given a marginally painful burning stimulation on the back of their hand rated the pain considerably lower when they were shown a picture of the Virgin Mary compared to a comparable but secular portrait. This effect was not observed in atheists. Moreover, the brain scans of the religious believers showed a different pattern of activation while they were observing the Virgin.

Religious participants showed stronger activation in a key area related to anxiety (the medial prefrontal cortex, mPFC), when they looked at the non-religious compared to the religious image. However, there was evidence that when they could look at an image of the Virgin Mary while they experienced physical pain, the religious might recruit a brain

Leonardo's *Lady with Ermine* (left) was less effective than Battista Salvi's Madonna (right) in relieving pain for religious participants in tests

area related to coping, the right anterolateral prefrontal cortex (alPFC). The findings of this group of researchers suggest that a religious belief can perhaps work as a placebo, and that therefore the two broad types of belief – the secular belief that something can alleviate suffering, and a religious belief – are *not* mediated by an entirely different brain mechanism. In any event it is possible that a secular picture, say of your mother, could also serve to bring relief from pain.

So what, basically, distinguishes the believing brain? If no particular pattern of brain activation is unique to belief, as seems to be the case, perhaps we should take a completely different tack and look instead at the defining key features of the mindset of fundamentalists: how might they be catered for at the level of neurons? Certainly, defining oneself primarily by full-time subscription to a fundamentalist ideology appears to change the emphasis within the portfolio of human emotions. For example, the neuroscientist/psychologist Kathleen Taylor has made an extensive study of belief systems in fundamentalist societies and communities. By examining writings from these extreme movements, Kathleen has reached a surprising and fascinating conclusion. She has discovered that the over-riding emotion is not one of blind rage, or even anger, but disgust.

Psychologists and anthropologists acknowledge six basic human emotions: surprise, anger, happiness, fear, sadness and disgust. Of these, disgust is perhaps the most sophisticated in that it only appears after the first few years of life. Indeed, the psychologist Paul Rozin at the University of Pennsylvania has shown that an infant will happily drink apple juice from a brand-new, pristine bedpan or eat chocolate shaped as faeces, while older children will not – despite reassurances that the fluid concerned really *is* apple juice. Disgust is an important emotion in that it prevents us from ingesting or even allowing close to us anything that might be harmful. Dirty kitchens, putrid food, coprophagia (eating faeces), other people's spit – all would be bad for our health, and all would evoke feelings of disgust. However, it is only once we have had some experience of the world that we are able to differentiate the dangerous from the innocuous.

But this same basic survival mechanism has now been hi-jacked to help enforce group membership. Belonging to a group immediately differentiates you from others, from those who don't belong. The more pervasive the collective identity, the stronger this exclusion will need to be, and the more invaluable will prove the primeval yet learnt emotion of disgust at those not in the group. According to Kathleen Taylor, the anti-Semitic phrases suffusing Hitler's *Mein Kampf* are redolent mainly of disgust: the text employs a vocabulary that would normally be associated with some stealthy and elusive infection.

The anti-Semitism of the Nazis in particular, and the hatred of others outside one's own belief system in general Kathleen argues, are based therefore on the notion that the non-believer, the non-subscriber, the dissident, is like an invisible virus – and all the more dangerous for it. So combatting such a difficult enemy in the struggle for racial 'hygiene' cannot be achieved by a simple punch-for-punch process, a clear-cut form of warfare; after all, you cannot identify the enemy that easily. This enemy is more like a sickness against which you have to be on constant guard, and against which you have to take preventative action. But you don't get angry with putrid food – you just have to destroy it as efficiently as possible with minimal fuss. Hence the most appropriate retaliation isn't a fight in which the enemy is killed, but a cold-blooded campaign as a result of which they are 'exterminated', as in a plague or pandemic.

Following the work of the American psychiatrist Robert Lifton, Kathleen has suggested that this rational, 'therapeutic' attitude dominates in strong ideologies against the non-subscriber, who is perceived as far worse than a conventional enemy. While a traditional enemy might invade your territory, this invisible viral foe could invade your body and, most importantly, your brain. 'They' could infiltrate your mind and influence what you believe, and in so doing jeopardize your very identity. Interestingly enough, this is precisely the vocabulary that is also employed by the renowned atheist Richard Dawkins, who has developed non-belief into a belief system all of its own and who persistently refers to religion as a 'virus': 'Like computer viruses, successful mind viruses will tend to be hard for their victims to detect. If you are the victim of one, the chances are that you won't know it, and may even vigorously deny it. Accepting that a virus might be difficult to detect in your own mind, what tell-tale signs might you look out for?'

So disgust is a way of differentiating very clearly the desirable from the non-desirable. But just how do you stop the repugnant virus from infiltrating? Obviously, you'll need strong brain defences: you'll need to close your mind.

You may well by now be raising the objection that many extreme religious sects, such as the Amish or Jehovah's Witnesses or monks in silent orders, are not driven by disgust. True; and do remember that from the outset we were clear about not exploring religion as such but were looking at ideologies. The all-important difference is whether you perceive that everyone outside your system is hostile or utterly misguided: quite often the one implies the other! And it is then, when the need for an active defence strategy seems necessary and hence a belief becomes politicized, that disgust and anger come into play.

One clear difference between an individual identity versus this type of collective identity might be its degree of malleability. As we keep seeing, the hallmark of the individual human brain is its dynamism, its ability to respond to individual experiences and in so doing to generate a personalized brain, a mind. Because the individual is constantly evolving, constantly in dialogue with the outside world and therefore constantly modified by it, your identity could be quite precarious; you could be all things to all people. One way of ensuring that your personalized mind developed from the *tabula rasa* of the infant into a more consistent and robust entity that wasn't immediately swayed by distracting inputs and diverse experiences in the external world, would be to ensure that some internal counter-defences were in place – strong associations relatively impervious to subsequent outside influence. We call these defences beliefs. Beliefs would enable you to navigate the world without recourse to the time-consuming exercise of reasoning from first principles of logic, or having to wait for first-hand empirical evidence.

But beliefs are surely forged, as are all aspects of the personalized brain, through personalized neuronal connections? And, as we have seen again and again throughout this book, connections are enforced and maintained by experience. So how can beliefs, here defined as *not* dependent on experience, be embedded so effectively and persistently in the brain?

An alternative way of ensuring that beliefs endure might be the knowledge that they are shared, that the belief system is collective: 'Everyone says so' and 'But everyone knows that' are common, even if hardly persuasive, justifications of a point of view. Mere endorsement by others as you mix with them in your group might enforce the underlying neuronal connections as strongly as if you were witnessing the same experimental result over and over again first-hand. The multiple feedback from others around you will serve in the same way as the enforced piano playing, both real and merely imagined, did in the scenario of the non-pianist volunteers that we encountered in Chapter 2: a mere thought can change the size of certain areas of neuronal territory. And if that can happen by imagining you were playing five-finger exercises over just five days, how much more effective would years of comparable mental exercise be in shaping the configuration of your neuronal connections?

That's not to say that a mind so configured is incapable of change: indeed, there are many stories of believers who lost their faith or became disillusioned with a particular political ideology. Yet such large-scale transformations aren't usually spontaneous and much more likely to be the result of some experience or change in circumstance. The neuronal circuits of Anyone's brain might be more robustly wired than, say, that of Nobody; but that's not to say that they are completely impervious to modification by inputs. After all, that's what the brain does all the time.

Yet taken to extremes – and the extreme is our prime interest here – the collective ongoing endorsement of beliefs is a vital form of protection for them. And the corollary to ongoing endorsement would be the exclusion of any competing alternative: the non-believer. The overt hostility towards those who dissent, the unfaltering conviction of being utterly right and the simplistic black/white outlook are all reminiscent of extreme fundamentalist movements which claim a monopoly on the Truth.

An extreme collective 'Anyone' identity, then, appears to be characterized by two phenomena that feature more prominently than in the portfolio of the individual persona: disgust and intolerance. This combination serves as a means of identifying, nurturing and protecting a robust set of beliefs that form part of a common narrative, a collective identity, in turn enforced by prescribed and regulated experiences.

Anyone's brain, then, is not qualitatively different from that of Someone or Nobody: there are no special, specific and unique features. The difference is most likely one that is quantitative: it varies in degree. Disgust and intolerance, which we all experience some of the time, here work overtime as strategies that harness the normal plasticity of the brain. But there must also be some positive pay-off. Let's now look at the benefits of extreme belief systems and how the positive aspects of such a mindset combine with what we have seen so far, to shape strong belief systems at the level of actual brain mechanisms. Just how do you become Anyone?

BEING ANYONE

When you believe in something, you are going beyond what your senses tell you. Perhaps you can see some sort of pattern or connection in a temporal sequence of events, or between a group of objects, that is not immediately obvious from the literal actions or physical properties within those events or objects: perhaps some outcome or object has a 'meaning' that wouldn't be apparent to the casual, non-believing observer. Or perhaps you don't need your senses at all to 'know' that something or someone exists, does something, and that it is good or bad. All humans have belief systems: after all, we would be unable to get on in life if we waited for first-hand evidence or had to start from scratch with logical argument to determine the best course of action each moment of our lives.

We have just seen that there are no brain regions activated uniquely in the believing brain, but rather that certain brain regions could be under- or overworking in an exaggeration of normal brain function. A more appropriate question to ask, then, is not how belief is fixed in the brain as some distinct phenomenon but how a 'normal' human process of belief can be so exaggerated as to lead to a collective identity that eclipses the private individual. The question we are asking here is this: what are the basic neural mechanisms interacting with what environmental requirements that would enable an otherwise individual identity to be subsumed into Anyone?

In order to preserve a collective identity, the relevant, underlying brain mechanisms would need to be stable; and to be stable they would need to be more impervious than usual to the caprices of individual experience. So the potential for any varied, chance or idiosyncratic external influences in the environment would have to be minimized, as would the usual flexibility of the brain in response to those events. At the same time, the belief systems that were the basis of a collective world-view would need to be constantly reinforced by ongoing experience within the group, most readily through the statements, actions or shared activities of other members.

Such ongoing support would protect against any displacement or distortion by discordant inputs, while at the same time increasing the notion of 'significance' through strengthening the relevant neuronal connections. In the end, an extreme and by no means normal outcome would be that the connections in the brain underlying the belief, and hence the shared view and a collective identity, would be so established and pervasive as to be self-perpetuating, determining what you do to such an extent that alternative, chance or individual behaviours would be minimized. In this way a chicken-and-egg cycle would be set up whereby a predetermined environment – one in which little that was novel or unexpected occurred – reinforced a pre-existing neuronal connectivity, and vice versa.

So what must happen in the brain, and therefore in the mind, to shape a prescribed, collective identity? As we have seen, the normal situation is for beliefs, one's mindset, to be constantly modified and updated by experience. In every-day life these experiences will typically influence our ongoing 'attitude' – the first stage in forming a belief. Psychologists define attitudes as providing 'a simple structure for organizing and handling an otherwise complex and ambiguous environment'. This structure is assembled on accessible information, both long-term and temporary. In turn the accessibility of such information will depend on its organization in memory, namely how many associations it triggers, along with the frequency and recency of its activation. Beliefs or attitudes will be determined by the associations they trigger within a framework of weak and strong, direct and indirect associations, known as a semantic network, as demonstrated below.

The activation level of each node will slowly decay with time if it doesn't receive inputs from activation spreading through the network. A network of associations with varying degrees of strength from node to node fits well with current knowledge of the development of neural networks within the physical brain. This description could easily be accommodated with what we know about neuronal plasticity. For several decades now, neuroscientists have been investigating the underlying neuronal nuts and bolts for the 'use it or lose it' principle that, as we have seen, personalizes the brain into a mind through personal experience. This now well-established and well-understood brain mechanism, called long-term potentiation or LTP for short, operates at the level of the synapse, enabling, as the term suggests, a connection to be 'stronger' the more it is made to work. Although the concept was introduced by the visionary psychologist Donald Hebb as far back as the mid-twentieth century, it was only several decades later that the physico-chemical basis of the phenomenon was actually demonstrated: the more a synapse is active, the more effective it becomes, just as muscle becomes stronger through exercise. Through LTP, then, we can establish neuronal connections of varying strength – a strength that is ceaselessly modified by how much the neurones are being stimulated and used.

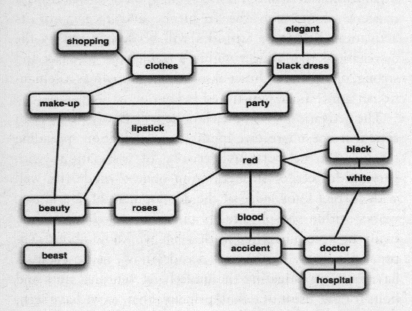

A network of linguistic associations is a good model for the development of neuronal connections

So attitudes are realized through neuronal connections, and those connections are dependent upon experiences. Now imagine what might happen if the dialogue between brain and outside world were much more one-sided.

'Attitudes' become beliefs when they are so strong that they are not as malleable as normal to updates from individual experience. How could such super-neuronal connectivity be established?

Although we are investigating the brain mechanisms of belief in general, not of religion in particular, studies of religiosity none the less provide valuable insights that could eventually be generalized to secular belief systems. The anthropologist Harvey Whitehouse and his colleagues have studied patterns of variation among religious traditions around the world, and conclude that religious ideas are learned and passed on in two contrasting yet complementary ways. It turns out that these anthropological phenomena can translate directly into the terminology and concepts of neuroscience as two broadly distinct patterns of brain activation and processing.

The first mode of learning relies upon repetition. Many religious traditions are founded upon extremely frequent transmission of core concepts, involving regimes of routinized oral transmission that are markedly more intense and prolonged over a human being's lifespan than most other kinds of information exchange: they occur as part of everyday life. Whitehouse has summarized this mode as 'low arousal, high frequency'. By contrast, the second mode involves unusual excitement and elevated arousal. Some religious traditions, ancient and modern, place great store on rarely performed rituals that, almost without exception, involve exceedingly high levels of emotional and sensory stimulation: this mode is, according to Whitehouse, 'high arousal, low frequency'.

Harvey suggests that these patterns would, in turn, be linked to different forms of memory. Not only in humans, but also in a wide range of other species with complex nervous systems, learning and memory are the building-blocks of behavioural flexibility. These sophisticated cognitive feats depend upon the twin strategies of 'rehearsal', repeating particular behaviours, and 'arousal', being able to recall exceptional events associated with strong emotional associations. The classic example (for those old enough) is that everyone remembers what they were doing, however banal, on the night John F. Kennedy was shot. Memories, then, result from biologically ancient strategies of learning through a combination of repetition and emotional arousal.

We saw a while ago that Pick's disease was an impairment in memory for facts, Alzheimer's for events. This same distinction for different types of memory holds true in the healthy brain: in general, psychologists divide human memory into memory for facts, known as semantic memory, and memory for specific events with certain time-space points of reference, called episodic memory. Whitehouse's idea is that the repetition of particular experiences many times over favours semantic memory: this type of memory is characterized by general knowledge about the world, based on experiences so numerous that we can seldom recall when or how we first learned a particular fact, and there is no one single, conspicuous episode.

This type of memory would be most appropriate for the high-frequency, low-arousal type of belief systems. For example, the daily repetition of the set prayers that characterize so many forms of worship would be an excellent way of ensuring a specific high-frequency input for driving neuronal connections into a certain generic or semantic pattern.

Whitehouse has assembled considerable evidence that this type of rehearsal/repetition is necessary for the stable transmission of doctrinal orthodoxies and, moreover, that routinization of religious practices serves to suppress creative innovation at the same time as it enhances recall for authoritative teachings such as the Bible. Nevertheless, patterns of heavy repetition can also induce tedium under certain circumstances, and thus lower motivation, thereby risking the temptation of opening up the mind to the novelty of non-prescribed inputs. One way in which many religious traditions solve this problem is through the evolution of relatively low-frequency, high-arousal rituals.

Unusual and unexpected experiences, such as the assassination of JFK or more recently the death of Diana, Princess of Wales, come with a strong emotional tag and thus produce a clear 'episodic' memory; such distinct moments in our lives, which usually consist of somewhat lower-key and far more frequent experiences, cannot of course, by definition, be relied upon for the strengthening of belief systems. Paul's epiphany on his famous journey to Damascus may be a good example of a belief driven by a highly emotive and special event, but the number of believers would be far smaller if such occurrences were the only route to the 'low frequency, high arousal' mode of learning! How could the environment be contrived to deliver such moments more systematically?

Virtually all low-frequency rituals involve comparatively high levels of emotional arousal. Collective chanting, singing and moving in synchrony might offer excitement comparable to that of fast-paced sports, raves, drugs and sex: indeed, many low-frequency, high-arousal rituals aim specifically at a blurring of waking/dreaming boundaries and a heightening of emotional salience. This time the individual isn't obliterated as in the Nobody scenario, but sublimated to a gripping narrative – one, however, that is not individual but collective: Anyone.

The big difference is that, in contrast to the Nobody scenario, the senses themselves are not at a premium – it's the 'meaning' which they carry that's all-important. Although it might be risking an oversimplification, the analogy would be not so much with a mindless rave as with chanting at a football match or being transported by the pageantry of a Nazi rally, where the narrative of the storyline, a collective one, was all-important. Interestingly enough, participation in such rituals appears capable of triggering long-term rumination on questions of 'meaning' in a way that participation in more humdrum, routinized rituals does not. In traditional religions involving traumatic initiation rites, for instance, novices assume that there has to be a good reason for having to endure the initiatory ordeals, while the meanings of the ritual procedures are tantalizingly opaque. Somewhere in the details of what occurs and the cryptic murmurings of the initiators, clues must surely be buried. The devotee thus embarks on a lifetime of potentially irresolvable ruminations, a process of reflection that may unfold in fits and starts but never entirely fades.

Harvey Whitehouse dubs this phenomenon 'Spontaneous Exegetical Reflection'. He and his colleagues have conducted a number of experiments to investigate the effects of frequency and arousal on the ways in which we reason about the 'meanings' of religious experiences. The conclusion has

been that increasing arousal levels during ritual perfor-
mances not only increase the longevity, vividness and detail
of episodic memory but also stimulate this Spontaneous
Exegetical Reflection with regard to ritual episodes. In other
words, the more exciting a ritual is, the more frequently and
elaborately participants reflect on its possible meanings.
This idea is consistent with the impression that high-arousal
rituals contribute to meaning-laden, personalized religious
experiences that routinized, unexciting ceremonies alone
might not sustain. And the more you are reflecting – just
as we saw in Chapter 2 with people who imagined they were
playing the piano – the more you are strengthening certain
connections, to the exclusion of potentially opposing inputs
from the outside environment.

The inter-relationship at the level of neurological mechanisms between ritual, arousal and Spontaneous Exegetical Reflection still needs to be worked out in much more
detail. But one specific factor that clearly plays an important role in ritual, as well as having a huge effect on arousal,
is music. Music is found throughout human culture and has
a powerful role in personal, social, cultural and religious
experience. In creatures as diverse as birds, whales and
fruitflies, certain mating signals can be melodic and rhythmic in structure. But the human experience of music
appears to transcend the sound itself: it has even been
referred to by the poet Francis Sparshott as 'an alternative
reality' and by the neuropsychologist Chris Frith as an
'ideal time which is more pleasurable than real time'.

Although this quality of music can be important in a
broad spectrum of experience, from a concert performance
of a Mahler symphony to a rave, it is particularly relevant

in religious ritual, from singing the Lord's Prayer to reciting the Koran to the dancing of Dervishes. There is a growing body of evidence that listening to music can improve memory for a ritualistic experience, through modifying arousal levels. The physiological measures used as indicators of arousal might be heart rate, breathing, the way the skin conducts electricity, and blood pressure, which can increase or decrease depending on the type of musical experience – respectively, relaxing or stimulating. It seems that the speed of the music, the tempo, is the major factor.

In addition, we know from neurological measures as well as behaviour that music does indeed improve attention and aid memory. For example, one fascinating investigation has shown that rats exposed to Mozart run mazes more successfully than their counterparts. Frances Rauscher and her colleagues at the University of Wisconsin studied four groups of rats exposed *in utero*, as well as sixty days after birth, to complex music (a Mozart sonata), minimalist music (a Philip Glass composition), white noise or silence. They were then tested for five days, three trials per day, in a multiple T-maze. By the third day, the rats exposed to the Mozart work completed the maze more rapidly and with fewer errors than the rats assigned to the other groups. The difference increased in magnitude up to and including the fifth day.

This result suggests that repeated exposure to complex music induces improved spatial-temporal learning in rats, resembling results found in humans. We can only assume that this effect is not due to rats being connoisseurs of good music: indeed, John Hughs from the University of Illinois has shown that a critical factor in whether or not music enhances cognitive prowess in this way is how often the volume rises and falls. One suggestion is that the music of Mozart is characterized by the volume rising or falling in repeating sequences of twenty to thirty seconds, and that this may coincide with, even drive, brain wave patterns of thirty-second cycles.

Moreover, brain scans reveal that listening to music can cause neural activation in regions of the brain strongly related to emotional processing. The neural structures of particular interest are the right temporal lobe, which is involved particularly in melodic processing and singing, the amygdala and hippocampus, well-known regions linked to emotion and memory that are activated during intensely pleasurable music, and the orbitofrontal cortex and sub-callosal cingulate, both activated during singing and associated with emotional processing. By now I am sure you are well rehearsed in not over-interpreting these data to mean that the brain regions in question are the 'centres for' aspects of music processing. But we can conclude, in a sense, the opposite: music activates many brain areas, in turn therefore probably influencing the holistic landscape of the brain and hence one's consciousness.

Aside from the strong and repetitive stimulation of music and rituals there are other, though much less commonplace, ways in which religious experience may be triggered. A state of delirium, a brain seizure, a close shave with death or an apparently miraculous intervention or visitation can induce similar effects: these events are all 'low frequency', but are the kinds of episodes that one tends to remember and reflect upon. Like high-arousal rituals, they may have puzzling components triggering a search for intentional meaning: why did this happen to me, at that particular time and place, with such-and-such a set of consequences? People commonly assume that these experiences are shaped and directed by some powerful presence, which may be construed, for example, as disembodied agents. The low-arousal, high-frequency doctrinal systems, based on routinized transmission, often provide a convenient – arguably in extreme cases the only – framework for the interpretation of such experiences. Thus Whitehouse's two 'modes of religiosity' probably serve to reinforce each other.

However, since we are trying to map these phenomena on to actual, identifiable brain processes, the real appeal of the two modes is that they depend on an inter-relationship between arousal and frequency of inputs, both of which can eventually be translated into physical events in the physical brain. But we must now be careful to distinguish between the laying down of belief systems and subjective momentary spiritual experience. While heightened spiritual experiences are one-off, or at least very rare, events, what we are really exploring here is what could be happening more long-term in the brain. How might we ensure that such events will be accorded 'meaning' rather than just being pleasant or frightening or exciting sensory experiences? And that's not all: this 'meaning' will be different, stronger, compared to normal learning, in that the formation of connections that these events drive will have to be particularly robust and relatively inflexible. We return, then, to our initial, basic question: what are the special features of the mindset of a believer?

One clue might be that religion and other belief systems are usually associated with reports of subjective states of wellbeing and happiness; religious rituals and even everyday worship, or rallies and parades, may therefore somehow trigger the release of the brain's naturally occurring opiates, endorphins. But what is actually happening in the brain during a ritual, or indeed a political rally or parade, which might cause this effect? In answer to this question, the placebo effect could provide some valuable insights: after all, it is a 'pure' belief dependent on no other context or system, and with no grounds for validity whatsoever. The sugar pill really does contain nothing else.

This astonishing yet very familiar phenomenon, whereby a patient may feel better after a 'treatment' with an inert substance, has been acknowledged for hundreds of years. However, the placebo effect only started to be taken seriously after World War II, when a physician named Henry Beecher noticed that the therapeutic effects of morphine could in many cases be replicated by administering a saline injection, so long as the patient remained under the impression that they had in fact received this powerful analgesic – which happened at that time to be in short supply.

For the next fifty years, careful and controlled investigation of this unlikely effect has revealed that it is indeed a robust phenomenon, but only under certain circumstances. Perhaps not surprisingly, placebos work via the immune system – but only up to a point. Our immune system can be classified into a general defence mechanism to tissue injury, and an evolutionarily more sophisticated and specific one by which highly selective agents called antibodies target specific chemical invaders. Conditions involving the latter, bacterial and viral infections, are not responsive to a placebo. However the more primitive, basic component, the first stage in the immune system response, can be suppressed by placebo treatment. Whether caused by internal or external triggers, this first phase consists of swelling, fever, redness and pain; such effects in turn lead to nausea, tiredness, depression and loss of appetite. Illnesses that are primarily due to a continuation of this 'acute phase' response are those that can be suppressed most effectively by inert agents.

The underlying biochemical chain reaction of the immune system is now well established, if highly complex. The chemicals released from damaged cells act as messengers to stimulate nerves to cause the subjective sensation of pain, so that you withdraw from the site of the injury; in addition there is a widening of the blood vessels (hence redness) to increase the transport of white blood cells (as pus) which in turn combat bacteria, as well as enabling the removal of cellular debris. All the extra energy required is met by calories made available from the conversion of fat to glucose by glucocorticoids, more specifically the stress chemical cortisol which is released from the adrenal gland. But calories can be optimized by events in the brain too. As well as this local action, the white cells trigger a powerful substance called prostaglandin to flood into the brain and create a sense of apathy and loss of appetite in order to conserve energy, as well as fever to combat the proliferation of more bacteria. This action of prostaglandin in the brain can be over-ruled by an agent known to combat pain, the naturally occurring opiates endorphin and enkephalin.

We know that in some way the placebo effect works via enkephalin, since a blocker of that substance, naloxone, also blocks the placebo effect. We also know that the effect works not via the inert chemical itself, but due to *belief* about the inert chemical. So how might we link a biochemical event, release of enkephalins, with a psychological one, the formation of a belief? If religious/ritual or rally/parade experiences cause the release of natural opiates, and if a placebo belief causes the release of these same substances, could the final mechanism in both cases be one and the same?

We saw in Chapter 12 that the answer might well be 'Yes': Catholic subjects found that pain decreased when they were contemplating a picture of the Virgin Mary. In addition, the observations from brain scans suggested that this common mechanism would involve the right anterolateral prefrontal cortex, activation of which has already been shown to be linked to suppression of pain sensations. This area also shows lowered glucose use, in other words it is less active, in depression, which is in turn linked to excessive pain sensations (hyperalgesia). So it might be that in some way the anterolateral prefrontal cortex is sensitive, even if indirectly, to the actions of naturally occurring opiates which, as with morphine itself, not only suppress pain but also generate feelings of wellbeing.

As well as starting to throw light on the salient brain regions, the more insightful clues come from what the neurons might be doing within those brain areas that will predispose Anyone to experience a ritual or rally in a certain way and imbue it with a certain 'meaning', as well as living their whole life in a certain way and ultimately seeing themselves as they do. We have established that arousal and repetition are important in an inter-related fashion, the precise balance of which will be determined by the particular doctrine to which you are subscribing. But in order to attain the final holistic believing state – one characterized by unusually strong neuronal connectivity, the activation of which somehow leads to a concomitant feeling of wellbeing – a variety of inter-related neuronal mechanisms will have to be operating across a variety of brain regions. All we can do at this stage is list them: raised levels of endorphins caused by an exaggerated neuronal mechanism of long-term potentiation in as yet unspecified neuronal networks, related in turn to intense repetition and sporadic high arousal levels, in turn linked to release of modulating agents such as dopamine and serotonin, themselves also linked respectively to 'reward' and alleviation of depression.

This final reward/wellbeing state would act as a reinforcer to perpetuate the behaviour which in turn perpetuated the connections. Although it is impossible as yet to link these features into a realistic model that distinguishes Anyone's brain, the predisposing factors would be the same as for plasticity in general and the mechanisms of LTP: young age, intense repetition, lack of competing input and reinforcement of consistency – only much more exaggerated.

In any event, the brain somehow achieves a clear end result: a very strong mindset relatively impervious to the happenstance and caprices of a life narrative. As such, the brain of Anyone could differ from that of Someone in that the neuronal connections, once formed, would imbue minimal sensory input with much more idiosyncratic salience, both positive and negative, and be far less dependent on, and sensitive to, feedback from that outside world. Events, people and objects in the outside world would have a 'meaning' that might be less obvious than it would be if extrapolated from the sensory features alone. This profile, however, is not qualitatively different to that of Someone's life, but more an exaggeration, a quantitative difference.

In situations where happenstance is minimized in favour of a highly structured, routine life, then clearly the plasticity of the brain will take on a certain configuration unopposed. The occasional ritual or high-arousal experience will then be imbued with the relevant associations that will further reinforce the existing mindset. By contrast, in the caricature scenario of Someone there will be a life narrative dominated by many high-arousal, one-off events – but they will be far more idiosyncratic, with an insufficient pre-existing shared conceptual framework, for those events to have a commonly held 'deep' significance. Rather, each event will have a personal relevance to the individual concerned, which may or may not be consistent with other occurrences but which does not fit into the widely held conceptual framework that characterizes the believer's brain: the pay-off for sublimating an individual identity to a more public, collective one. Hence the plaintive cry of Someone that their life is 'meaningless' or that they don't 'understand' what it all 'means'.

Anyone could also be the flip-side to Someone, when it comes to symbols of status, those vehicles of Oliver James's dreaded 'Affluenza' virus. Back in Chapter 8, I suggested that Someone's behaviour has transcended its original biological function to symbolize something essential about us as individuals, and hence our relative status to each other. As we saw, the Seven Deadly Sins could be viewed as the behaviours through which we each establish that we are unique individuals; it would follow that they would have been/are perceived as undesirable, indeed 'deadly', in societies where individuality is not at a premium. Conversely, in societies where extreme individuality and self-obsession are applauded, such as the caricature scenario of the West Coast of the USA, such behaviours are encouraged.

Status is important for defining our individuality, and such status can be derived by the exercise of the Seven Deadly Sins. But if this holds for a private, individual identity of Someone, could we define the public collective persona of Anyone in a similar way? Yes, I think we can; but the portfolio of sins is different. Whereas Western values place more premium for the private Someone on the symbolism of lust, gluttony, avarice, sloth, vanity and envy, the collective status of fundamentalism, of a public identity, could not be so easily realized via these conduits; in fact, they would be condemned. The narrative of the public Someone, from the Nazis to Al Qaeda, is much more readily a David-and-Goliath storyline. For the Nazis, they were the hapless minority overwhelmed by a global Jewish conspiracy; Osama bin Laden and his like, meanwhile rail against an omnipresent and omnipotent USA. Assuming that, as in politicized ideologies, there *is* a Goliath, then for such a public Someone, the sin of anger is the most obvious and easiest means for defining identity: 'Men's *collective* [my italics] passions are always evil,' warned Bertrand Russell. Of all the ways of asserting status, anger for a David-and-Goliath storyline is the most obvious course against an otherwise higher-status society.

As such, we can draw parallels between the individual Someone and the collective identity (Anyone) mandated by extreme ideologies. The current conflict of Western societies, in particular the USA, with fundamentalism could be interpreted as a struggle between these two types of identity – a private Someone versus a public Anyone. Perhaps the violence seen, for example, on 9/11 was not an act of primeval, 'mindless' aggression with territorial analogies in the animal kingdom, but rather a bid for higher status, in turn a means of asserting an identity, albeit a collective one.

But to what extent has a 'natural' urge to have an individual identity been suppressed by such cultures, where a collective storyline predominates? Or is the opposite true? Is it the concept of a unique self that is an unnatural artefact of the last two centuries or so? The question is impossible to answer because the critical point is that the human brain, and hence the mind, is not a self-contained, isolated entity. Human nature and the 'self', being rooted in the human brain, are inextricably interlinked in incessant dialogue with the outside world and the passage of events within it. The human brain, and hence identity, are locked into a chicken-and-egg relationship with the outside world. Needless to say, at the present time the mind and its life narrative, and hence the ultimate expression of human nature, are engaged in interplay with two very different external world forces.

On the one hand, we have seen that an increasingly pervasive information technology, coupled with an ever more invasive biotechnology, might lead to a culture of passivity and hedonism that obliterates the individual altogether. The excessive materialism that has provided such an easy expression of the Seven Deadly Sins in the twenty-first-century could now, paradoxically, be hastening their extinction: the Nobody scenario.

On the other hand, fundamentalism is suppressing the uniqueness of the individual and imposing a collective narrative. If this collective identity of Anyone prevails, then the dominant and defining 'sin' may well be a continual anger, as was encouraged in the populace in collective sessions in Orwell's *1984*; meanwhile, the individual identity of Someone might in any event be jeopardized by a sanitizing and homogenizing raft of high technologies. The central question will be whether human nature, defined here as predicated on individual status, could evolve in a way that survived fundamentalism and technology respectively by being independent of external status symbols and especially symbolic behaviours.

If so, we would need to develop a means of 'internal' status, where the self could applaud itself. In the next chapter we shall look at what kind of changes in education, work, lifestyle, thinking and relationships would be needed for such a basic and large-scale change in our identity, and see whether they are, after all, what we would want.

14

BEING CREATIVE

'It is suicide to live in a society dependent on science and technology, where virtually no one knows anything about science and technology.' These were the sombre thoughts of the astronomer Carl Sagan as he contemplated a future inseparable from the remorseless march of technology. Let's hope that no one would argue with the current urgent need of the twenty-first-century citizen for empowerment through a passing familiarity with science and technology: after all, it's changing everything we care about – the climate, reproduction, nutrition, health. But by the same token the whole message of this book is that, with equal urgency, we need to understand the reverse: could those same innovations actually be changing our minds as never before in human history? Only once we have appreciated how our malleable brains are interacting with the current and imminent technologies will we be able to plan the kind of education, as well as the goods and services, which we shall both want and need by the mid-twenty-first century. This chapter is all about the options before us, and about optimizing the kind of life that the future could hold.

Someone, Nobody or Anyone: are they truly useful ways of thinking about the brain, or rather the mind? If the ideal is that each of us should be fulfilled and have a unique sense of self, then the dismal conclusion of the previous chapters is that none of these scenarios meets *both* these goals. In sound-bite summary: Someone offers individuality without fulfilment; Anyone fulfilment without individuality; and Nobody neither individuality nor fulfilment.

Somehow there must be a means of acquiring status, not in the snobbish *Affluenza* sense but simply as a means of distinguishing yourself from everyone else, and hence in a way that would be truly fulfilling. Ideally, each of us would have a sense of being unique, but *independent* of external situations based on aspiring superiority to the appearance, belongings and behaviour of others. And this internally driven, non-comparative way of defining our uniqueness would be fulfilling in a way that dependency on the views, actions and attitudes of others inevitably falls short of.

But is this such a novel suggestion? After all, in the third century BC in ancient Athens the Stoic movement advocated an inner autonomy freed from and unperturbed by the slings and arrows of what life and our fellow men – or women – can throw at us. Am I saying any more than that Stoicism is the only way of surviving the twenty-first century with one's sanity and sense of self intact? Yes, I am. Because while Stoicism might be a good defence mechanism against a techno-laden, clamouring and intrusive outer world, it's just that. In itself, developing a means of being impervious to the cruelty or stupidity of others, or to the strident demands of the screen and the mobile, is not in itself very fulfilling. We need not just to minimize the second-hand agenda of the outside world, but to develop an internal one of our own.

Most of us at some stage in our lives have had the thrilling experience of seeing a new solution to a problem, not necessarily in lofty theories or the professional world but perhaps in DIY, cooking or a social conundrum. You don't have to be Mozart or Einstein to experience that wonderful feeling of a strong sense of uniqueness through a new insight or idea – making a connection that has never been made before. Not only are such 'Eureka' moments extremely exciting, they also reinforce an inner conviction that *you* are special because only *you* have had that certain thought. Creativity is surely the ultimate expression of individuality, and a characteristically human activity: it is deeply fulfilling for those who achieve it, and usually of some kind of incidental benefit to wider society. Creativity, then, might offer an ideal way forward: the 'Eureka' scenario. This form of identity would be both private *and* fulfilling!

Unfortunately, for most of us ordinary mortals such moments are at best rare and certainly cannot be dialled up from the nervous system on demand; but there is no obvious reason why such occasions might not be increased, and indeed in everyone's repertoire. If only we knew more about the brain and the creative process.

In this one short chapter it will be impossible to survey all the work and ideas that have been generated with regard to creativity. Not only is it a truly multidisciplinary phenomenon, but investigations themselves can harness many disciplines. So we shall have to narrow down our exploration. Since this book is all about the personalization of the physical brain into a mind we shall concentrate almost exclusively on what neuroscience, or rather neuroscientists, have to say on the subject.

Perhaps as good a place as any to start is with a case study of creative individuals, such as Howard Gardner's

Extraordinary Minds. While it appears that creativity can often run in families, so, with apparent equal frequency, does creativity often surface out of the blue. Not only do we now know that genes and environment are so interconnected as to render the old 'Nature vs Nurture' debate futile, but it would be particularly hard while exploring creativity to disentangle the all-important environmental social factor of families exposed to similar influences: for example, both Leonardo da Vinci and Michaelangelo had to contend with the arguable disadvantage of the time, that of low social status. Then again gifted children, such as piano-playing prodigies or mathematical whizzes, exhibit from a very early age behaviours not displayed by most of their peers, perhaps practising or studying for many hours a day; so surely there must be some sort of a genetic, inherited, link.

But we have seen from the outset that the notion of a single gene 'for' intelligence, say, is just not realistic. A more likely scenario is a particular genetic cocktail that might predispose a child, via a highly indirect and complex chain of neuronal events, to play the piano six hours a day. But in any case, such a package of genes switching each other on and off according to the vagaries of the environment would still be extremely remote in relation to what was actually happening in the holistic brain of a five-year-old turning away from the sun streaming through the windows and transfixed instead by the dull black and white keys silently waiting.

Moreover, we must be cautious about conflating prodigious skills or talents with creativity. Skilled sensory-motor coordination – the finely honed interaction between hand

and eye deployed by a painter or fine-tuned mathematical reasoning is not necessarily 'creative'. That said, creativity is usually equated with exceptional skills expressed through particular media, such as music or art, and/or the rarefied ways of thinking characterized by the poet, the philosopher or the Nobel prizewinning scientist.

But surely these are just extreme examples of all of our much more humdrum 'Eureka' moments. There is no evidence that exceptionally creative individuals have some additional biological feature unavailable to the rest of us ordinary mortals; as far as we know, not only is there is no special gene but no extra brain area either, nor exotic transmitter. If anything, the difference is highly likely to be not *qualitative* but *quantitative* – some individuals would indeed be more creative than others. But it would be all about a difference in degree. And if it's a difference in degree, then it should be possible to discover eventually what common-or-garden ordinary processes in the brain are at work, to greater or lesser extents.

However, it's not obvious where to start to understand the creative process in neuronal terms: it's as hard to study scientifically as it is even to define in the kind of operational way that would be a prerequisite to such an investigation. In 1999 a report from the UK Department of Education entitled *Creative and Cultural Education* suggested that: 'Creativity is an imaginative activity fashioned so as to produce outcomes that are both original and of value.' The report went on to list the key factors: 'First, they always involve thinking or behaving *imaginatively*. Second, overall this imaginative activity is *purposeful*: that is, it is directed to achieving an objective. Third, these processes must generate something *original*. Fourth, the outcome must be of *value* in relation to the objective.'

Yet while this definition might be helpful in providing a checklist to evaluate whether something or someone is creative, it doesn't really get to grips with the actual brain process(es) that result in these desiderata. Such an approach appears to lack any rooting in actual, perhaps novel, neurobiological mechanisms or processes and, most importantly, doesn't seem to be operating under any overarching theory or testable hypothesis/es.

Creativity presents a special problem in that, quintessentially, it involves a *unique* activity or outcome that we need inevitably to generalize to some kind of set principles or uniform formula. Still, one way forward could be to attempt to characterize societies or groups of individuals where creativity is more prominent than usual.

Different societies throughout history that were characterized by unusually creative outputs include fifth-century Athens, the Renaissance in Europe, Elizabethan England, the eighteenth-century Enlightenment; nineteenth-century Paris and early twentieth-century America. Irrespective of the era, all these societies shared the feature of generating a sense of freedom and of being on the edge, as well as enabling a critical mass of creative individuals to work in a competitive but convivial atmosphere. The support of mentors and patrons and the all-important issue of economic prosperity would also be ideal conditions for creativity to thrive and to ensure that the greatest numbers could be creative to the greatest extent.

Yet this shopping list is really just permissive: it describes an environment where you wouldn't be troubled by more basic issues of survival, nor worried when, inevitably, you were attacked or suppressed for original views. Indeed, you might well be part of a group, as with the French Impressionists, where originality was the accepted, 'normal' way of life, and where friends would act as sounding-boards, providing the checks and balances that so characterized the prototype Socratic dialogue. Such an approach then tells us what is necessary, but not necessarily sufficient.

An alternative strategy could be to look directly at the brains of particularly creative individuals. For example, some twenty or so years ago a Berkeley professor, Marion Diamond, conducted a post-mortem study of Einstein's brain and discovered that the great creative scientist displayed only three possible differences from his less gifted counterparts. First, he had a significantly higher than normal proportion of glial cells, the housekeeping cells in the brain, relative to neurons in a particular area (the left inferior parietal cortex) which, surprisingly, was due to a disproportionate lack of neurons; secondly, he had a greater packing of neurons due to a cortex that was, again surprisingly, thinner than usual. The third difference was that a particular fold known as the Sylvian fissure on the surface of the brain was smoother than normal in Einstein's case, possibly enabling more effective communication across wide areas of cortex.

Whatever the possible explanations of these anomalies, they must clearly remain anecdotal due to a sample size of one! None the less, this approach highlights the difficulty of generalizing features from the unique cases that perforce characterize creativity. In addition, such studies also demonstrate the problem of extrapolating from a neuro-logical feature any of the myriad cognitive characteristics that constituted Einstein's, or anyone else's, mental state. For example, as well as being a scientific genius Einstein exhibited schizotypal traits (he was predisposed to schizo-phrenic thought but not diagnosed as suffering from the disease), while his son actually suffered from schizophre-nia. Could schizophrenia itself be a predisposing factor for creativity?

'Madness need not be all breakdown. It may also be breakthrough,' claimed the legendary psychiatrist R.D. Laing, who famously studied the insights that might be gained from studying schizophrenic thought. Evidence has indeed suggested a reliable relationship between creativity and psychosis, although the observations are largely anec-dotal: few studies have examined this relationship using rigorous empirical methodology. None the less, it is the 'association areas' of the cortex (the areas related directly to neither sensory inputs nor motor outputs) which become disturbed in chronic schizophrenia. These evolutionarily more sophisticated regions would therefore be essential brain areas in human creativity. In addition other brain regions, the thalamus and cingulate, are over-active in short-term schizophrenics, while a laundry list of other regions (the associative frontal, parietal, temporal gyri) are under-active in long-term schizophrenics. All that can be deduced here, however, is that schizophrenia is a complex and sophisticated impairment in a variety of cognitive functions that will inevitably be reflected in a wide range of brain regions, be they under- or over-active. And although creativity will involve the kinds of functions linked to the association cortex, so too will non-creative workaday cognition.

None the less, in one study using behavioural and brain imaging methods psychologists at Vanderbilt University investigated in detail the creative thinking process in relation to schizotypal personality, schizophrenia and activity of the prefrontal cortex on each side of the brain. Subjects were divided into three groups: those diagnosed as schizophrenic; those ascertained psychometrically as schizotypal; and healthy control subjects. All were then set a novel 'alternate uses' task designed to assess divergent thinking ability. As its name suggests, this task required subjects to generate 'uses' for conventional and ambiguous objects, arguably as a straightforward test of creative thinking.

It turned out that schizotypes had enhanced creative ability, as measured on the task, compared with the diagnosed schizophrenic and healthy control subjects who showed similar performance to each other overall. The imaging data revealed that the creative thinking was associated with prefrontal cortex activation, with that on the right-hand side in particular contributing to the enhanced creative thinking observed in the psychometric. Creative thinking, then, seems to be involved with a schizophrenic *predisposition*; perhaps, once the disease becomes full-blown, other problems such as paranoia and ready distractibility might intervene to offset the creative train of thought. Yet we would still need to know what is special about schizotypal thought patterns and why they relate, in particular, to the right prefrontal cortex.

Other brain imaging studies, of individuals with epilepsy, aphasia (loss of speech) or mania, have attempted to reveal a common pattern that might be a factor in the creativity that can characterize these cases. Temporal lobe changes as in excessive writing (hypergraphia) often lead to an increase in idea generation, though sometimes at the expense of quality. This emphasis on quantity of words generated roughly parallels the pressured communication of temporal lobe epilepsy, mania and Wernicke's 'jargon' aphasia – a condition, as its name suggests, in which the patient speaks volubly but incomprehensively. Meanwhile, frontal lobe deficits can be associated with a decrease in idea generation, comparable to the sparse speech of Broca's aphasia, the obsessive thoughts that can characterise depression, and other frontal lobe lesions, where speech itself is hard. But, impressive and painstaking though these studies may be, the bottom line is that there is no simple, stereotyped brain scan that would belie the creative mind at work.

A completely different clinically defined group that has problems with words and a tendency to be left-handed, and, most significantly, tends to display more creativity than the general population, is people with dyslexia. At the Laboratory of Physiology at Oxford, the neuroscientist John Stein has developed an intriguing explanation as to why the dyslexic brain might be different. Reading requires the acquisition of good writing skills for recognizing the visual form of words, which allows one to access their meaning directly. It also requires the development of good phonological skills for sounding out unfamiliar words using knowledge of letter–sound conversion rules. In the dyslexic brain, certain language areas in the temporo-parietal on the two sides are unusually symmetrical, without the normal left-sided advantage.

Stein has also found that, in dyslexics, the development of part of the visual system is impaired: this so-called magnocellular system is responsible for timing visual events when reading. It signals any visual motion that occurs if unintended movements lead to images moving off the central area of vision; these signals are then used to bring the eyes back on target, to focus on each letter. It seems that this sensitivity to visual motion helps determine how well literacy skills can develop in both good and bad readers.

It turns out that in dyslexia development of this all-important magnocellular system is abnormal: since motion sensitivity in dyslexics is reduced, many show unsteady focusing with both eyes and hence poor visual localization, particularly on the left side (known as 'left neglect'). This can cause the letters they are trying to read to appear to move around and cross over each other.

But the problem isn't a purely visual one: many dyslexics also have auditory/phonological problems. Distinguishing letter sounds depends on picking up the changes in sound frequency and amplitude that characterize them. Thus, high frequency and amplitude modulation sensitivity help the development of good phonological skill, while low sensitivity impedes the acquisition of these skills – also seen with an impaired magnocellular system, this time as part of the hearing process.

Now the provenance of both visual and auditory mag-nocellular systems, which contribute to binocular fixation and to inner speech for sounding out words, is a particular brain area called the cerebellum. This is a small, cauli-flower-like structure at the back of the brain and almost distinct from it: indeed, some dub it the autopilot of the brain because it's linked to many automatic movements involving sensory-motor coordination. Since there's evidence that most reading problems have a fundamental sensory-motor cause, it's perhaps not surprising that this crucial region, the cerebellum, is clearly defective in dyslexics.

Stein's suggestion is that the magnocellular systems in the cerebellum have failed to develop properly: but why? Interestingly, this time there's a clear genetic basis, and surprisingly it's in the immune system. The best-understood linkage is to the control of production of antibodies – specific chemical enemies directed at highly specific molecular targets. In this case, the development of the magnocells may be impaired by antibodies expressed inappropriately and thus affecting the developing brain. In any event, these magnocells also need high amounts of polyunsaturated fatty acids: so one possible way of helping dyslexics might be to nurture the genetically deficient cells with foods high in these fatty acids, such as fish oils.

But what has all this to do with creativity? In evolutionary terms, the genes that underlie magnocellular weakness and characterize dyslexia wouldn't be so common unless there were also compensating advantages. Hence Stein suggests that in dyslexics there may be heightened development of the complementary parvocellular systems, the second half of the sensory systems. While magnocellular systems enable precise differentiation of component sounds or letters, this parvocellular system is more global in function. Hence unfettered, unopposed exercise of the parvocellular system, as in the brains of dyslexics, might underlie their frequent holistic creative ability for 'seeing the whole picture' that extends from art itself right through to entrepreneurial talents. Indeed, a link has already been shown between dyslexia and the simplest expression of this ability on a global visual-spatial task – speed of recognition of impossible figures.

Another neurological condition in which creativity is an unexpected side-effect is dementia. What might be happening in the brain in this case? Just as with dyslexia, it seems that the critical factor might be the dominance of one system that's normally counterbalanced in dynamic equilibrium with another. For example, loss of function in the anterior temporal lobes may lead to the 'facilitation' of artistic skills. Pick's disease, which we first discussed back in Chapter 4, is a particularly good example. Perhaps a breaking down of traditional classifications and definitions, as characterizes Pick's disease, could also be a prerequisite for creativity. The critical issue may be to achieve the appropriate dynamic balance between frontal and temporal lobe activity, mediated by mutually inhibitory interactions across the different regions of cortex.

In any event, it's important to consider not just relevant regions of brain but the transmitter systems that they use to communicate with each other. The observations that creativity often occurs during levels of low arousal, and that many people with depression, such as Van Gogh, are creative, suggest that chemicals such as the transmitters serotonin and norepinephrine might be important factors in facilitating creativity when they are unusually low. By contrast, another transmitter that, like serotonin and norepinephrine, fountains up from the primitive parts of the hub deep in the brain to the higher centres is dopamine. We have already seen that dopamine is in functional *excess* in schizophrenia: it can apparently influence novelty-seeking and creative drive, and thus perhaps account for the alleged link between schizophrenia and creativity. Such a link might also explain the possible influence of drugs, such as those that simultaneously increase dopamine availability and, allegedly, creativity.

Creative individuals may use psychoactive drugs in the belief that they are enhancing their ability to produce highly original work, but a major obstacle is that their life circumstances are at the same time jeopardized, so the causal relationship of drugs to creativity is uncertain. One study some ten years ago examined this question through an experiment in which the effects of alcohol were investigated on subjects who were asked to combine pictures of wild flowers that were implicitly organized around a set of three dimensions: colour, shape and number. The results showed no pharmacological effect of alcohol on the creative combinations that the subjects produced. However, the most interesting finding was that the novelty and structural recombination of the wild flower arrangements were enhanced when subjects *thought* they had consumed alcohol, whether or not they had actually done so. Perhaps, then, the critical issue is a predisposition, as we saw with the 'creative' societies, to feel uninhibited and free. The assumption that you were under the influence of alcohol might provide the necessary excuse to let your mind range free without fear of criticism.

In any event, data on brain chemicals, and the drugs that manipulate them, must be interpreted with caution. Just as there is no gene 'for' a function, nor any brain region as the exclusive centre 'for' a sophisticated trait, so specific transmitters are not exclusively dedicated to any one specific mental process. Rather, these chemicals will pervade many brain regions and have powerful yet indirect effects on a host of emergent functions and dysfunctions. Transmitters such as dopamine may, for example, merely modulate arousal levels, and in so doing make a marked yet non-specific difference. Once again, if levels of particular transmitters are important in particular areas, then at most it would be a necessary rather than a sufficient condition.

In any case, the common factor in all these different approaches is that studies of human subjects with aberrant minds/brains focus on the *potential* for creativity, not the momentary act of creativity itself. While no one brain area, not surprisingly, has a monopoly on creativity, it seems that a crucial theme is the often unusual balance *between* brain areas. Then again, it might simply be that 'seeing the whole picture' or, even more loosely, 'feeling uninhibited' is just the first step, the necessary but not sufficient requirement. After all, not all dyslexics, drug users, schizophrenics or neurodegenerative patients are conspicuously creative. So let's differentiate two equally valid but distinct questions, the first of which we have already pondered: (1) What quasi-permanent features of the brain predispose an individual to be creative? But then (2) What is actually happening in the brain during a creative moment?

One experiment that deals with this second question was devised by Paul Howard-Jones and his team at Bristol University, where they scanned the brains of normal subjects in order to identify those areas of the brain associated with a creativity test on generation of a story. The subjects had to build into a story a set of words that were unrelated to each other. The results suggested that areas of the right prefrontal cortex are critical to the types of divergent semantic processing involved with creativity in this context. You will recall that it was the right prefrontal cortex, interestingly enough, that seemed unusually active in the schizotypal group who showed greater potential for creativity when asked to think up different uses for everyday objects. In a sense the two tasks have more than a passing similarity: thinking up multiple different uses, and thinking of different ways in which one word can be used in relation to others, may well both be related to activity in the right prefrontal cortex.

But we know better, by now, than to say that this sophisticated function is 'localized' there, or, worse still, that the right prefrontal cortex is the 'centre for' this aspect of creativity. None the less, whatever the intermediary process there does appear to be some kind of association between activity in the right prefrontal cortex and appreciating the full flexibility of either words or everyday objects. The bigger question, though, would be to what extent such an ability was pivotal to creativity.

People sometimes solve problems via a unique process regarded objectively as insight, and experienced subjectively as an 'Aha!' moment: perhaps it is *this* process that we need to track in the brain. No psychologist has ever clarified whether or not different cognitive and neural processes lead to solutions based on insight, or if solutions differ only in subsequent subjective feeling. Certainly, recent behavioural studies indicate distinct patterns of performance and suggest differential involvement of the two brain hemispheres for insight versus non-insight solutions.

At Northwestern University the cognitive neuroscientist Mark Jung-Beeman has observed two distinct, objective neural patterns relating to insight. Subjects were set verbal problems, and after each correct solution indicated whether they had solved them with or without insight. Brain imaging revealed increased activity in a particular area (the right hemisphere anterior superior temporal gyrus) for insight relative to non-insight solutions. Moreover, scalp EEG recordings revealed a sudden burst of high-frequency neuronal activity in the same area beginning a third of a second *prior* to those insight solutions. This right anterior temporal area has been associated with making connections across distantly related information during the process of comprehension. The conclusion, then, is that the sudden flash of insight, as indicated by the sudden activity, occurs when solvers engage connections that had previously eluded them. Again, then, although this time it's the temporal rather than the frontal lobe, it's the right-hand side of the brain that seems to be particularly prominent and the ability to make new connections that seems crucial.

So here might be the kind of crucial difference we have been trying to hunt down: the 'Eureka' brain could contrast with that of Anyone's as regards its potential plasticity. We saw earlier that, whatever the predisposing factors might be, we could characterize the brain of the fundamentalist as one where the neuronal connectivity was particularly ro-bust and more impervious to the influence of chance or haphazard inputs and experiences. Meanwhile, the 'Eur-eka' brain would have to be the exact opposite: existing connectivity would need to be disabled, and the means for novel connections to form would need to be maximized. We have seen both in Chapter 13 and here that such flexibility or persistence of neuronal connectivity is possible as a result of the various conditions ensuing in each case. Arousal levels, in turn reflected in levels of various neurochemicals; frequency of input; consistency and type of input – all will play their part, in ways as yet not documented in detail by neuroscience in determining the configuration of connections in the brain, and the resultant sustainability/malleability of those connections – one's mind.

Yet the idea that a fundamentalist mindset, Anyone's brain, is the polar opposite to a creative one has an intuitive resonance. Creativity is obviously a complex process, manifesting in various ways and to differing extents, and generating a number of questions and approaches. Take the creative predisposition. It isn't sufficient to invoke the mindsets of drug-takers or the mentally ill, such as Van Gogh, to 'explain' a brain with a predisposition to creativity: after all, not all drug-takers and mentally ill people are creative, nor, conversely, do all artists, writers and composers necessarily suffer mental illness or take drugs. None the less, from the brief, non-exhaustive outline above several basic principles emerge.

As might be expected, the brain areas (the association cortex) most linked to sophisticated mental functions light up in most studies; more specifically, a persistent theme appears to be the interaction between two such regions, the frontal and temporal lobes. It's impossible, given the range of cases studied and the variation in experimental procedures, to develop any precise descriptions; however, it could be that a mutually inhibitory relationship between remote parts of the cortex and other brain areas somehow, paradoxically, predisposes the brain to 'make new connections' more readily and 'see the big picture'. The under-function of the schizophrenic prefrontal cortex, for example, and/or a dysfunctional dyslexic cerebellum might have similar *net* effects on an all-important parameter such as the functioning of the temporal lobe or levels of dopamine, which might feed back on the functioning of its counterpart frontal lobe and Stein's magnocellular systems. These processes would in turn be under the long-term modulatory influences of transmitters, particularly ones such as dopamine and norepinephrine which emanate from the primitive hub of cells deep in the brain.

Please don't worry if this all seems far too technical and incomprehensible – because it is, even to me and other professional neuroscientists. These neural interactions, spanning as they do both the macro-anatomical level and the level of micro-synaptic signalling, are currently too complex and too fragmented to have been analyzed and described in detail by any of us: the current picture still defies any attempt at a serious, holistic, computational-type model of the creative mindset. And yet a critical question is whether, and of so how, such unusual scenarios do indeed influence brain plasticity – the ability to form connections generally. This is an important question because, irrespective of the actual brain processes and the anatomical areas in which they occur, the ability to break and make connections is clearly key.

We have just seen that it isn't sufficient to invoke the

mindsets of drug-takers or individuals such as Van Gogh, in all his instability, to 'explain' creativity. None the less, I'm suggesting that the mindless mindset that characterizes, but isn't exclusive to, the drug-taker, the psychotic, the patient with dementia or indeed the child is a prerequisite for deconstructing the world, and with it the dogmatic, accepted ways of viewing and understanding it. Creativity, therefore, might result from a series of steps.

The first step would be to devise ways for dismantling the most obvious and accepted of connections, be they between words, colours, shapes or ideas. The next step would be to bring together elements (be they word, colours, shapes or facts) that have never been linked before. Then follows a crucial third step: mere novel linkages are insufficient, as witnessed in many drug-takers' meaningless ramblings or schizophrenics' neologisms – nonsense words. And after all, a child's painting is no work of art. What is the difference, then, between four-year-old Phoebe's painting of a highly novel purple-coloured sheep with turquoise legs, and Damien Hirst's somewhat more famous pickled counterpart? The critical third issue – the all-important necessary and sufficient condition – is that the new combination of colours/words/ideas triggers new extensive connections: new 'meaningful' associations in both the creator and, ideally, others. We see the world, thanks to the creation in question, in a new way because new and extensive and therefore 'meaningful' associations have formed in our brains, triggered by these novel juxtapositions of previously disparate elements. So, while Phoebe's version of a sheep may display novel colours, they are, literally, meaningless. Meanwhile,

An unusual interpretation of a sheep, by Phoebe Collins aged four –
but is it creative?

Hirst's more conventionally coloured creation raises in the
mind issues of mortality, the transience of a moment
trapped in infinity, and so on.

However, there is also a critical precondition. If we are
about to deconstruct or challenge an existing set of connections, we must accept a degree of risk that the end result
may not meet the criteria for the three steps: deconstruction; novel pairings; new meaning. So the most basic
condition of all in the creative process may well be to
foster an environment and mindset that isn't risk-averse. I
suggested much earlier that the new, unprecedented environment brought about by the current technologies might
enhance a tendency for recklessness: if so, in the future we
shall need to manage that environment to encourage just
the appropriate degree of risk-taking.

Although the predisposition to risk-taking and creativity itself can be studied, in both cases, from many different

stances – anthropological, humanities, sociological, psychological, psychiatric, neurological – the neural mechanics of the act of creativity itself, the exhilarating experience of that special moment, can surely only be approached directly by invasive studies of the brain. By definition, the creative process is often instant, 'Aha' or 'Eureka', as a crucial connection is made. Even within neuroscience, non-invasive brain imaging, such as MRI, has a time resolution (seconds) that is far too slow to capture the essential, instantaneous process online. The alternative is to use EEG recordings to monitor, for example, the all-important third of a second prior to an 'Aha' moment. However, such recordings lack any spatial resolution and offer no true insight as to the precise neuronal mechanisms, neither within the cortex nor with any inter-related subcortical or cerebellar systems, nor indeed with the transmitter systems that enable such cerebral coordination.

In order to develop a scientific approach to creativity we need, first, experimental tools for studying both the question of the creative mindset and the actual creative process; secondly, a neuroscientific model that could actually link these two questions; and thirdly, a general theory that could incorporate the neuroscientific, three-step model suggested here into other disciplines in which the behaviour, though not the brain processes, of creative individuals is studied directly. Perhaps scientists in the future will make some headway with these potential experimental projects.

But for the purposes of our current journey we need to look further still, beyond the present and future of neuroscience, and place the individual back into society. Let's see how both the creative predisposition, and indeed the creative process itself, could fit into the lives of our children and grandchildren, to make the mid-twenty-first century the most exciting time ever to be alive.

15

AN IDEAL IDENTITY FOR
THE TWENTY-FIRST CENTURY?

Yes, of course the scenarios that I've been outlining are crass caricatures. But, like all caricatures, they might enable us to appreciate key issues stripped to their most basic. The defining feature in the Someone identity would be *relations* with others: behaviours that symbolize, and are reactive to, one's own status vis-à-vis others in any particular society. The brain would be characterized by extensive neuronal networks that were malleable enough to be constantly updated and changed in response to shifting values and status as a result of ongoing experience. Identity would always be conditional on the situation at any one time.

Meanwhile the defining feature of the Anyone identity would be *actions*: the ritualized motions and prescribed patterns of living out each day. We saw that the connections here would be as extensive as in the Someone brain, yet less changed by the happenstance of the moment. The stronger, more rigid neuronal network would on the one hand allow for a more robust, internally derived and less conditional identity, but also one that was more uniform and predictable.

The Nobody brain would be the antithesis of this extensive yet rigid network that could in turn confer unequivocal checks and balances. Here instead there would be no frames of reference. This time the brain would be maximally receptive to incoming stimuli, but with relatively less neuronal networking to assign any 'meaning': the emphasis would be more on sensation than on cognition. The defining feature of the Nobody identity would be raw *feelings*.

Another big health warning: I'm not for one moment suggesting that the brain, say, of someone who works for much of the time on the screen has hardly any neuronal connections, nor that the neuronal connections in a fundamentalist's brain are utterly unchangeable. It's all a question of degree – the extent to which brain connections can be strengthened and weakened, and the *relative* extent to which they have been formed and are operational in the first place. The only point to make is that neuronal plasticity, and the factors that contribute to it – modulation by transmitters, in turn determined by arousal levels, strength and repetition of stimuli etc. – might be a useful neuroscientific framework for at least starting to conceptualize, at a physical level, these subtle potential differences in the human mindset.

Moreover, the central issue is not whether humanity will divvy up neatly into Someone, Nobody or Anyone stereotypes, but rather the extent to which such discrepant outlooks and agendas will chart the course of succeeding generations for the rest of this century. From the Russian Revolution to the Nazis to the Cold War to Al Qaeda, the passage of the twentieth century was dominated by the tension between self-centred consumerism on the one hand and collective fundamentalist doctrines on the other: Someone versus Anyone.

But the deluge of technologies in just the last few years

has introduced a possible third option: Nobody. Could the unprecedented pervasion of our time by what some might simply see as harmless gadgets really make such a big difference to the way our children and grandchildren will live their lives? At the extreme, just imagine a society in which each person no longer defines themselves as separate entities. In such a scenario information, bio- and nano-technologies will have obliterated the traditional means of individual demarcation, from the familiar firewall of the physical body and brain to our notions of external 'reality', to third party access to our innermost body processes, to homogenization of generations through homogenized health, appearance and reproductive potential, to a blurring of the daily narrative of work and leisure: in short, a transformation of the entire traditional, unique life story which defines each one of us, and which makes life so fulfilling.

If only some of these predictions become reality, mid-twenty-first-century society might look, and feel, very different. Not only would people appear more similar, in terms of a uniform age and with more standardized faces and bodies, but they would be more uniform in outlook, tending to the reactive, interactive disposition characterized by the Nobody scenario. And if so, the mentality of the future could be to have a shorter attention span, a tendency to think in terms of visual icons rather than abstract ideas, and at the same time to be less risk-averse. Future generations would thrive on hectic fact-fielding activities, but no longer be so well equipped as their predecessors to place isolated events in a context. Moreover, their sense of personal identity might well not be so developed and they would consequently co-exist more effectively than their twentieth-century predecessors as anonymous enablers, untroubled by issues of ego and self-image. In any event, their motivation for daily life would be more on the process, more on the feel of the momentary experience of what they were actually doing, than on the longer-term implications or the significance of those actions. In short, life would be more comfortable and more fun, but would have less meaning.

Already such possibilities are showing signs of coming to pass, even if only on a small scale. What we buy is coming closer to what we do: we are already shifting, at least in Western society, from merely owning goods to placing increasing emphasis on services and the feelings they pro-duce – to sensations. As the design of products becomes optimized and standardized, and as costs fall to the degree that they are available to the mass market and no longer have in themselves an elitist cachet, the differentiation of brands is relying increasingly on the *experience* associated with those goods: from a sense of wellbeing and content-ment engendered by the nurturing of an after-sales relation-ship, to the thrill at the convergence of a wide choice of music or words or sights in a way that was previously unimaginable but is now assured by the iPhone, for ex-ample. And as the trend in Western society for the Nobody scenario poses an ever more tempting alternative to being Someone, goods will become more and more synonymous with services *per se*. At the limit, the 'product' will be increasingly comparable to current computer games – purely the wherewithal to have a particular experience.

So just think of this century indeed witnessing the breakdown in the Western world of the traditional compartments of life, and bringing with it a life that's relatively unchanging from one day to the next, a life lived out of the context of a sequential narrative: nothing less than the demise of a life story. In some respects, such an existence might not be so different from the more traditional alternative offered by the Anyone scenario: in both cases there would be few surprises, but while the appeal of fundamentalist doctrines is to be a small part of a great and significant storyline, the momentary experience for those locked into the screen, in a world devoid of meaning, would be fragmented and an end in itself. As such these isolated moments would need to be as engaging as possible in themselves in order to provide the necessary degree of all-consuming sensory stimulation. Yet these screen experiences are currently somewhat passive: they are appealing to the Nobody scenario in that they foster strong – literally sensational – feelings.

Now imagine the appeal of being able to make the transition from the generic glow of rescuing the princess – essentially of solving a series of precedented algorithms – to achieving something unique for the first time ever. Merely solving a problem to which the answer is known would surely pale in comparison to the incandescent excitement of the creative process. So, as goods and services continue to blur into each other, perhaps the most successful commodities in the future might be those that offer the consumer not just an experience, but a *creative* experience. Now you would feel not only a sense of fulfilment, but also a sense of individual identity.

We've seen that the creative process itself might have to

consist of three steps: first, deconstruction or challenge; secondly, bringing together new elements; thirdly, attaching a significance or new insight to that novel synthesis. Such steps might be realized in many obvious products ranging from toys to computer games, and, perhaps less obviously, in certain types of carefully designed environments. If these innovations could then have significance about how you see yourself, or the society in which you live, or the world in general, or if they help you and others see things in a new way, then they would be even more rewarding.

If indeed we can evolve from twentieth-century-type goods via current turn-of-the-century-type services to mid-twenty-first-century creative experiences, then society in general, as a cause-and-effect dialogue of brains with the environment, would inevitably be morphing correspondingly towards a more creative disposition. Not everyone would be a Mozart or a Picasso, but they might be more confident and at ease about their unique identity. Let's assume, just for the moment, that this trend is a positive step to be welcomed.

So here we are, living in a society in which people are more fulfilled as individuals than when they were caught in an arms race of owning more and more branded but inert objects, and when latterly they slumped in front of a screen playing games with predictable endings. How might a creative mindset be achieved on a wide scale, given the technologies at our disposal, for the next generation, who may have grown up spending six hours a day in two dimensions?

I'm sure many parents and grandparents would welcome

hard statistics on critical factors such as hours spent in front of a screen, critical age ranges, the offsetting influences of other activities and, above all, knowledge as to what abilities – compared to the ones possessed by those of us educated in the last century – may now be lost and also what may now be gained with this new way of processing information. Many admirable projects are in train but the public need to know about them, and they need to know about each other. Now is the time to ensure public engagement in the process. We shall need to consider how twenty-first-century technology can help deliver a twenty-first-century education system, not by turning the clock back, and not by picking off small or specific projects, but by coordinating on a nationwide scale, within both the public and private sectors, the best of the science and technology initiatives.

The Foresight Programme, for instance, based in the British Government Office for Science within the Department for Innovation, Universities and Skills, uses science-based methods to provide visions of the future. Their website explains: 'Although we can't predict the future, our research methods are useful in helping us to identify potential risks and opportunities in relation to science and technology, which can enable policymakers to develop strategies to manage our future better.' This programme has already made a significant impact upon our thinking about the future of a number of issues in society; perhaps the government should now consider a similar in-depth project to explore the future of new technologies on learning and education in the next few decades. In particular, surely we need some kind of analysis and national, or even international, survey of shifting trends in the whole portfolio of learning and thinking skills? There are some big questions needing urgent answers. What are the influences on children today? Where is the actual evidence of a new type of impact? What do we actually want children to learn? And, most importantly, how do we deliver these desiderata using the new technologies?

No one independent institution or organization, no one single project, can take on such a challenge. We need, at government level, to spearhead a large-scale public debate, and thereby to ensure that the citizens of the mid-twenty-first century have the most fulfilling lives possible, in the most successful society possible. There are already some valuable initiatives underway which have brought together different sectors: for example, the Economic and Social Research Council-funded seminar series 'Collaborative Frameworks in Neuroscience and Education' have been a catalyst for bringing together neuroscientists and educators to help us start to understand learning and create an evidence base upon which twenty-first-century education can be built. It is still very early days, but here are some specific ideas of my own with which we could start.

A key issue, as we saw in Chapter 10, is the possible demise of a conceptual framework, a means of evaluating current experience against ideas and generalizations previously elaborated and modified by reading books and endlessly cross-referencing them. But we should not assume that all children nowadays, and particularly in the future, will be so well equipped. We have access to unlimited and up-to-date information at the touch of a button, and soon, probably, at a simple utterance; but in this new, answer-rich world, surely we must ensure that we are able to pose appropriate, meaningful questions.

As an essential basic intellectual requirement, we need a way of providing conceptual frameworks that can be delivered in an engaging format by harnessing screen technologies. A high priority would be to develop the notion of abstract concepts, such as freedom or free will or love, above and beyond visual icons, perhaps by the presentation of many varied examples in wide-ranging contexts, inviting the user to work out and reflect on the common link. The development of conceptual frameworks could then be encouraged by intensive cross-referencing, perhaps as a condition before progressing further with a navigation. Such an exercise could benefit 'working memory' – the ability to keep many ideas and rules in play all at once.

Such an exercise would have to include a time for the essential consolidation that occurs naturally as you turn the pages of a book, but then pause to stare at the wall as the ideas 'sink in'. This is a time when you will be measuring up the new idea against the checks and balances of your own idiosyncratic conceptual framework – trying out the idea in a variety of different contexts and against different questions to see if it can stand up. Perhaps software could be developed that at least has built-in pause times, but in addition could attempt to nurture this checks-and-balances process against the nascent framework that has been built so far.

These are just some ideas that attempt to realize, via the screen, the types of abilities that would have resulted more readily from reading books. In both cases having a here-and-now experience would give way to thinking in a sequential narrative, but not just a narrative where the thrill was on the process towards finding a meaningless answer, like freeing the princess. Ideally, learning to think beyond icons and being encouraged to place that thinking in an ever more complex context would reprioritize *content* over mere cognitive *process*.

But even so, even were software to be developed along these lines, we would at best be ensuring that the new technologies were optimizing the learning process that fosters, in turn, a content, a meaning to life. Such an endpoint might well be laudable; however, the proposal here is not to look back to a time that never was, but to make the most of the exciting and unprecedented possibilities opening up. Someone, Nobody and Anyone: if as it seems, the three types of identity could not deliver the ideal means to achieve fulfilment and a sense of self in the twenty-first century, then we should be exploring ways in which the new technologies might enhance the 'Eureka' mindset for the first time on a mass scale.

We have just seen that there is no consensus on what creativity actually is – no tidy operational definition that would enable a line to be drawn objectively between a merely good idea/solution and a 'creative' one, or between a 'creative' person and the rest of us who might none the less occasionally have our 'Aha' moment. And since it's so hard even to identify in neutral terminology what, say, Mozart and Shakespeare and Picasso and Chanel might have had in common, it's particularly challenging to try to devise a means to forge this same unidentifiable process in the developing brain.

If none the less we adopted the three steps I've suggested, then we could at least stipulate certain basic prerequisites. First, the confidence to challenge the existing assumptions/associations: we know already that emotion, especially negative emotions such as fear of failure, can have a huge impact on a child's performance. For example, the psychologist James Bryan and his colleagues at Northwestern University recently reported that there was a correlation between 'learning disabled' children and a fear of failure – they were more anxious than their 'non-disabled' counterparts.

Secondly, we need to be appropriately unencumbered by the constraints of existing conceptual frameworks in order to countenance bizarre and novel associations. This skill is, of course, based partly again on having confidence – but both the confidence and imagination to ask the question: 'What if?' Imagination, as we saw in Chapter 9, might best be developed in the absence of literal visual input, such as when a parent is reading their toddler a story, and therefore might be in jeopardy as the icons of the screen pervade more and more hours of each day. However, as I keep pointing out, even the unfettered, imaginative mentality – the one that characterizes, arguably, most children, some schizophrenics and many drug-takers – is only halfway there.

The critical third step to coming up with a novel output *with a meaning* entails checks-and-balances thinking, though ticking off against a much wider and more flexible system of boxes than is normal. Only then can we ensure that the new association, the new link is indeed significant, enabling oneself or others to see the world in a new way.

The ability to think in such a wide style, where a new idea or phenomenon or sound or sight is placed in a context to evaluate its 'meaning', is all dependent on a robust working memory – holding many rules and ideas in play simultaneously.

In an ideal situation, then, we would need an environment in which children and adults alike felt confident and thus emotionally secure come what may, in which they were trained to visualize unseen scenes, and in which they were given whatever mental exercises aided working memory. But there is of course no single endpoint or measure that would determine whether your child was creative. The best we can do is to work out what the stages of the creative process might be, attempt to translate those stages into brain processes, then organize the environment so that those brain processes are realized to their fullest potential.

Yet if we could define creativity so precisely, and if we could manipulate the brain into a desired 'creative' mind, would it actually be ethical? Perhaps we would be delivering the very fears of Orwell's *1984* and Huxley's *Brave New World* – the manipulation of the individual in such an invasive and targeted manner as to obliterate their personality, their individuality. But not to worry: the answer, or at least the reassurance, lies in what we have learnt about the brain. There is no single gene for a complex mental trait, no simple chemical that can be increased or decreased by a drug that will enable us to cherry-pick and plan the mental portfolio that constitutes either our own mental state and prowess or that of our unborn children.

However, manipulation of the environment has – most famously since the time the Jesuits emphasized the first seven years of life – proved particularly powerful in narrowing the human mind along standardized lines that converge into a collective, uniform narrative. But that same sensitivity to external inputs can now, arguably for the first time on a large scale, be exploited to engender creativity and with it the most individual brain possible. The wonderful point about creativity is that it cannot be contrived, because it is not a specific trait, a set of beliefs, an operationally defined skill or a corpus of knowledge. We have seen that the best we might be able to do is to set up predisposing influences; the rest is up to the interaction in each case with the individual brain, the individual time and space coordinates.

But just say that such a policy really did deliver an entire society of individuals who were much more creative than any previous one. What would it actually be like to have a community where everyone was fired up, excited by the act of revelation and discovery, with such a strong and robust sense of self that each was impervious to the needs or reactions of others? We might be facing the caricature of the West Coast mentality, one of unconstrained selfishness, self-obsession and egocentricity: a community that wasn't in fact a community because creativity in itself may well enable a wonderful feeling of self-realization and fulfilment but doesn't necessarily bring with it an ability to form successful relationships and interact successfully with others. Some might say, looking at the numerous highly creative yet dysfunctional exemplars throughout history, that the exact opposite was the case.

One answer might be to limit the number of those in society who were creative. This prospect is redolent of

Brave New World but without any genetic engineering, though still drawing forth the obvious ethical objection to disadvantaging the individual for the benefit of the whole society. But imagine, none the less, if we could simply allow some individuals unsupervised access to screens all day, or to low-arousal, high-frequency monotonous chanting, or to endless possessions that they were told made them better than others: just imagine that we could skew things respectively in favour of lots of distinct little Nobodies, Anyones or Someones. The problem is that we have already seen that these personas, taken to the extreme, are not best fitted to make for a vibrant, interactive or stimulating community. The impossibility of the balance between the needs of the individual and the greater good of society stretches back for millennia.

So how could a balance be achieved? How could people's brains/minds be so manipulated during the environment of their formative years that they were nice and cooperative and altruistic, but at the same time realized their full potential and were intellectually fulfilled? Some might say that this is precisely what we have at the moment – a minority of dysfunctional but valuable eccentrics and a much larger majority of mediocre (by definition) but content and well-socialized citizens. Yet that's the whole issue: we *don't* have that in any current society and probably never have had; and we are less and less likely to have it if the predictions of the previous chapters come to pass.

Let's take a different tack. Perhaps the answer might lie, not in contriving different stereotypes, but in drawing on the advantages that each offers society. True, a creative mindset can be of use both in providing exciting inputs intellectually and in pointing to new developments for living healthier, longer, more comfortable and ecologically sustainable lives. But then again, sometimes we need to work collectively, to sublimate our personal needs and wants for a cohesive team effort: Anyone. At other times we need, in ways a chimp would never appreciate or understand, to ritualize or symbolize our actions and identity with physical objects or behaviours that thus give a 'significance' to what is happening around us, and a 'meaning' to our very existence: Someone. Finally, we sometimes need to be mind-less, to 'let ourselves go' on the ski slope, on the dance floor, in the bedroom or at the dining table: Nobody.

In short, all four scenarios – Someone, Nobody, Anyone and Eureka – have their time and place in the narrative of a human life story, as well as in enabling a fully functional and successful society. The problem until now has been that the balance hasn't been right – neither for the individual nor for the particular society in which they live. But now, for the first time in human history, the technology is there to enable us to have not just the technological toolkit but also the time and space to shape a world that creates an environment where all four personas can be developed into an integrated portfolio. Perhaps then our children and grandchildren will have the potential to be truly fulfilled individuals and useful to society.

Of course such a prospect, I'm suggesting, is at the moment utterly hypothetical and entirely lacking in any practical detail or application: but even so, it immediately begs the question as to whether future generations could or should use science to work towards realizing the combined portfolio of all four personas as a basic feature of future society. If neuroscience can so deconstruct, analyze and understand the human mind as to enable meaningful manipulation of the environment, might we be robbing successive generations of that most precious attribute of the individual, Free Will? Yet the issue of the determinism or otherwise of the vagaries of genes, proteins, synapses, neuronal networks and brain regions, as of the brain that they constitute and of the way that brain interacts with the world, remains open for debate and relentless speculation. Just as the issue of the ultimate desirability of an 'ideal' society – of an arguably sanitized community of healthy, well-adjusted and fulfilled individuals – might still be somehow, in some intangible way, deficient.

As we grow, as our brains become personalized into 'minds', so we cease to take the world at face value and place it instead in the context of our own life stories, our own highly individual experiences that make up a unique narrative. We have seen that the astonishing sweep of human individuality is a direct consequence of this dynamism of our brains, from the incessant modification of brain processes by the happenstance of the environment.

The deep, ancient and relentless questions of Free Will and an ideal society remain, it would seem, a world away from the daily mechanical drudge of the lab. Indeed, many believe that scientists should only be experimental pragmatists: they should just get on with generating data unguided by any driving falsifiable hypothesis, applying the techniques they have learnt and reporting in specialist/technical journals whatever they find within reductionist and established paradigms. Given this thankless rat-race, upon which depend grants for the individual and income for their university department, it isn't hard to see why few would ever contemplate placing their findings in a wider philosophical or ethical or political context.

But surely the whole rationale for neuroscience is that brain scientists should start, not so much with the unconditional acceptance and application of an experimental technique, but with a truly meaningful question. Surely we neuroscientists should be grappling to formulate hypotheses, for example about human nature, the mind and consciousness; tough though it is, we should then be prepared to take the most difficult challenge of all to *translate those hypotheses into the physico-chemical context of the brain itself.* Little did I realize as I awaited my plastic pot and its pungent contents so long ago that, on the brink of the future which was opening up, it might one day be possible to do just that.

FURTHER READING

The Future (Ch 1)

Bloom, F.E. (Ed) (2007) *The Best of the Brain from Scientific American: Mind, Matter, and Tomorrow's Brain*. Dana Press

Greenfield, S.A. (2003) *Tomorrow's People*. Penguin

James, O. (2007) *Affluenza*. Vermilion

Kaku, M. (1999) *Visions: How science will revolutionize the twenty-first century*. OUP.

Martin, J. (2006) *The Meaning of the 21st Century: A vital blueprint for ensuring our future*. Eden Project Books

The Brain (Chs 2–4)

Bateson, P. and Martin, P. (2000) *Design for a Life: How behaviour develops*. Vintage

Diamond, M. Johnson, R. Protti, A. Ott, C. and Kajisa, L. Plasticity in the 904-day-old male rat cerebral cortex *Exp. Neurol.* 87: 309–317. 1985.

Escorihuela, R.M. Tobena, A. and Fernandez, T. (1994) Environmental enrichment reverses the detrimental action of early inconsistent stimulation and increases the beneficial effects of postnatal handling on shuttlebox learning in adult rats *Behav. Brain Res.* 61: 169–173. 1995.

Greenfield, S.A. (2000) *The Human Brain: A guided tour*. Basic Books

Greenough, W.T. McDonald, J.W. Parnisari, R.M. and Camel, J.E. Environmental conditions modulate degeneration and new dendrite growth in cerebellum of senescent rats *Brain Res.* 380: 136–143. 1986.

Hockly E, Cordery PM, Woodman B, Mahal A, van Dellen A, Blakemore C, Lewis CM, Hannan AJ, Bates GP. (2002) Environmental enrichment slows disease progression in R6/2 Huntington's disease mice. *Ann Neurol.* 2002 Feb;51(2):235–42

Huttenlocher, P.R. (2002) *Neural Plasticity: The effect of environment on the development of the cerebral cortex*. Harvard University Press.

Maguire, EA. Gadian DG, Johnsrude IS, Good CD, Ashburner J, Frackowiak RS, Frith CD. (2000) Navigation-related structural change in the hippocampi of taxi drivers. *Proc Natl Acad Sci U S A.* Apr 11;97(8):4398–403.

Pascual-Leone, A. Nguyet D., Cohen, L.G., Brasil-Neto, J.P., Cammorata, A. & Hallett, M. (1995). Modulation of muscle responses evoked by transcranial magnetic stimulation during the acquisition of new fine motor skills. *J.Neurophysiology*, 74:3 1037–1045

i.d.

Restak, R. (2001) *The Secret Life of the Brain*. Dana Press & Joseph Henry Press

Ridley, M. (2004) *Nature via Nurture: Genes, Experience, and What Makes Us Human*. HarperCollins

Whalley, L. (2001) *The Ageing Brain*. Weidenfeld & Nicolson

Drugs, Brain Disorders, Biotechnology & Nanotechnology (Chs 5 – 6)

Baker, R. (1999) *Sex in the Future: Ancient urges meet future technology*. Pan

Claridge, G Ed (1997) *Schizotypy: Implications for Illness and Health*

Duncan, D.E. (2005) *The Geneticist Who Played Hoops with My DNA And other masterminds from the frontiers of Biotech*. Morrow

Frith, C. and Johnstone, E.C. (2003) *Schizophrenia: A Very Short Introduction*

Fukuyama, F (2002) *Our Posthuman Future: Consequences of the Biotechnology Revolution*

Goodman and Gilman (Eds) (2001) *The Pharmacological Basis of Therapeutics* 10th Ed. McGraw-Hill

Gosden, R. (1999) *Designer Babies: The brave new world of reproductive technology*. Pheonix

Greenfield, S. A. and Vaux, D.V. (2002) Parkinson's disease, Alzheimer's disease and motor neurone disease: identifying a common mechanism. *Neuroscience*. 113(3):485–92

Hochberg, L.R. et al., (2006) Neuronal ensemble control of prosthetic devices by a human with tetraplegia. *Nature* Vol 442

Human Genetics Commission (2006) Making Babies: reproductive decisions and genetic technologies.

Jones, RAL (2004) *Soft Machines: nanotechnology and life*. OUP

McGaugh, J.L.(2003) *Memory & Emotion: The making of lasting memories*. Weidenfeld & Nicolson

Nestler, E.J. (2002) From neurobiology to treatment: progress against addiction. *Nature* Vol 5

Ozin, GA and Arsenault, AC. (2005) *Nanochemistry: A chemical approach to nanomaterials*

Renneberg, R. (2007) *Biotechnology for Beginners*. Academic Press

Rossi, S. and Rossini, P.M. (2004) TMS in cognitive plasticity and the potential for rehabilitation. *Trends in Cognitive Sciences* Vol 8.

Stock, G. (2002) Redesigning Humans: Choosing our children's genes

Turner, D.C. et al., (2003) Cognitive enhancing effects of modafinil in healthy volunteers. *Psychopharmacology* 165, 260–269

Human Nature & Identity (Chs7 – 8)

Deacon. T. (1997) *The Symbolic Species* W.W. *Norton & Co*.

De Botton, A. (2004) *Status Anxiety*. Hamish Hamilton

Greenfield, S.A. (2000) *The Private Life of the Brain*. Penguin

Hobson, P. (2002) *The Cradle of Thought: Exploring the origins of thinking*. Macmillan

Kass, L.R. (2003) *Beyond Therapy: Biotechnology and the Pursuit of Happiness*. Dana Press

Lodge, D. (2002) *Consciousness and the Novel*. Secker & Warburg

Marmot, M. (2004) *Status Syndrome* Bloomsbury

Medina, J. (2000) *The Genetic Inferno: Inside the seven deadly sins*. Cambridge University Press.

Miller, P. and Wilsdon, J. Eds (2006) *'Better Humans': The politics of human enhancement and life extension*. Demos.

Mithen, S. (1996) *The Prehistory of the Mind*. Thames and Hudson

Neuroethics: Mapping the Field (2002) Conference Proceedings *Dana Press*

Palmer, S. (2006) *Toxic Childhood*. Orion

Tallis, F. (2004) Love Sick: *Love as a Mental Illness*. Century

Wilson, E.O (1978) *On Human Nature*. Penguin

Wahrman, D. (2004) *The Making of the Modern Self*. Yale University Press

Impact of IT (Chs 9–11)

Green, H. and Hannon, C. (2007) Their Space: Education for a digital generation. Demos.

Hyman, S.E., Malenka, R.C. and Nestler, E.J. (2006) Neural Mechanisms of Addiction: The role of reward-related learning and memory. *Ann. Rev. Neurosci.* 29 565–598

Johnson, S. (2005) *Everything Bad is Good for You*. Penguin

Livingstone, S. and Bober, M. (2005) UK Children Go Online. ESRC

Restak, R. (2003) *The New Brain: How the modern age is rewiring your mind*. Rodale

Turkle, S. (1995) *Life on the Screen*. Simon & Schuster

Belief (Chs 12–13)

Bohner, G. and Waenke, M. (2002) *Attitudes and Attitude Change*. Psychology Press

Coles, R. (1999) *The Secular Mind*. Princeton University Press

Dawkins, R. (2006) *The God Delusion*. Bantam Press

Dunbar, R. (2006) Beyond Belief. *New Scientist* Vol 28

Evans, D. (2003) *Placebo: The belief effect*. HarperCollins

Taylor, K (2004) *Brainwashing: The science of thought control*. OUP

Whitehouse, H. (2004) *Modes of Religiosity: A cognitive theory of religious transmission*. Altamira Press

Creativity (Chs 14–15)

Andreasen, N. (2005) *The Creating Brain*. Agrupacion Sierra Madre

Flaherty, A.W. (2005)Frontotemporal and dopaminergic control of idea generation and creative drive. *J Comp Neurol*. 493. 147–53.

Folley BS, and Park S. Verbal creativity and schizotypal personality in relation to prefrontal hemispheric laterality: a behavioral and near-infrared optical imaging study.

Gardner, H. (1997) *Extraordinary Minds*. Basic Books

Howard-Jones, P. (2007) Neuroscience and Education EPSRC/TLRP

Jung-Beeman M, Bowden EM, Haberman J, Frymiare JL, Arambel-Liu S, Greenblatt R, Reber. P.J, Kounios J. (2004) Neural activity when people solve verbal problems with insight. *PLoS Biol*. 2(4):E97.

Howard-Jones PA, Blakemore SJ, Samuel EA, Summers IR, Claxton G (2005)

Semantic divergence and creative story generation: an fMRI investigation. Brain Res Cogn Brain Res. 2005 240–50.

Kishimoto H, Yamada K, Iseki E, Kosaka K, Okoshi T. (1998) Brain imaging of affective disorders and schizophrenia. *Psychiatry Clin Neurosci.*;52 Suppl:S212–4.

Lapp WM, Collins RL, Izzo CV. (1994) On the enhancement of creativity by alcohol: pharmacology or expectation? *Am J Psychol.* 107,173–206

Miller BL, Cummings J, Mishkin F, Boone K, Prince F, Ponton M, Cotman C.(1998) Emergence of artistic talent in frontotemporal dementia. *Neurology*;5, 978–82

Sandri G. (2004) Does computation provide a model for creativity? An epistemological perspective in neuroscience. *J Endocrinol Invest.* 27, 9–22

Smale R. (2001) Addiction and creativity: from laudanum to recreational drugs. *J Psychiatr Ment Health Nurs.* 8, 459–63.

Stein J. (2001) The magnocellular theory of developmental dyslexia. *Dyslexia* 7, 12–36.

Turner, D.C. and Sahakian, B.J. (2006) Neuroethics of Cognitive Enhancement, *BioSciences* Vol 1.

Walker RH, Warwick R, Cercy SP (2006) Augmentation of artistic productivity in Parkinson's disease. *Mov Disord.* 21, 285–6.

Witelson SF, Kigar DL, Harvey T. (1999) The exceptional brain of Albert Einstein. *Lancet.* 353, 2149–53.

Vinge V (2006) 2020 computing: the creativity machine. *Nature.* Mar 23;440(7083):411.

von Karolyi C, Winner E, Gray W, Sherman GF(2003) Dyslexia linked to talent: global visual-spatial ability. *Brain Lang.* 85,427–31

SOURCES OF ILLUSTRATIONS

Page 29: Pascual-Leone A, et al. Modulation of muscle responses evoked by transcranial magnetic stimulation. Reproduced by permission *Journal of Neurophysiology* 74: 1037–1045, 1995, figure 6. Page 40: Rube Goldberg *Self-Opening Umbrella*. Rube Goldberg is the ® and © of Rube Goldberg Inc. Page 47: Zeck G, and Fromherz P. Noninvasive neuroelectronic interfacing with synaptically connected snail neurons immobilized on a semiconductor chip. *PNAS*, 2001, August 28 Vol 98 (18):10457–62. Copyright 2001 National Academy of Sciences USA. Page 95: Adapted from Woolf N J. The 'hub' of brain cells primarily affected in Alzheimer's Disease, Parkinson's Disease, and motor neurone disease. *Journal of Neuroscience* 1996 Vol 74:625-651. Page 225: Left *The Lady with the Ermine* (detail) by Leonardo da Vinci, Czartoryski Museum Cracow Poland/photo Bridgeman Art Library. Right *Virgin Mary* (detail) by Giovan Battista Salvi, Cesena Municipal Art Gallery Italy. Page 235: Association Network Diagram adapted from *Attitudes and Attitude Change (Social Psychology: A Modular Course)* by Gerd Bohner and Michaela Wanke, 2002 Psychology Press. Page 273: Reproduced by permission.

INDEX

Figures in italics refer to diagrams.